Clinician's Guide to the Assessment Checklist Series

The Assessment Checklist series, created by Michael Tarren-Sweeney, provides the world's first standardized caregiver-report measures of a range of attachment- and trauma-related mental health difficulties experienced among children growing up in foster, adoptive, kinship and residential care. This clinical manual provides essential guidance for child and adolescent mental health clinicians who use the Assessment Checklist measures, including the Assessment Checklist for Children (ACC), the Assessment Checklist for Adolescents (ACA) and the Brief Assessment Checklist (BAC), as part of their specialized assessments of children and adolescents in care.

Comprised of three parts, the book explores all aspects of using and interpreting the Checklist series. Part 1 provides an overview of the Assessment Checklist measures, the rationale for their development and instructions on how to use the measures for clinical assessment, screening and treatment monitoring. Part 2 provides expert guidance to clinicians on interpreting Assessment Checklist score profiles and provides detailed information about several specific types of mental health difficulties measured by them. Part 3 describes the development and psychometric properties of the various Assessment Checklist measures, including information about their validity and reliability. It also introduces several new measures that are under development.

Ideal for clinical child psychologists, child and adolescent psychiatrists, child psychotherapists and clinical social workers looking to improve the quality and depth of their clinical assessments with children and adolescents, this book provides essential guidance on professional use of the Assessment Checklist measures.

To request a copy of the checklists, please follow the instructions provided at the start of Chapter 2, under the headings *'Who can use the Assessment Checklist measures?'* and *'How to obtain the measures and become a registered user'*. Please also see www.childpsych.org.uk.

Michael Tarren-Sweeney is a clinical child psychologist, epidemiologist and child developmental theorist. He is Associate Professor of Child and Family Psychology at Canterbury University in New Zealand as well as a consultant clinical psychologist for government and charitable children's agencies in Australia.

Clinician's Guide to the Assessment Checklist Series

Specialized mental health measures for children in care

Michael Tarren-Sweeney

Routledge
Taylor & Francis Group
LONDON AND NEW YORK

First published 2014
by Routledge
27 Church Road, Hove, East Sussex, BN3 2FA

and by Routledge
711 Third Avenue, New York, NY 10017

Routledge is an imprint of the Taylor & Francis Group, an informa business

British Library Cataloguing in Publication Data
A catalogue record for this book is available from the British Library

Library of Congress Cataloging in Publication Data
Tarren-Sweeney, Michael
Clinician's guide to the assessment checklist series : specialized mental health measures for children in care / Michael Tarren-Sweeney.
pages cm
Includes bibliographical references.
1. Child Behavior Checklist. 2. Behavioral assessment of children 3. Mentally ill children–Institutional care–Psychological aspects. 4. Foster children–Psychological testing. 5. Child mental health services. I. Title. II. Title: Assessment checklist series. III. Title: Specialized mental health measures for children in care.
RJ503.7.C48T37 2014
618.92'89–dc23
2013021858

ISBN: 978-0-415-83608-1 (hbk)
ISBN: 978-1-315-85820-3 (ebk)

Typeset in Times
by FiSH Books Ltd, Enfied

For my darling Georgie,
and our three wonderful children.
With all my love.

Contents

Figures

Tables

Preface

The story of how and why the Assessment Checklist measures were developed, and how they later came to be used by clinicians around the world, began in 1989 when I started working as a child and family psychologist with a statutory social care agency. Before then I had a brief and fitful career as a psychologist, interspersed by a musical career. My new job in a front-line child welfare office proved to be a profound and life-altering experience. I was confronted by the reality of so many children in our community having such great need for psychological assistance, but with so little empirical knowledge on how best to provide this. Yet, there was something very different about this work that could (and should) not be readily dismissed for want of specialized knowledge. I felt this in the passion and commitment of my fellow clinicians and social workers, as well as in the people who care for these vulnerable children. And I felt inspired by the children themselves, and also privileged at having the opportunity to contribute in small ways to improving their well-being. I also began to understand some of the impossible dilemmas faced by child welfare systems, and of how, despite so many people's best intentions, these systems repeatedly initiate actions that adversely impact on children's development and felt security. I expect that many people who read this book will have had similar experiences and realisations.

While I was fortunate to have very experienced clinical supervisors, their knowledge base was largely derived from child developmental theories (especially attachment theory) and a body of anecdotal clinical experience shared amongst those who specialized in working with maltreated children and children in care. In the 1990s there were enormous gaps in research-generated knowledge, and almost no empirical basis for assessment and psychological interventions. Despite considerable advancements in our understanding of the mental health of children at large (gained largely through neurobiological and large-scale epidemiological studies), the nature of mental health difficulties experienced by many children in care remained a mystery to even the most experienced clinicians who worked in this field.[1]

For these reasons I decided that I should try to learn more about the mental health of children in care, initially by way of a longitudinal, epidemiological study called the Children in Care study (CICS). It was as much focused on learning about the determinants, predictors and developmental course of mental ill-health experienced by children in care, as it was on the nature of their symptomatology. Nevertheless, a critical aim was to obtain population estimates of the nature and prevalence of mental health symptoms experienced by children in long-term care. More than twenty previous studies had estimated the mental health of representative populations of children in care (i.e. not clinical samples) using the Child Behavior Checklist (CBCL), which effectively was the reference standard caregiver-report measure for psychiatric epidemiological research. I chose to include the CBCL in the study so that the findings could be compared with those obtained for other samples of children in care, as well as normative and other risk groups.

The next task was to select additional measures that could estimate those mental health difficulties manifested among children in care that are not adequately measured by the CBCL. This presented four main challenges. First, I located several niche instruments that measure very specific types of mental health difficulties (e.g. sexual behaviour problems, dissociation), but none that adequately measure multiple types of difficulties. Second, I found that combining the CBCL with a number of additional niche measures generated a survey questionnaire that was far too long for a population study. Third, many of the available measures were not well validated, and/or were deductively designed to measure pre-determined constructs, such as psychiatric diagnoses (unlike the CBCL, which has empirically-derived syndromes scales). And finally, there appeared to be no existing measures for some of the problems that the study sought to cover (e.g. abnormal pain response, food maintenance behaviours).

In light of these challenges, my Ph.D. supervisor and I concluded that the only satisfactory solution was to design a single caregiver-report instrument to measure most of the mental health difficulties manifested by children in care that are not adequately measured by the CBCL. The new instrument was termed the Assessment Checklist for Children (ACC), so as to avoid any direct reference to children's care status (as I knew from experience that children often lay eyes on mental health checklists sent to their caregivers, and I wanted to avoid contributing to these children's perceptions of being different to other children). The instrument's content and format were developed in the second half of the 1990s, with an early version being included in the 1997 CICS pilot study. A final 132-item research version was included in the CICS baseline survey between 1999 and 2002. In the late 2000s a follow-up survey and related cross-sectional adolescent survey of the CICS was carried out, piloting an adolescent version of the ACC, which became the Assessment Checklist for Adolescents (ACA).

Like many psychometric instruments, the ACC and ACA were thus initially designed for research. After the ACC performed well in the Children in Care study, it was distributed to some clinicians working in this field; initially my Australian colleagues who had contributed to the design of the ACC in some way (either informally or through the clinician survey and focus group). This led to requests for more information about the instrument's psychometric properties, as well as scoring and reference information that might help clinicians better interpret the ACC scores. Normative reference data and clinical ranges were derived from the CICS score distributions, and included on ACC score profile sheets. In this way the ACC transitioned from a population survey instrument to a clinical assessment measure. Since details of its development and psychometric properties were first published (Tarren-Sweeney, 2007), it has been distributed to many hundreds of specialized clinical services for children in care and those adopted from care, in every corner of the developed world. At the last count the ACC has also been employed in around 25 research studies! In late 2012 the ACA was finally developed to the point where it too could be used as a clinical assessment measure, and the Brief Assessment Checklists were derived from the ACC and ACA for use as mental health screening and treatment monitoring measures. This brings the story of the Assessment Checklists up to the time of writing this clinical manual. Hopefully the story will continue further, as ventured in this book's final chapter.

I do hope that you find this manual and the Assessment Checklist measures contribute usefully to your mental health assessments of children and young people in care, and those adopted from care.

Note

1 For example, there was no explanation for why more than half of the children in care with whom we were working had inattention/overactivity, when at that time most theorists and researchers proposed that ADHD was a developmental disorder that did not have social determinants.

Acknowledgements

The content of Chapter 5 was first published in Tarren-Sweeney, M. (2008). Predictors of problematic sexual behaviour among children with complex maltreatment histories. *Child Maltreatment*, 13, 182–98.

The content of Chapter 6 was first published in Tarren-Sweeney, M. (2010). An exploratory investigation of abnormal pain response among pre-adolescent children in foster care. *Clinical Child Psychology and Psychiatry*, 15(1), 65–79.

The content of Chapter 7 was first published in Tarren-Sweeney, M. (2006). Patterns of aberrant eating among pre-adolescent children in foster care. *Journal of Abnormal Child Psychology*, 34, 623–34. It is reproduced here by kind permission of Springer.

Much of the content of chapters 9, 10 and 11 was first published in the following two articles:

Tarren-Sweeney, M. (2013) The Assessment Checklist for Adolescents – ACA: a scale for measuring the mental health of young people in foster, kinship, residential and adoptive care. *Children and Youth Services Review*, 35, 384–93;

Tarren-Sweeney, M. (2007) The Assessment Checklist for Children – ACC: a behavioral rating scale for children in foster, residential and kinship care. *Children and Youth Services Review*, 29, 672–91.

Much of the content of Chapter 12 was first published in Tarren-Sweeney, M. (2013). The Brief Assessment Checklists (BAC–C, BAC–A): mental health screening measures for school-aged children and adolescents in foster, kinship, residential and adoptive care. *Children and Youth Services Review*, 35(5), 771–9.

List of abbreviations

ACA	Assessment Checklist for Adolescents
ACA-SF	Assessment Checklist for Adolescents – Short Form
ACC	Assessment Checklist for Children
ACC–SF	Assessment Checklist for Children – Short Form
ACC+	Assessment Checklist for Children – Plus
ACP-SF	Assessment Checklist for Pre-schoolers – Short Form
APR	Abnormal Pain Response
AUC	Area under the curve
BAC–A	Brief Assessment Checklist for Adolescents
BAC–C	Brief Assessment Checklist for Children
BPM	Brief Problem Monitor
CAMHS	Child and Adolescent Mental Health Service
CBCL	Child Behavior Checklist
CICS	Children in Care Study
CIS	Client Information System (an early version of the NSW state child welfare database)
CSA	Child sexual assault
DSM	Diagnostic and Statistical Manual for Mental Disorders (various editions)
HSS	Hyperphagic Short Stature
ICD	International Classification of Diseases
LAAC	Looked after and adopted children
NSW	New South Wales (Australian state)
OOHC	Out-of-home care
RAD	Reactive Attachment Disorder
ROC	Receiver Operating Characteristics
SBP	Sexual behaviour problems
SDQ	Strengths and Difficulties Questionnaire
STI	Subject to item ratio
TFC	Treatment foster care

Part I

Overview and user information

Chapter 1

Introducing the Assessment Checklist measures

ACC, ACA and BAC

The Assessment Checklist measures are a series of empirically-derived caregiver-report rating instruments that measure mental health difficulties observed among children and young people in alternate care ('out-of-home care', 'looked after children), those who are subsequently adopted from care, and maltreated children at large. While the Assessment Checklist measures were initially developed for use in epidemiological and clinical research, they are also standardized for use as clinical assessment and screening instruments.

The Assessment Checklist measures were designed to measure mental health symptoms that are characteristically observed among these groups, and which are not adequately measured by standard parent-report checklists, such as the Child Behavior Checklist (CBCL) and the Strengths and Difficulties Questionnaire (SDQ). Comprehensive coverage of the psychiatric symptomatology of children and young people in care is thus obtained when an Assessment Checklist measure is used in combination with an instrument that measures more common difficulties observed among children at large, such as the CBCL.

The Assessment Checklist measures are:

- The Assessment Checklist for Children (ACC, 120 items), for use in comprehensive mental health assessment of children aged 4 to 11 years, with user restrictions.
- The Assessment Checklist for Children – Short Form (ACC-SF, 44 items), for use in mental health reviews and treatment monitoring of children aged 4 to 11 years, with user restrictions.
- The Assessment Checklist for Adolescents (ACA, 105 items), for use in comprehensive mental health assessment of young people aged 12 to 17 years, with user restrictions.
- The Assessment Checklist for Adolescents – Short Form (ACA-SF, 37 items), for use in mental health reviews and treatment monitoring of young people aged 12 to 17 years, with user restrictions.
- The Brief Assessment Checklist for Children (BAC-C, 20 items), for mental health screening and casework monitoring of children aged 4 to 11 years, without user restrictions.
- The Brief Assessment Checklist for Adolescents (BAC–A, 20 items), for mental health screening and casework monitoring of young people aged 12 to 17 years, without user restrictions.

Assessment Checklist measures that are under development or consideration:

- Assessment Checklist for Children Plus (ACC+). A relatively brief 'green shoots' measure of behaviours suggesting adaptive, pro-social functioning and well-being, for use in comprehensive mental health assessment and treatment monitoring of children and young people aged 4 to 17 years, without user restrictions.

- Assessment Checklist for Preschoolers – Short Form (ACP-SF). A short form caregiver-report checklist designed to measure the mental health difficulties of children in alternate care and adoption, in the second half of their first five years of life (that is, from age 30 to 60 months). Long form (ACP) and screening (BAC-P) versions will be developed further down the track after the ACP-SF has been piloted in population studies.
- Assessment Checklist for Adolescents – Self-report (ACA-SR). The viability of developing a relatively brief (fewer than 50 items) self-report version of the Assessment Checklist for Adolescents is presently being considered. This measure would need to be restricted to ACA items that young people are able to accurately reflect on, and which are relatively non-confronting.

Table 1.1 The Assessment Checklist series: measures that are completed, under development and awaiting development

Informant	*Purpose*	*Age range* 2.5 to 4 years	*Age range* 4 to 11 years	*Age range* 12 to 17 years
Caregiver-report	Clinical assessment, restricted use	ACP awaiting development	ACC (120 items)	ACA (105 items)
	Clinical review, treatment monitoring, restricted use	ACP-SF (< 40 items) under development	ACC-SF (44 items)	ACA-SF (37 items)
	Screening, casework monitoring, administrative tool, unrestricted use	BAC-P awaiting development	BAC-C (20 items)	BAC-A (20 items)
	'Green shoots' measure, clinical assessment, treatment monitoring, unrestricted use		ACC+ 4 to 17 years (< 40 items) under development	
Self-report	Clinical assessment, clinical review, treatment monitoring, restricted use			ACA-SR (< 50 items) awaiting development

Overview

The Assessment Checklist for Children – ACC

The ACC is a 120-item carer-report psychiatric rating instrument, measuring behaviours, emotional states, traits and manners of relating to others, as manifested by children in care and those adopted from care. The ACC's content was developed systematically, with a view to measuring all clinically significant problems experienced by children in alternate care that are not adequately measured by standard parent-report checklists. Ten clinical and two low self-esteem scales were empirically derived via factor analysis. Initial data indicate that the instrument has good content, construct and criterion-related validity. Comprehensive survey estimates of the mental health of children in care can be obtained using the ACC in parallel with the CBCL. The instrument also provides a means for studying the characteristics and determinants of complex psychopathology manifested by child welfare populations. The ACC has ten clinical scales and two low self-esteem scales that were empirically-derived through factor analysis.

The ACC clinical scales are:

I Sexual behaviour
II Pseudomature interpersonal behaviour
III Non-reciprocal interpersonal behaviour
IV Indiscriminate interpersonal behaviour
V Insecure interpersonal behaviour
VI Anxious–distrustful
VII Abnormal pain response
VIII Food maintenance behaviour
IX Self-injury
X Suicide discourse

The ACC low self-esteem scales are:

I Negative self-image
II Low confidence

The ACC Clinical Scale I measures age-inappropriate sexual behaviour. Scales II to V measure various forms of maladaptive interpersonal relatedness that are suggestive of attachment disorder behaviours and/or attachment-related social difficulties. Scale II describes a pattern of precious pseudo-maturity and role reversal. Scale III describes emotionally withdrawn, avoidant and non-reciprocal social behaviours, with high scores being suggestive of a severely avoidant-insecure attachment style and/or inhibited form of reactive attachment disorder. Scale IV describes a pattern of indiscriminate overfriendliness, affection-seeking and attention-seeking behaviours, resembling the disinhibited form of reactive attachment disorder. Scale V measures a range of social behaviours and emotional difficulties suggestive of felt insecurity that is likely to reflect both trait insecurity (insecure attachment, temperament) and state insecurity (e.g. as a response to severe stressors, such as impermanent care). Scale VI measures a pattern of trauma-related anxiety and distrust. Scale VII measures a pattern of abnormal responses to physical hurt suggestive of pain insensitivity or failure to communicate felt pain. Scale VIII measures a pattern of excessive eating and food acquisition (termed food maintenance syndrome), that appears to be primarily triggered by acute stress, and which resembles the behavioural correlates of Hyperphagic Short Stature. Scale IX primarily measures various types of self-injurious behaviour, but also measures three pica-type behaviours. Scale X measures suicidal talk, attempted suicide and some other behaviours indicating risk for self-harm. The ACC Low Self-Esteem Scale I measures self-evaluations that suggest a profoundly negative self-image, while Scale II measures self-evaluations suggesting discouragement and low confidence in one's social, educational or other abilities.

Non-putative labels

The naming of scales is problematic, as it can inadvertently infer causality, or underlying theoretical constructs. Non-putative terms were selected for the ACC and ACA scales because they were largely derived empirically, and because maltreatment and attachment syndromes are as yet inadequately conceptualised. For example, 'abnormal pain response' was used in preference to 'pain dissociation' or 'pain agnosia', since the latter terms imply specific mechanisms.

Translations

At the time of this book's publication, the ACC response forms had been translated into German, Norwegian, Romanian and Spanish, while a number of European researchers were working on Portuguese, Russian, Serbian and Swedish language translations.

The Assessment Checklist for Children – Short Form – ACC–SF

The Assessment Checklist for Children – Short Form (ACC–SF) is a 44-item short form of the ACC that was developed primarily for use as a research instrument and as a relatively brief treatment monitoring measure. It excludes the low self-esteem scales, the suicide discourse scale and the pica index from the self-injury scale. The full version of the ACC is recommended for comprehensive mental health assessment, and the Brief Assessment Checklist for initial mental health screening.

The Assessment Checklist for Adolescents – ACA

The ACA is a 105-item, caregiver-report, psychiatric rating scale that measures behaviours, emotional states, traits and manners of relating to others, as manifested among 12 to 17 year-old young people in care, as well as young people who are adopted from care or who have a history of maltreatment. The ACA was designed to measure a broad range of mental health difficulties observed among young people in various types of care, that are not adequately measured by standard rating instruments, such as the CBCL, SDQ and Conners scales.

The ACA has seven clinical scales and two low self-esteem scales that were empirically-derived through factor analysis.

The ACA clinical scales are:

I Non-reciprocal interpersonal behaviour
II Social instability/behavioural dysregulation
III Emotional dysregulation/distorted social cognition
IV Dissociation/trauma symptoms
V Food maintenance behaviour
VI Sexual behaviour
VII Suicide discourse

The ACA low self-esteem scales are:

I Negative self-image
II Low confidence

The ACA Clinical Scale I describes emotionally withdrawn, avoidant and non-reciprocal social behaviours, with high scores being suggestive of a severely avoidant-insecure attachment style and/or inhibited form of reactive attachment disorder. Scale II describes a complex combination of unstable, attachment-related social relatedness difficulties and behavioural dysregulation. This scale incorporates the majority of items contained in the ACC Pseudomature and Indiscriminate scales. Scale III describes a pattern of highly dysregulated emotion and affective instability, coupled with distorted social cognition (negative attributions, paranoid beliefs). Scale IV measures a pattern of trauma-related dissociation and anxiety symptoms. Scale V measures a pattern of excessive eating and food acquisition (termed food maintenance syndrome), that appears to be primarily triggered by acute stress, and which resembles the behavioural correlates of Hyperphagic Short Stature. Scale VI measures age-inappropriate sexual behaviour. Scale VII measures suicidal talk, attempted suicide and some other behaviours indicating risk for self-harm. The ACA Low Self-Esteem Scale I measures self-evaluations that suggest a profoundly negative self-image, while Scale II measures self-evaluations suggesting discouragement and low confidence in one's social, educational or other abilities.

The Assessment Checklist for Adolescents – Short Form – ACA–SF

The Assessment Checklist for Adolescents – Short Form (ACA–SF) is a 37-item short form of the ACA that was developed primarily for use as a research instrument and as a relatively brief treatment monitoring measure. It excludes the low self-esteem scales and the suicide discourse scale. The full version of the ACA is recommended for comprehensive mental health assessment, and the Brief Assessment Checklist for initial mental health screening.

Brief Assessment Checklists (BAC–C and BAC–A)

The Brief Assessment Checklist for Children (BAC–C), and the Brief Assessment Checklist for Adolescents (BAC–A) are 20-item caregiver-report psychiatric rating scales designed to: (a) screen for and monitor clinically-meaningful mental health difficulties experienced by children and adolescents in various types of care; and (b) be safely administered and interpreted by health and social care professionals other than child and adolescent mental health clinicians. The BAC–C/A were also designed to be used as brief casework monitoring tools by foster care and adoption agencies, and for treatment monitoring in CAMHS. The BAC–C and BAC–A were derived from the Assessment Checklist for Children (ACC, 120 items) and Assessment Checklist for Adolescents (ACA, 105 items) respectively.

The Brief Assessment Checklists are highly accurate in screening for clinical range ACC and ACA scores, as well as for CBCL clinical range scores. They are moderately accurate in screening for children that caregivers reported had been referred to mental health services. Initial estimates of their psychometric properties compare favourably with that of existing screening instruments, including the Strengths and Difficulties Questionnaire and the Brief Problem Monitor (CBCL short form).

Why are there presently no teacher- and self-report versions of the Assessment Checklists?

A structural limitation of the Assessment Checklists relative to the other screening measures is the lack of teacher- and self-report versions. In regards to the BAC–C/A, a lack of multi-informant data is less critical for screening purposes than it is for comprehensive assessment.

Teacher versions of the ACC, ACA and BAC have not yet been developed because these instruments measure a range of difficulties that are unlikely to be reliably observed and reported on by teachers. Consequently, considerable new work needs to be carried out to develop valid and useful teacher-report versions of the Assessment Checklists.

Adolescent self-report versions of the ACA and BAC–A have not been developed because some of its items are likely to be very emotionally confronting for young people (may cause some people undue distress), and also may not be reliably measured through self-report. However, there is scope to develop a self-report shortened version of the Assessment Checklist for Adolescents, consisting of those items that young people are most able to reflect on, and which are least emotionally confronting.

Rationale and background to the development of the Assessment Checklist measures

Population research with children in alternate care, and those adopted from care, has focused on their presentation of commonly-observed psychopathology, as measured by standard parent-report rating scales, such as the Rutter scales (Elander and Rutter, 1996), the Child Behavior Checklist (CBCL) (Achenbach and Rescorla, 2001) and the Strengths and Difficulties Questionnaire (SDQ) (Goodman, 2001). The reliability of foster parent reports of children's problems remains somewhat uncertain, although there is evidence that in respect of children in long-term care, foster parents are at least as reliable as parents (Tarren-Sweeney *et al.*, 2004). To date, more than 20 studies have published CBCL scores for children in care, mostly in North America (Armsden *et al.*, 2000; Heflinger *et al.*, 2000; Horan *et al.*, 1993; Pilowsky, 1995), while the Rutter scales have been used extensively in alternate care research in Europe (Lambert *et al.*, 1977; Roy *et al.*, 2000; Rushton *et al.* 1997; St Claire and Osborne, 1987; Vorria *et al.* 1998; Yule and Raynes, 1972).

The mental health of such children has thus tended to be framed in terms of the problems measured by these scales, specifically aggression, inattention and emotional problems, whilst relationship and trauma-related difficulties have been overlooked. Yet, this was not always so! Early accounts of children in institutional care emphasised their grossly disturbed relationship styles, accompanied by aggressive behaviour, low empathy and hyperactivity (Wolkind and Rushton, 1994). This was variously described as 'affectionless psychopathy' (Bender and Yarnell, 1941), 'the affect hungry child' (Levy, 1937), and 'institutional syndrome' (Goldfarb, 1949). More recently, research on the problems of Romanian adoptees has revived an interest in the nature of attachment difficulties and inattention/hyperactivity among infants raised in residential care (Kreppner *et al.*, 2001; O'Connor *et al.* 1999).

The Rutter scales provide global estimates of psychopathology and identify emotional disorders, conduct disorders and hyperactivity (Elander and Rutter, 1996). The CBCL similarly yields global estimates of psychopathology, as well as measures of depressive and anxiety symptoms, somatic complaints, social and thought problems, inattention/overactivity, defiance, aggression and other anti-social behaviour (Achenbach and Rescorla,

2001). The scales do not adequately measure a range of problems manifested by children in care, most notably their attachment and peer relationship difficulties, dissociative and anxiety responses to trauma, self-injury and age-inappropriate sexual behaviour.

The Assessment Checklist for Children

The ACC was developed in the late 1990s for use in the baseline survey of the Children in Care Study (CICS), a prospective epidemiological study of the mental health of children in long-term foster and kinship care, in New South Wales (NSW), Australia (Tarren-Sweeney and Hazell, 2005, 2006). The ACC was designed to measure those problems manifested by children in care, which are not adequately measured by the CBCL (which was also administered in the study), including low self-esteem. While a number of instruments measure relevant problems, such as attachment disturbances (Minnis *et al.*, 2002), dissociation (Steinberg, 1996), and sexual problems (Friedrich *et al.*, 1991), no single instrument was suitable for the task. The ACC was also designed for use in clinical assessments of children in care, addressing a need for more comprehensive and specific clinical data (Garwood and Close, 2001).

Since 2007, the ACC has been employed in over 20 studies in Europe, North America and Australasia, and is increasingly used, particularly in Britain and Australia, as a clinical assessment tool by specialized mental health services for children and young people in care.

The Assessment Checklist for Adolescents

The ACC's content was derived for a wide age range (4 to 17 years), with a view to: (a) employing a single set of items for baseline and follow-up studies; and (b) comparing the factor structure of this common set of items at different developmental stages. This plan was subsequently revised following examinations of what the ACC appears to measure among children and young people at different ages, and with different developmental pathways. A developmental perspective suggests that clinical phenomena are likely to evolve in complex ways in the context of both age-sensitive developmental stages, and maladaptive developmental trajectories. For this reason it was thought that, prior to embarking on a 7- to 9-year follow-up of the CICS cohort (who would then be aged 11 to 18 years), there should be closer investigation of the validity and comprehensiveness of the ACC item pool for measuring those mental health symptoms manifested by adolescents in care that are not adequately measured by the CBCL, SDQ, Conners, etc. This preliminary investigation located a number of items that appear unsuitable for an adolescent population, suggested a need to modify some ACC items for an adolescent population, and suggested that some clinical phenomena manifested by young people in care are not adequately captured by the ACC. These findings prompted the formal development of an adolescent-specific measure for young people in the care system, the Assessment Checklist for Adolescents.

The Brief Assessment Checklists

Existing screening measures for school-aged children and adolescents

While there are many child and adolescent mental health assessment measures, there are relatively few brief measures designed to provide a broad screen for mental health difficulties (as distinct from screeners for single symptom categories). Most of the measures that fit this description are designed for early detection of emotional and behavioural difficulties among infants and pre-school children. Three measures that fit this description for school-aged children and adolescents are the Strengths and Difficulties Questionnaire (SDQ), Brief Problem Monitor (BPM), and the Behavioral and Emotional Screening System (BESS). The SDQ is a brief screening measure of mental health difficulties and prosocial behaviour (Goodman, 2001), that utilises parent-report (ages 3–4 and 4–16), teacher-report (ages 3–4 and 4–16), and adolescent self-report (ages 11–17) forms. The SDQ has 25 items, consisting of 20 symptom items that constitute a total difficulties scale and four clinical sub-scales (emotional symptoms, conduct problems, hyperactivity-inattention and peer problems) and five prosocial behaviour items. The instrument also includes questions designed to measure how a child's mental health difficulties impact on their functioning and well-being, and the burden they place on others. Despite its brevity, the SDQ has strong psychometric properties (particularly for the teacher version) and has demonstrated screening utility (Stone *et al.*, 2010). It is also readily accessible in that it has no user restrictions and is distributed freely as a non-commercial instrument. For all of these reasons the SDQ has become the most widely used and well recognised child and adolescent screening measure.

The BPM is a 22-item cross-informant version of the CBCL (and its equivalent teacher- and self-report forms), that was developed recently to monitor children's functioning and response to therapeutic interventions (Achenbach *et al.*, 2011). Nineteen items were derived from the CBCL internalising (6 items) and externalising (7 items) broadband scales, and the attention problems syndrome scale (6 items), and three are respondent-nominated 'additional items'. Although it was not expressly designed for use as a screening instrument, the BPM's brevity will likely see it increasingly used for that purpose, particularly if it is shown to have comparable or better screening utility to the SDQ. However, the BPM contains no items from the Social problems and Thought problems syndrome scales, which children and young people in care score highly on.

The BESS is also a relatively new screening instrument. The BESS Parent form is a 30-item short form version of the BASC-2 Parent Rating Scale (Dowdy *et al*, 2012). The BESS provides a single total problems score for screening purposes for preschool aged children through to age 17. The BESS also has teacher-report and self-report (from Grade 3) versions. The BESS's screening utility is not yet well established.

Rationale for developing the Brief Assessment Checklists

Available mental health screening instruments for school-aged children and adolescents are designed to screen for the symptoms and disorders most commonly endured among the population at large, particularly anxiety, depression, peer socialisation difficulties, inattention/overactivity, aggression and other conduct problems, and oppositional-defiant behaviour. No instrument has been designed to screen for additional characteristic difficulties experienced by children and young people in care (described earlier in this chapter) that the ACC and ACA were designed to measure. Just as there is a need for clinicians to have tools that contribute to their comprehensive assessment of these difficulties, there is also an evident need for tools that accurately screen for these difficulties.

There are two reasons why the ACC and ACA are not suitable for use as screening and casework monitoring measures. Firstly, they have too many items (120 and 105 respectively) to qualify as brief, easy-to-complete measures. Secondly, given the nature of some of the problems measured by these checklists and the labels given to their empirically-derived scales, it is the developer's belief that the ACC and ACA cannot be safely used by people other than qualified child and adolescent mental health professionals. Without adequate training in clinical and psychosocial-developmental formulation, users are likely to misinterpret the meaning of high scale scores, and children are more likely to be labelled as having particular attachment- and/or trauma-related difficulties, based on a single source of information. Consequently, use of the ACC and ACA is restricted to qualified clinicians and researchers. Yet, child welfare and social care agencies have a legitimate need to carry out mental health screening and monitoring for vulnerable children and young people in their statutory care, particularly in jurisdictions that do not have a proactive primary care mental health service for children in care. Furthermore, primary health care workers who are responsible for carrying out health screening may not have adequate training in mental health assessment to interpret the meaning of ACC and ACA score profiles.

Together this constitutes a rationale for developing brief screening versions of the ACC and ACA that: (a) have high screening accuracy; (b) provide a single total difficulties score, i.e. without any constituent sub-scales; and (c) can be safely used and interpreted by social care and health professionals other than child mental health clinicians.

Universal comprehensive assessment is preferable to screening

While the Brief Assessment Checklists have the potential to increase the accuracy and relevance of mental health screening for children and young people in care, we should be mindful that this does not legitimise universal mental health screening as representing unqualified *best practice*, as distinct from best practice *within the constraints of limited mental health resources*. There is compelling evidence to support the argument that, given the availability of an adequately trained and specialized workforce, children in care would be better served by universal, comprehensive assessment, bypassing the need for mental health screening (with the exception of screening for immediate risk of harm). Almost all children in care are exposed to systemic, adverse pressures on their development and well-being, and they have vulnerabilities that are not necessarily revealed by their mental health presentations. Many of these pressures can be profoundly distressing and undermine children's felt security. Much of this risk can be identified and intercepted, and their effects prevented and remediated, through thorough assessment.

I would argue that we need to shift towards a new standard of psychological practice, informed by more detailed assessment of attachment- and trauma-related problems, and a wider developmental and contextual focus than that typically employed in mental health clinical assessments, within what might be termed a *clinical/psychosocial-developmental* scope of practice. In essence, specialized assessment of these children requires a shift from a relatively narrow, 'mechanical' focus on identifying children's symptoms and disorders, to seeking a comprehensive understanding of their felt experience, their relationships, family/placement processes, and systemic and care-related pressures on their development.

Chapter 2

Using the Assessment Checklist measures for clinical assessment, screening and treatment monitoring

Who can use the Assessment Checklist measures?

The ACC and ACA were designed to be used within *comprehensive mental health and psychosocial-development assessments* of children and young people, and for clinical research. There is a danger that ACC and ACA scores can be inappropriately interpreted or misused by non-clinicians. They thus should not be employed as a screening or evaluative tool by agencies without direct oversight by qualified clinicians. It is important to emphasise that the developer does not agree to these measures being used primarily for administrative purposes by children's or health agencies.

The Brief Assessment Checklists (BAC–C and BAC–A) were primarily derived from the ACC and ACA for use as mental health screening measures by primary health, social care and adoption agencies. The Brief Assessment Checklists may also be used for case monitoring and administrative purposes by such agencies. While the developer places no restrictions on who may use the Brief Assessment Checklists (they can be freely downloaded from www.childpsych.org.uk), we should be mindful of the potential for individuals or agencies to misuse these measures, or misinterpret their scores.

User qualifications for the ACC, ACC–SF, ACA, and ACA–SF

Use of the ACC and ACA (including the short form versions) is restricted to:

1 researchers and research teams carrying out relevant research;
2 appropriately qualified child and adolescent mental health professionals and supervised trainees, such as those having qualifications in (or being trained in) child and adolescent psychiatry, clinical psychology, child psychotherapy and clinical child social work;
3 developmental, educational and/or paediatric psychologists.

These measures are distributed freely to registered individuals or to a nominated person within a registered clinical or developmental/educational agency, within the terms of a limited licence agreement. Approved individuals and agencies agree to comply with user restrictions set out in the licence agreement, and to not pass the measures on to non-approved users. If you have colleagues who work outside of your service and wish to use the ACC/ACA, then please direct them to www.childpsych.org.uk, where they will find information about how to obtain these measures.

These restrictions are primarily designed to stop the measures being used for non-clinical/psychosocial-developmental purposes (e.g. as an administrative tool), and to reduce the risk of children and young people being harmed or disadvantaged due to incorrect clinical formulation and labelling of their difficulties.

Limited licence for the ACC, ACC–SF, ACA, and ACA–SF

"A limited licence to use the Assessment Checklist for Children (ACC) and the Assessment Checklist for Adolescents (ACA) and their short form versions (ACC–SF, ACA–SF) is presently granted to people who register their use with the instrument's developer. Only genuine researchers, qualified child and adolescent mental health clinicians (as well as developmental/educational/paediatric Psychologists),[a] and supervised clinical trainees are approved to use the ACC and ACA. Block approval can be sought by clinicians working in relevant agencies or services (e.g. a CAMHS team, or the Psychological Services division of a child welfare agency). In this instance, the Clinical Director of the agency or service should ensure that the instrument is only distributed to qualified users. Only registered users have approval to use the ACC and ACA for an appropriate purpose. Registered users may not distribute these materials without the developer's permission. All materials remain the copyright of the developer, who reserves the right to revoke this limited licence. Please email the developer michael.tarren-sweeney@canterbury.ac.nz to be registered as an ACC and ACA user, and to obtain the ACC and ACA materials (sent as PDF documents)."

[a] Includes Registered, Chartered or Board Certified Psychologists, Child and Adolescent Psychiatrists, Clinical Social Workers, Psychotherapists and Child Counsellors with training or experience in clinical and/or developmental child and adolescent assessment.

How to obtain the measures and become a registered user

To obtain the Brief Assessment Checklists (BAC–C and BAC–A)

Individuals and agencies may freely download and use the Brief Assessment Checklists without user restrictions or the need to be a registered user. The BAC–C and BAC–A forms can be downloaded at www.childpsych.org.uk and scoring and interpretation instructions are provided later in this chapter.

To obtain the ACC, ACC–SF, ACA, and ACA–SF

Registered users of these instruments are either individual clinicians or a team of clinicians working within an agency. For the latter, the team's clinical director or most senior clinician should request use of these measures on behalf of the team, and should ensure that all clinicians in their team read the limited licence agreement before receiving the measures. When a team is registered, there is no need for individual clinicians within that team to be separately registered (even if they wish to use the instruments in their separate private practice).

To obtain these measures, please email your request to michael.tarren-sweeney@canterbury.ac.nz, including details of your professional qualification and/or relevant training, a brief description of the purpose for using these measures in your work and whether you are applying as an individual user or on behalf of a team. If this appears to meet the user restrictions described above, then I will email the ACC, ACC–SF, ACA and ACA–SF checklists to you, as well as the limited licence agreement and ACC and ACA Excel scoring sheets. The hand-completed scoring profiles can be downloaded at www.childpsych.org.uk

without restriction. In the event that the email address listed above is ever deleted or becomes inactive, then my updated contact details will be listed at www.childpsych.org.uk

Checklist structure and response format

The Assessment Checklist measures share a common checklist structure and response format. Each Assessment Checklist item refers to an individual behaviour, emotional state, trait or manner of relating to others, that is observable by a child's or young person's carer. There are separate versions of the ACC and ACA for boys and girls containing gender pronouns (him/her, himself/herself, he/she). Items are otherwise identical for boys and girls. The BAC–C and BAC–A do not have gender-specific versions.

Response scale

The Assessment Checklists employ a three-point response scale (0-1-2), similar to the Revised Rutter Scales ('does not apply', 'applies somewhat', 'certainly applies') (Elander and Rutter, 1996), the CBCL and its companion instruments ('not true', 'somewhat or sometimes true', 'very true or often true') (Achenbach and Rescorla, 2001), and the Strengths and Difficulties Questionnaire ('not true', 'somewhat true', 'certainly true') (Goodman, 2001). Achenbach argues that a three-option scale is preferable to a dichotomous scale, because untrained raters (i.e. parents) have more difficulty in responding to a 'present/absent' scale (Achenbach, 1991; Achenbach and Edelbrock, 1978).Conversely, finer differentiations than that offered by three options are more vulnerable to bias by respondent characteristics (Achenbac *et al.*, 1991), and do not provide greater discrimination between mental health syndromes (Achenbach and Edelbrock, 1978).

Measurement of infrequent critical events

The Assessment Checklists were designed to detect infrequent events of critical problems such as suicide attempts and discourse, age-inappropriate sexual behaviour and self-injury. Detecting single or isolated behaviours is important if they are markers for risk of harm, or if the events have clinical significance. Conversely, it is not useful to detect isolated instances of less critical problems, such as peer conflict. The Assessment Checklists differentiate between these two types of items by assigning them to separate parts, each of which employs a different three-step response scale.

Part 1 uses the following instructions for less critical/higher incidence problems:

circle 0 if the statement is not true for your child,[1] in the last 4 to 6 months;
circle 1 if the statement is partly true for your child, in the last 4 to 6 months;
circle 2 if the statement is mostly true for your child, in the last 4 to 6 months.

Part 2 uses the following instructions for more critical/lower incidence problems:

circle 0 if the behaviour did not occur in the last 4 to 6 months;
circle 1 if the behaviour occurred once in the last 4 to 6 months;
circle 2 if the behaviour occurred more than once in the last 4 to 6 months.

Timeframe instruction

In the context of alternate care, the CBCL's timeframe 'now or within the past 6 months', might unduly confuse respondents. Temporary and short-term foster carers have less opportunity to observe their foster child's behaviour. In clinical practice, foster parents often query the CBCL timeframe if they have known the child for less than six months. It was also thought that the word 'now' might confuse respondents in Part 2, where an item is scored if the behaviour occurs only once within the timeframe. Hence it was decided that the timeframe instruction should be in the last 4 to 6 months.

Prompts to describe a scored item

A number of ACC and ACA items are potentially imprecise measures of maladaptive symptoms, either because they have greater scope for caregivers misinterpreting their intended meaning (e.g. has panic attacks), or because the behaviours measured by those items are not always maladaptive (e.g. cuts or rips her/his clothes). In the first example, a lay person's understanding of what constitutes a panic attack can differ quite markedly from the specific clinical phenomenon that clinicians understand. In the second example, older children sometimes cut or rip their clothes to follow a clothing fashion or to affiliate with a youth sub-culture (it is for this reason that this item was excluded from the ACA). To ensure these items retain validity, respondents are prompted to *describe* the behaviour (in space set out below the item) whenever these items are scored 1 or 2. Thirteen ACC items and ten ACC items have a 'describe' prompt.

Example of a completed Assessment Checklist record form

Figure 2.1 provides an example of an ACC record form completed by a foster mother of a fictional 8-year-old child. Sample Assessment Checklist record forms are also listed as Appendices 2 (ACC–SF, boys' form), 3 (ACA, girls' form), 4 (ACA–SF, boys' form), 5 (BAC–C), and 6 (BAC–A).

How to use the Assessment Checklists

Checklist respondents

The Assessment Checklists are designed to be completed by children's adoptive parents and alternate caregivers, including foster parents, kinship caregivers (such as grandparents) and residential care workers. Children's social workers and teachers *are not valid respondents*, because they do not have the opportunity to observe or learn in other ways about many of the difficulties measured by the checklists. While the instrument's content is valid for many maltreated children who are not in care, it has not been established that birth parents of maltreated children are reliable informants of their children's mental health.

The Assessment Checklists attempt to estimate children's mental health by asking caregivers to report their observations of the presence and frequency of children's symptoms. Whereas some items measure 'externalised' difficulties that can be readily observed by caregivers, others measure difficulties that are less directly observable. These latter symptoms are revealed to caregivers more through children's verbal communication than their non-verbal behaviour. The absence of a clear window to children's inner experiences accounts in

ACC **Assessment Checklist for Children** **GIRLS FORM**

PART 1 **Here are some statements that describe children's behaviour and feelings.**

For each statement, please circle the number that best describes your child in the **last 4 to 6 months.**

→ circle **0** if the statement is **not true** for your child in the last 4 to 6 months.
→ circle **1** if the statement is **partly true** for your child in the last 4 to 6 months.
→ circle **2** if the statement is **mostly true** for your child in the last 4 to 6 months.

Please do not check your answers with your child, as they may cause distress or embarrassment.

(0) 1 2	1.	Adjusts slowly to changes
0 1 (2)	2.	Attention-seeking behaviour
0 1 (2)	3.	Avoids eye contact, except if in 'trouble'
(0) 1 2	4.	Believes she is no good at anything
0 1 (2)	5.	Can't concentrate, short attention span
0 1 (2)	6.	Changes friends quickly
0 1 (2)	7.	Clingy
0 1 (2)	8.	Complains of not being likeable
0 (1) 2	9.	Craves affection
0 1 (2)	10.	Dislikes herself
(0) 1 2	11.	Distrusts adults
(0) 1 2	12.	Does not cry
(0) 1 2	13.	Does not share with friends
(0) 1 2	14.	Does not show affection
(0) 1 2	15.	Does not speak up for herself
(0) 1 2	16.	Easily discouraged at home
(0) 1 2	17.	Easily discouraged at school
0 1 (2)	18.	Easily influenced by other children
(0) 1 2	19.	Eats from garbage
(0) 1 2	20.	Eats things that are not food
0 (1) 2	21.	Eats too much
(0) 1 2	22.	Fearful of men in general
(0) 1 2	23.	Fearful or nervous at bedtime
(0) 1 2	24.	Fears she might be molested
0 (1) 2	25.	Fears she might do something bad
0 1 (2)	26.	Fears you will reject her
0 (1) 2	27.	Feels ashamed
0 (1) 2	28.	Feels worthless or inferior
(0) 1 2	29.	Finds it hard to make decisions
(0) 1 2	30.	Gets hurt a lot, "accident prone"
0 (1) 2	31.	Gives up too easily
(0) 1 2	32.	Gorges food
0 (1) 2	33.	Has a low opinion of herself
(0) 1 2	34.	Has an imaginary friend
0 (1) 2	35.	Has nightmares
(0) 1 2	36.	Hides feelings
(0) 1 2	37.	Hides or stores food
(0) 1 2	38.	Hugs men, other than relative or male carer
(0) 1 2	39.	Is convinced that friends will reject her
(0) 1 2	40.	Is fearful of being harmed
0 (1) 2	41.	Lacks confidence
(0) 1 2	42.	Lacks guilt or empathy
(0) 1 2	43.	Laughs when injured or hurt
(0) 1 2	44.	Lives in a fantasy world
0 1 (2)	45.	Low self-esteem
0 1 (2)	46.	Manipulates or 'uses' friends
(0) 1 2	47.	Play includes violent or frightening themes
(0) 1 2	48.	Possessive, can't share friends
0 (1) 2	49.	Precocious (talks or behaves like an adult)
(0) 1 2	50.	Prefers to be with adults, rather than children
0 (1) 2	51.	Prefers to mix with older children
(0) 1 2	52.	Refuses to talk
0 1 (2)	53.	Relates to strangers 'as if they were family'
0 (1) 2	54.	Resists being comforted when hurt
0 (1) 2	55.	Risks physical safety, fearless
(0) 1 2	56.	Says friends are against her
0 1 (2)	57.	Says she is "bad", or "no good"
0 (1) 2	58.	Secretive
0 1 (2)	59.	Seems insecure
(0) 1 2	60.	Startles easily
(0) 1 2	61.	Steals food
0 (1) 2	62.	Suspicious
(0) 1 2	63.	Thinks she is someone or something else
(0) 1 2	64.	Thinks other children are better than her
(0) 1 2	65.	Too compliant (over-conforms)
(0) 1 2	66.	Too dramatic (false emotions)
0 1 (2)	67.	Too friendly with strangers
0 1 (2)	68.	Too independent
(0) 1 2	69.	Too jealous
0 1 (2)	70.	Treats you as though you were the child, and she was the parent
0 (1) 2	71.	Tries too hard to please other children
0 (1) 2	72.	Tries too hard to please you
(0) 1 2	73.	Turns friends against each other
0 (1) 2	74.	Uncaring (shows little concern for others)
0 1 (2)	75.	Very forgetful
0 (1) 2	76.	Wants to be treated like a baby, or a toddler
0 (1) 2	77.	Wary or vigilant
(0) 1 2	78.	Withdrawn
0 (1) 2	79.	Won't attempt new activities
(0) 1 2	80.	Won't communicate with other children
(0) 1 2	81.	Worries that something bad will happen to you

Please turn over to complete part 2

Figure 2.1 Example of a completed ACC record form

ACC Assessment Checklist for Children

GIRLS FORM

PART 2 Please note that the instructions are different on this page.

On this page only

→ circle **0** if the behaviour **did not occur** in the last 4 to 6 months.
→ circle **1** if the behaviour **occurred once** in the last 4 to 6 months.
→ circle **2** if the behaviour **occurred more than once** in the last 4 to 6 months.

(0) 1 2 82. Asks to be physically punished
(0) 1 2 83. Attempts suicide
(0) 1 2 84. Bites herself
(0) 1 2 85. Causes herself to vomit
0 (1) 2 86. Causes injury to herself (describe): Hits head against wall until bruised/bleeding
(0) 1 2 87. Cuts or pulls out her hair (describe):
(0) 1 2 88. Cuts or rips her clothes (describe):
(0) 1 2 89. Describes how she would kill herself
0 (1) 2 90. Describes or imitates sexual behaviour
(0) 1 2 91. Distressed by traumatic memories
(0) 1 2 92. Does not show pain if physically hurt
0 1 (2) 93. Extreme reaction to losing a friend, or being excluded by other children (describe): Massive tantrums afterwards
(0) 1 2 94. 'Flirts' with strangers
(0) 1 2 95. Forces or pressures children into sexual acts
(0) 1 2 96. Has blackouts or periods of amnesia
(0) 1 2 97. Has panic attacks (when?)
0 1 (2) 98. Hits head, head-banging
(0) 1 2 99. Intentionally harms herself with knives or implements (describe):
(0) 1 2 100. Intentionally swallows dangerous substance to harm herself (e.g. medication, poison) (describe):
(0) 1 2 101. Kisses with open mouth
(0) 1 2 102. Masturbates at home in view of others
(0) 1 2 103. Masturbates at school, or in public
(0) 1 2 104. Picks at sores or injuries
(0) 1 2 105. Requests to be harmed
(0) 1 2 106. Rocks back and forth (describe):
(0) 1 2 107. Says her life is not worth living
(0) 1 2 108. Sexual behaviour not appropriate for her age (describe):
(0) 1 2 109. Sexual intercourse with another young person
(0) 1 2 110. Sexual relations with an adult (describe):
(0) 1 2 111. Shows sex parts to children (other than siblings)
0 1 (2) 112. Starts rude conversations, tells jokes about sex
(0) 1 2 113. Talks about suicide
(0) 1 2 114. Threatens to injure herself
0 (1) 2 115. Threatens to kill herself
0 (1) 2 116. Throws herself against walls, onto floors, etc (describe):
(0) 1 2 117. Touches or puts mouth on other person's sex parts
(0) 1 2 118. Tries to involve others in sexual behaviour (describe):
(0) 1 2 119. Unhealthy drinking (e.g. from discarded drink bottle, from toilet bowl) (describe):
(0) 1 2 120. Won't say when physically hurt

Please make sure you have answered each question on both sides of the page

ID:
Child's name: Carly Rogers
Child's age: 8
Your name: Jennifer Smith
Your relationship to the child: Foster Mother (e.g. mother, father, aunt, foster mother, grandfather)

Figure 2.1 continued

large part for poor (typically r is less than .30) parent–child inter-rater agreement on cross-informant measures of children's internalising difficulties (Tarren-Sweeney *et al.*, 2004). Given the nature and range of social and emotional difficulties measured by the Assessment Checklists, reliable estimates can only therefore be obtained from caregivers who have had sufficient opportunity to engage and interact closely with the child for a reasonable length of time, so that their reports are not just based on observations of non-verbal behaviour.

With this in mind, alternate care systems present two challenges to locating caregivers who can reliably report on the range of difficulties measured by the Assessment Checklists: (1) the amount, type and primacy of care provided by the respondent caregiver; and (2) the length of time the child has resided with the respondent caregiver.

The amount, type and primacy of care provided by the respondent caregiver

It is more difficult to obtain reliable caregiver-reported estimates of the mental health of children in non-family care settings, if they do not have the opportunity to engage with a primary, 'parental' caregiver. In larger residential facilities, children and young people's care can be shared across several shift-work staff, and the care model may only facilitate superficial 'non-parental-type' engagement. Conversely, some small group homes are staffed by live-in caregivers who are effectively foster parents, despite being employees rather than volunteer caregivers. Clinicians need to be mindful that the reliability of Assessment Checklist scores that they obtain for children and young people in non-family care settings will vary according to the respondent's caregiving role and level of engagement with the child.

> When assessing children and young people who reside in non-family type settings, it is very important that the clinician: (a) seeks to identify the caregiver who has greatest day-to-day contact with the child, and who the child engages most closely with; and (b) is mindful that the reliability of Assessment Checklist scores obtained for a child or young person in a large residential setting is highly dependent on the availability of a caregiver who has close, day-to-day involvement with the child.

Guidelines for selecting and instructing checklist respondents

- Ideally you should ask the caregiver who has the most day-to-day involvement with the child, to complete the checklist (note that 'most involved' does not necessarily equate to who the child 'gets on best with').
- It is sometimes useful to ask two caregivers to complete checklists. If so, the two respondents should be asked to complete the checklists independently of each other.
- When a child or young person is in residential or group care, attempt to identify and recruit the care worker who has the most involvement with, or knowledge of the child (see further discussion of this in the following section).
- Establish beforehand if the caregiver has sufficient reading age (around age 10) to respond to questions without assistance. If not, you may need to administer the checklist as an interview, or be on hand to provide assistance
- Provide respondents with a brief explanation of how to score the checklist. Point out the instruction to 'Please do not check your answers with your child, as they may cause distress or embarrassment'.

Timing and frequency of administration

Length of time child has resided with their caregiver

In recent years there has been a growing emphasis on assessing children as early as possible after they enter alternate care, with some protocols calling for screening and/or comprehensive assessment in the first weeks of care (Romanelli *et al.*, 2009). While there are good reasons for assessing children's physical and mental health, development and education status as early as possible, we are less likely to obtain reliable mental health assessment data for children during their first few weeks in a new care placement, whether that be in their initial placement or any subsequent one. We need to be mindful that being removed from one's parents and being placed with caregivers who are strangers is outside the range of normal childhood experience, and that this experience is likely to be bewildering and stressful in the first few weeks, even for children who have moved from an abusive home life to a safe, warm and caring alternate family. In such a context, many children show a marked reduction in disruptive behaviour in their first few weeks of being cared for by stranger adults (social workers refer to this as a 'honeymoon period'), while others manifest an increased range of symptoms indicative of felt distress, insecurity, anger, and fear.

> Wherever possible, children should not undergo formal or comprehensive mental health assessment until they have resided for at least six weeks with new caregivers. This includes administration of the ACC and ACA. This advice does not preclude carrying out earlier assessments of children's risk of causing harm to themselves or others.

Frequency of administration

As a general rule, the range of attachment- and trauma-related symptoms measured by the Assessment Checklists are fairly stable over short to medium timeframes, even where children experience radical changes in the developmental conditions that account for those difficulties. For these types of difficulties, the effectiveness of therapeutic caregiving and psychological interventions is likely to be evidenced through gradual symptom reduction over several years, rather than short-term dramatic changes. With this in mind, there is little to be gained from carrying out frequent administrations of the Assessment Checklists, even during treatment. Frequent administrations are *unlikely* to reveal dramatic changes in scores from one administration to the next, leaving clinicians and others with a possibly false impression that an intervention or placement is not therapeutic.

In Chapter 13 (in the context of describing the ACC+ measure), I speculate that early signs of therapeutic recovery might be more reliably detected through the emergence of behaviour that is contrary to symptoms of mental ill-health, what might be termed 'green shoots' adaptive behaviours. For example, a child who is typically callous, withdrawn and resists affection from his caregiver is likely to continue to manifest these attachment-related difficulties for some time after the first green shoots begin to emerge (such as a spontaneous, unsolicited hug), and may continue to score highly on problem scales long after his caregiver recognises qualitative changes to the child's attachment-related behaviours.

In instances where children are in stable long-term adoptive or foster placements, there is little to be gained from administering the Assessment Checklist measures more than once per year. Yearly re-administration provides greater scope for reliably detecting meaningful changes in children's mental health than more frequent administrations, especially when checklists are completed by the same caregiver.

More frequent re-assessment and 'monitoring' may be warranted when children and/or their caregivers are receiving intensive psychological interventions (such as Treatment Foster Care), or when children experience a change of placement. However, clinicians should be mindful that the absence of meaningful change in symptom scores over six-month or shorter timeframes provides a less reliable indication of the course of children's mental health difficulties, than a similar result measured over a 12-month timeframe.

Assessment of children with learning difficulties

The Assessment Checklist measures were developed and standardized using data obtained in the various stages of the NSW Children in Care study. The study samples included sizeable proportions of children having borderline to mild intellectual (around 22.4%) and other learning difficulties, comparable to that reported among other care populations (Klee, Kronstadt & Zlotnick, 1997; Leslie *et al.*, 2002), but the CICS excluded children having moderate to severe intellectual difficulties. The ACC and ACA item analyses did not reveal any validity concerns for using these instruments with children with mild intellectual disabilities or other types of learning difficulties (such as reading problems). However, these instruments are unlikely to provide valid measurement of the types of mental health difficulties manifested by children having moderate to severe intellectual disability.

The Assessment Checklist measures may be used for mental health assessment of children and young people who have a mild intellectual disability or other types of learning difficulties, but should not be used for assessment of children who have a moderate to severe intellectual disability.

The Assessment Checklist profile sheets

The Assessment Checklist profile sheets serve a number of purposes:

1 they provide a ready means for calculating and recording the various sub-scale and total scores;
2 they provide a graphical representation of normative score distributions as well as clinical and elevated score ranges, which allow the user to compare a child's present scores with various reference criteria;
3 they provide a graphical representation of a child's mental health score profile.

Examples of completed ACC and ACA profile sheets are provided as Figures 2.2 and 2.3 respectively. The ACC, ACC–SF and ACA have separate profile sheets for boys and girls, whereas the ACA–SF profile sheet serves both genders. The main difference between the

ACC/ACC–SF and ACA/ACA–SF profile sheets is that the ACC/ACC–SF profiles provide graphical representation of population normative data, while the ACA/ACA–SF do not. The ACC/ACC–SF profile sheets show gender-specific population normative score distributions for 5 to 10 year-old children in long-term alternate care. The profile sheets show the normative percentile and T-score for each raw score. Reference data for 4 and 11 year-olds were not included on the profile sheets because there were insufficient CICS subjects aged 4 and 11 to reliably estimate a population distribution.

The profile sheets are arranged in the following way:

- for the ACC and ACA, the clinical sub-scale scores and profile are laid out on the first page, and the low self-esteem scores and profile, total clinical score distribution, and some administrative information are set out on the second page. The short-form versions do not include low self-esteem scales;
- all checklist items are listed below their constituent sub-scale labels, or under the 'other items' label, with a space to write each item score. The sub-scale scores are recorded at the bottom of the columns containing the relevant item scores;
- the graphical score profiles are set out above the item and sub-scale scoring area, showing normative population distributions (ACC/ACC–SF only) and clinical and elevated score ranges;
- the first page of each profile also contains an area for calculating the total clinical (and where relevant) the composite low self-esteem scores.

Scoring the ACC and ACA (including short-form versions)

Step 1: respond to unanswered items

1. Identify any unanswered items, and where possible, ask the caregiver to score them.
2. If there are three or fewer unanswered items, allocate a zero score to each of them and proceed with scoring as usual.
3. If there are four or more unanswered items, identify which sub-scales they contribute to:
   i. if a sub-scale has two or more unanswered items, then refrain from calculating that sub-scale's score;
   ii. if a scale has one unanswered item, allocate that item a score of zero and calculate the scale score as usual.
4. Do not prorate ACC or ACA sub-scale or total scores to adjust for unanswered items.

Step 2: check for accuracy

1. Read all item descriptions (i.e. items that include the option to 'Describe: ________'). If a description indicates to you that the caregiver has interpreted the item to mean something different to what it is intended to measure, then it suggests the item has been scored incorrectly. In this situation, you should allocate a score of zero to that item.
2. Sometimes caregivers will circle two adjacent scores for an item as a way of indicating that they are either uncertain of the true score, or wish to create a mid-point between the two scores.

(0 1) 2 *or* 0 (1 2)

When this happens, do one of the following:

i. if only a few items are scored this way (say 3 or fewer), then allocate the higher score;

ii. if many items are scored this way (say 4 or more), ask the caregiver to score the checklist again, and to commit to one of the three score options.

Step 3: choose manual or electronic method for calculating scale scores

Most users will choose to derive checklist scores manually on paper profile sheets, so they can readily compare the child's scale scores to normative reference scores (ACC) and elevated and clinical ranges (ACC and ACA). This requires the user to manually transcribe each item score from a completed checklist on to a paper profile sheet, and then carry out a series of additions to calculate the various scale scores. Alternatively, users can enter the checklist item scores into an ACC or ACA Excel scoring spreadsheet that is distributed to registered users with the checklist forms. While the spreadsheet automatically calculates the various scale scores, it does not produce a graphic score profile. For this reason, the manual scoring method is more useful for individual clinical assessments, while the electronic scoring method is more useful for recording research checklist data.

Step 4: calculate the sub-scale scores and locate them on the profile sheet

1 Transfer the item scores to the appropriate boys or girls ACC, ACC–SF, ACA or ACA–SF profile sheet. Note that every item contributes to only one sub-scale, or is listed under other items.

2 Add together the item scores within each sub-scale to calculate the sub-scale scores (as well as the 'other items' score), and write these in the space provided below the item scores. You should then re-perform the additions to check they are correct. See example.

3 Once you have checked your calculations, locate and circle the equivalent sub-scale score on the profile section above the lists of items.

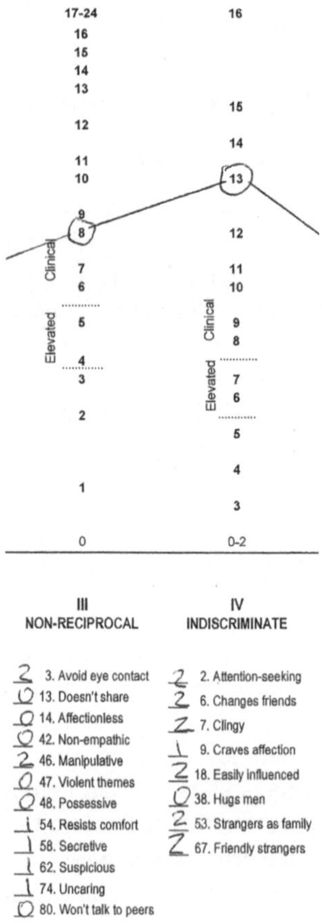

Step 5: calculate the total clinical score and the composite low self-esteem score

1 The total clinical score is calculated by adding the clinical sub-scale scores to the 'other items' score. To do this, transfer the clinical sub-scale scores and the 'other items' score to the relevant calculation box on the right hand side of the profile sheet. See example.

Add scores	
I	3
II	6
III	8
IV	13
V	8
VI	3
VII	0
VIII	1
IX	4
X	1
Other Items	5
=	52
Total Clinical Score **	

2 Once you have calculated the total clinical score, transfer it to the relevant Total Clinical Score profile box on the right-hand side of the second page of the ACC profile sheet. This step doesn't need to be done for the ACA, as its total clinical score is shown alongside the sub-scale scores on the first page of the ACA profile. See example.

Total Clinical Score = 52		
Raw	T	%ile
	Clinical range	
106-204	≥ 72	≥ 99
103-105	71	98
100-102	70	98
89-99	69	97
87-88	68	96
81-86	67	96
77-80	66	95
75-76	65	93
73-74	64	92
71-72	63	90
70	62	88
64-69	61	86
57-63	60	84
48-56	59	82
45-47	58	79
43-44	57	76
40-42	56	73
35-39	55	69

3 The ACC and ACA composite low self-esteem score is calculated by adding together the two low self-esteem sub-scale scores, as well as the item 'has low self-esteem'. See example.

4 Only calculate a total score if you were able to calculate all of the constituent sub-scale scores. If a sub-scale score cannot be calculated because of unanswered items, then a total score should not be calculated.

SELF-ESTEEM SCALES

I NEGATIVE SELF-IMAGE

0 4. No good at anything
2 8. Not likeable
2 10. Dislikes self
1 25. Fears might do bad
1 27. Feels ashamed
1 28. Feels worthless
1 33. Low self-opinion
2 57. Says is "bad"
0 64. Others are better

10 Total I

II LOW CONFIDENCE

0 1. Adjusts slowly
0 15. Doesn't speak up
0 16. Discouraged at home
0 17. Discouraged at school
0 29. Decision-making
1 31. Gives up
1 41. Lacks confidence
1 79. Attempt new activities

3 Total II

COMPOSITE

10 Total I
3 . Total II
2 45. Low self-esteem

15 Total COMPOSITE

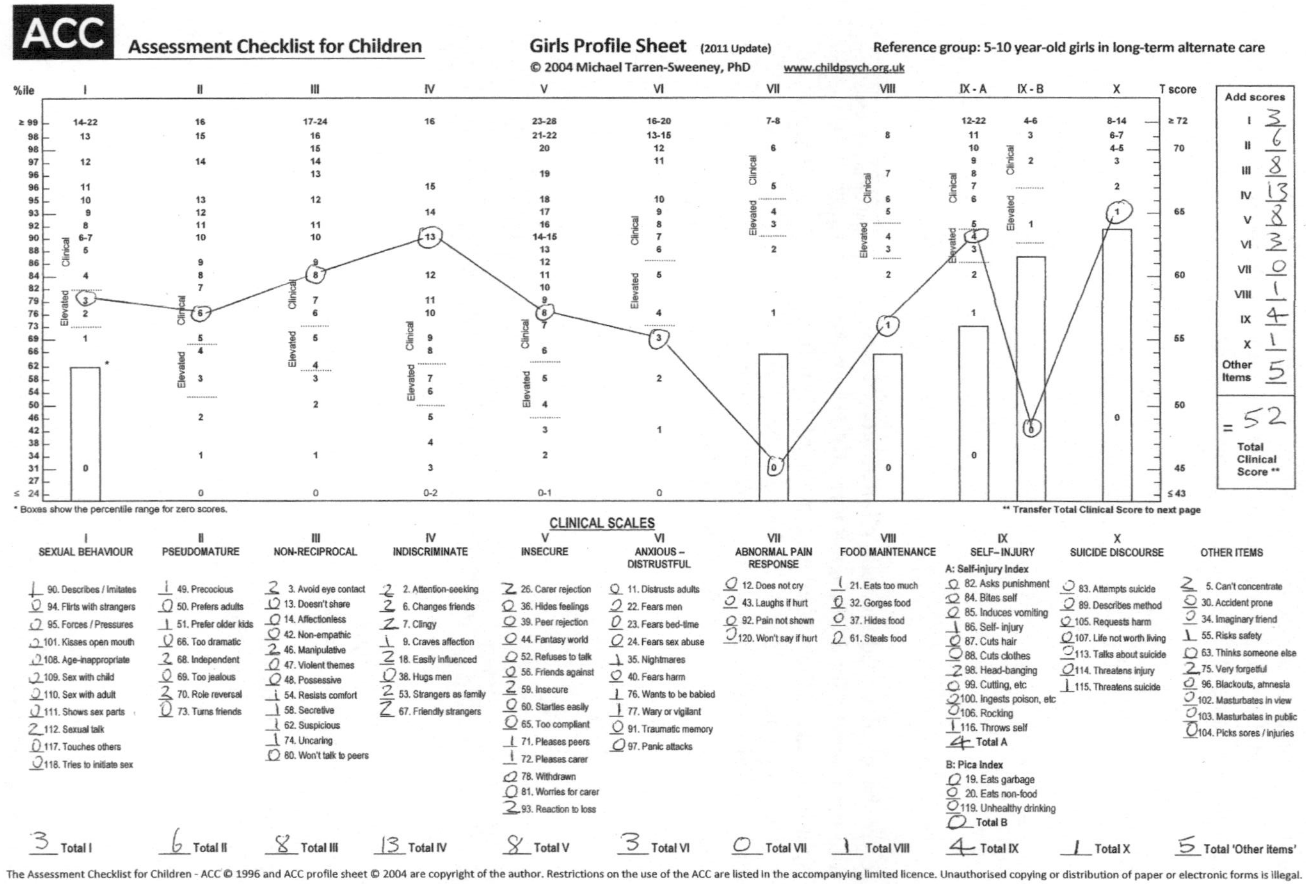

Figure 2.2 Example of a completed Assessment Checklist for Children (ACC) profile sheet

ACC Assessment Checklist for Children

Girls Profile Sheet (2011 Update)

© 2004 Michael Tarren-Sweeney, PhD

Reference group: 5-10 year-old girls in long-term alternate care

www.childpsych.org.uk

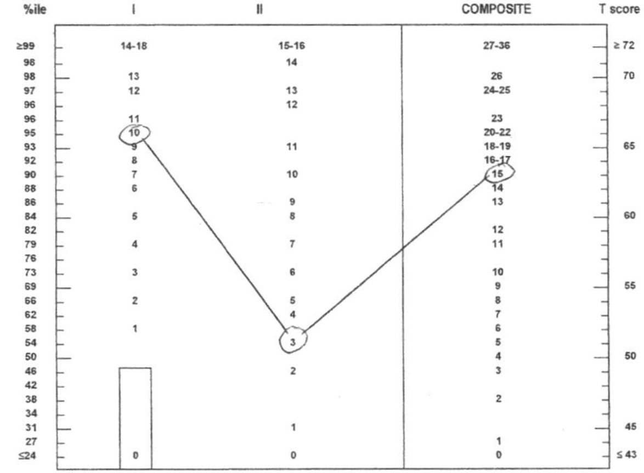

SELF-ESTEEM SCALES

I NEGATIVE SELF-IMAGE

0 4. No good at anything
2 8. Not likeable
2 10. Dislikes self
1 25. Fears might do bad
1 27. Feels ashamed
1 28. Feels worthless
1 33. Low self-opinion
2 57. Says is "bad"
— 64. Others are better

10 Total I

II LOW CONFIDENCE

0 1. Adjusts slowly
0 15. Doesn't speak up
0 16. Discouraged at home
0 17. Discouraged at school
0 29. Decision-making
1 31. Gives up
1 41. Lacks confidence
1 79. Attempt new activities

3 Total II

COMPOSITE

10 Total I
3 Total II
2 45. Low self-esteem

15 Total COMPOSITE

ID:

Child's Name: CARLY ROGERS

	Year	Month	Day
Date of Birth:	2004	11	23
Date of Assessment:	2013	9	15
Age:	8	9	22

Carer's name: JENNIFER SMITH
(the person who completed the ACC)

Carer's gender: Female ☑ Male ☐

Length of time carer has known child: 3 years

Carer's relationship to child
- ☐ Birth parent
- ☐ Step-parent
- ☐ Grandparent
- ☐ Other relative
- ☐ Adoptive parent
- ☑ Foster parent
- ☐ Group home staff
- ☐ Large residential staff
- ☐ Youth worker
- ☐ Other (describe): ____________

Care Status
- ☐ Not in care (resides with parents)
- ☐ Adoption
- ☐ Kinship care (resides with relatives)
- ☑ Permanent or long-term foster care
- ☐ Temporary or short-term foster care
- ☐ Group or residential care
- ☐ Other (describe): ____________

Referral Details:

Total Clinical Score = 52

Raw	T	%ile
Clinical range		
106-204	≥ 72	≥ 99
103-105	71	98
100-102	70	98
89-99	69	97
87-88	68	96
81-86	67	96
77-80	66	95
75-76	65	93
73-74	64	92
71-72	63	90
70	62	88
64-69	61	86
57-63	60	84
48-56	59	82
45-47	58	79
43-44	57	76
40-42	56	73
35-39	55	69
33-35	54	66
28-32	53	62
27	52	58
Borderline clinical range		
25-26	52	58
23-24	51	54
21-22	50	50
Normal range		
19-20	49	46
16-18	48	42
13-15	47	38
12	46	34
11	45	31
9-10	44	27
8	43	24
7	42	21
	41	18
6	40	16
	39	14
5	38	12
	37	10
4	36	8
	35	7
3	34	5
2	33	4
	32	4
1	31	3
	30	2
	29	2
0	≤ 28	1

ACC scores should be interpreted and reported by qualified child clinicians.

Figure 2.2 continued

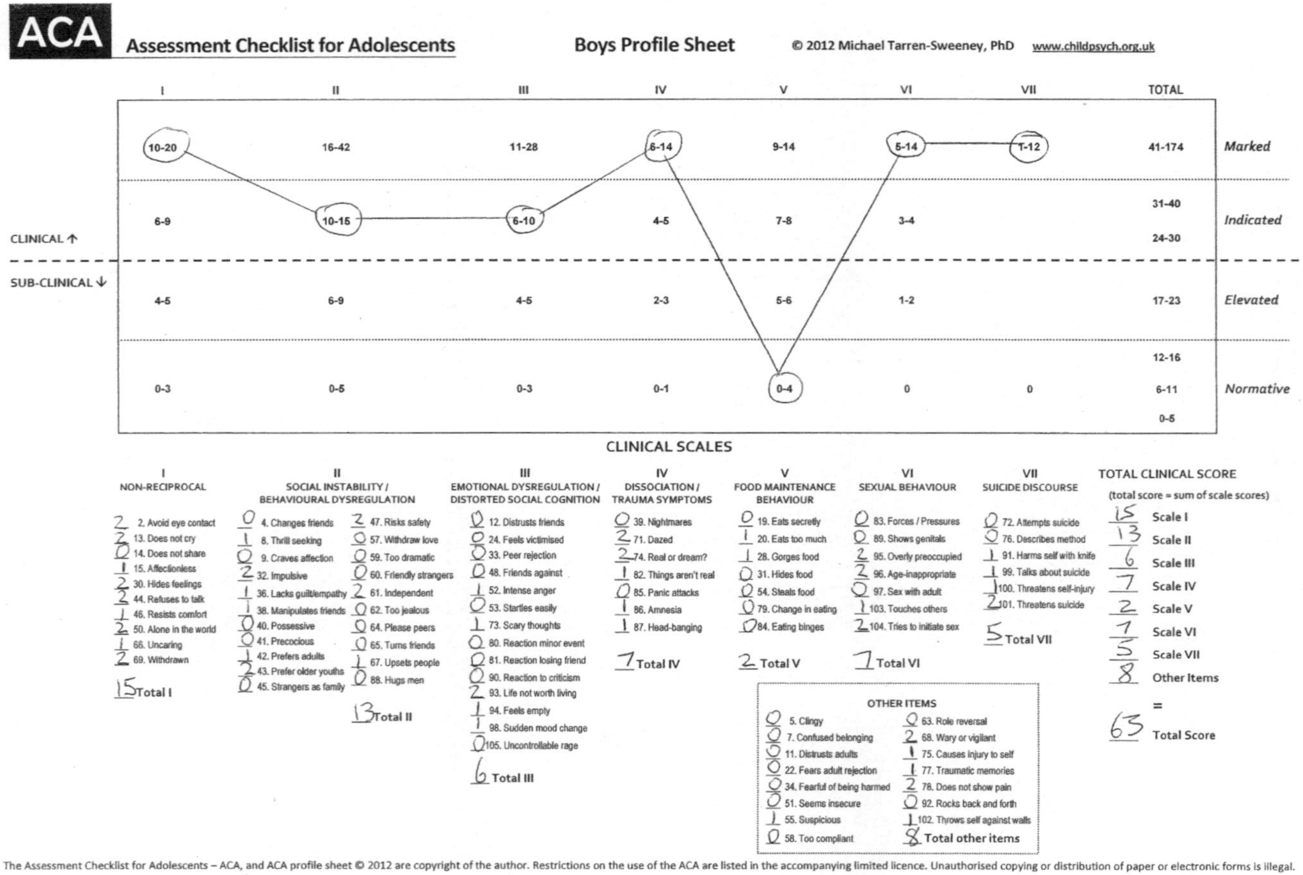

ACA Assessment Checklist for Adolescents — Boys Profile Sheet — © 2012 Michael Tarren-Sweeney, PhD — www.childpsych.org.uk

	I	II	III	IV	V	VI	VII	TOTAL	
CLINICAL ↑	10-20	16-42	11-28	6-14	9-14	5-14	1-12	41-174	*Marked*
	6-9	10-15	6-10	4-5	7-8	3-4		31-40 / 24-30	*Indicated*
SUB-CLINICAL ↓	4-5	6-9	4-5	2-3	5-6	1-2		17-23	*Elevated*
	0-3	0-5	0-3	0-1	0-4	0	0	12-16 / 6-11 / 0-5	*Normative*

CLINICAL SCALES

I NON-RECIPROCAL
2 2. Avoid eye contact
2 13. Does not cry
0 14. Does not share
1 15. Affectionless
2 30. Hides feelings
2 44. Refuses to talk
1 46. Resists comfort
2 50. Alone in the world
1 66. Uncaring
2 69. Withdrawn
15 Total I

II SOCIAL INSTABILITY / BEHAVIOURAL DYSREGULATION
0 4. Changes friends
1 8. Thrill seeking
0 9. Craves affection
2 32. Impulsive
1 36. Lacks guilt/empathy
1 38. Manipulates friends
0 40. Possessive
0 41. Precocious
1 42. Prefers adults
2 43. Prefer older youths
0 45. Strangers as family
2 47. Risks safety
0 57. Withdraw love
0 59. Too dramatic
0 60. Friendly strangers
2 61. Independent
0 62. Too jealous
0 64. Please peers
0 65. Turns friends
1 67. Upsets people
0 88. Hugs men
13 Total II

III EMOTIONAL DYSREGULATION / DISTORTED SOCIAL COGNITION
0 12. Distrusts friends
0 24. Feels victimised
0 33. Peer rejection
0 48. Friends against
1 52. Intense anger
0 53. Startles easily
1 73. Scary thoughts
0 80. Reaction minor event
0 81. Reaction losing friend
0 90. Reaction to criticism
2 93. Life not worth living
1 94. Feels empty
1 98. Sudden mood change
0 105. Uncontrollable rage
6 Total III

IV DISSOCIATION / TRAUMA SYMPTOMS
0 39. Nightmares
2 71. Dazed
2 74. Real or dream?
1 82. Things aren't real
0 85. Panic attacks
1 86. Amnesia
1 87. Head-banging
7 Total IV

V FOOD MAINTENANCE BEHAVIOUR
0 19. Eats secretly
1 20. Eats too much
1 28. Gorges food
0 31. Hides food
0 54. Steals food
0 79. Change in eating
0 84. Eating binges
2 Total V

VI SEXUAL BEHAVIOUR
0 83. Forces / Pressures
0 89. Shows genitals
2 95. Overly preoccupied
2 96. Age-inappropriate
0 97. Sex with adult
1 103. Touches others
2 104. Tries to initiate sex
7 Total VI

VII SUICIDE DISCOURSE
0 72. Attempts suicide
0 76. Describes method
1 91. Harms self with knife
1 99. Talks about suicide
1 100. Threatens self-injury
2 101. Threatens suicide
5 Total VII

TOTAL CLINICAL SCORE (total score = sum of scale scores)
15 Scale I
13 Scale II
6 Scale III
7 Scale IV
2 Scale V
7 Scale VI
5 Scale VII
8 Other Items
=
63 Total Score

OTHER ITEMS
0 5. Clingy
0 7. Confused belonging
0 11. Distrusts adults
0 22. Fears adult rejection
0 34. Fearful of being harmed
0 51. Seems insecure
1 55. Suspicious
0 58. Too compliant
0 63. Role reversal
2 68. Wary or vigilant
1 75. Causes injury to self
1 77. Traumatic memories
2 78. Does not show pain
0 92. Rocks back and forth
1 102. Throws self against walls
8 Total other items

Figure 2.3 Example of a completed Assessment Checklist for Adolescents (ACA) profile sheet

ACA Assessment Checklist for Adolescents

Boys Profile Sheet

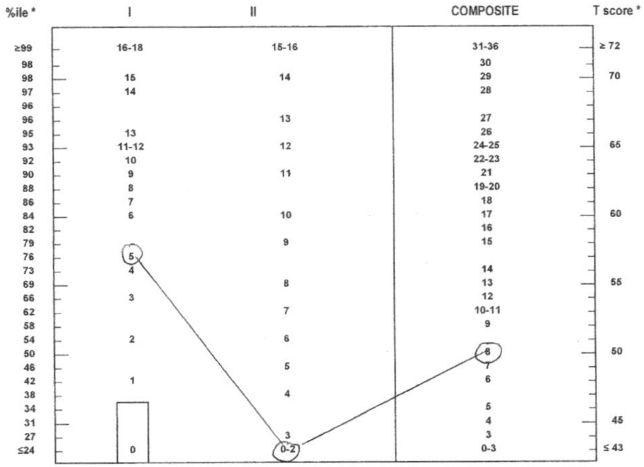

SELF-ESTEEM SCALES

I NEGATIVE SELF-IMAGE	II LOW CONFIDENCE	COMPOSITE
0 3. No good at anything	0 1. Adjusts slowly	5 Total I
0 6. Not likeable	0 16. Doesn't speak up	2 Total II
0 10. Dislikes self	0 17. Discouraged at home	1 37. Low self-esteem
0 21. Fears might do bad	0 18. Discouraged at school	
0 23. Feels ashamed	0 26. Decision-making	
1 25. Feels worthless	0 27. Gives up	
1 29. Low self-opinion	1 35. Lacks confidence	
2 49. Says is "bad"	1 70. Attempt new activities	
1 56. Others are better		
5 Total I	2 Total II	8 Total COMPOSITE

* Normative profiles derived from a mixed reference group of 125 adolescent males in regular foster care and 76 in Treatment Foster Care

ID:

Young person's name: FRANK BROWN

	Year	Month	Day
Date of Birth:	2000	5	1
Date of Assessment:	2013	7	4
Age:	13	2	3

Carer's name: JUDITH MOORE
(the person who completed the ACA)

Carer's gender: Female ☑ Male ☐

Length of time carer has known young person: 6 months

Carer's relationship to young person
- ☐ Birth parent
- ☐ Step-parent
- ☐ Grandparent
- ☐ Other relative
- ☐ Adoptive parent
- ☐ Foster parent
- ☑ Group home staff
- ☐ Large residential staff
- ☐ Youth worker
- ☐ Other (describe): ____________

Young Person's Care Status
- ☐ Not in care (resides with parents)
- ☐ Adoption
- ☐ Kinship care (resides with relatives)
- ☐ Permanent or long-term foster care
- ☐ Temporary or short-term foster care
- ☑ Group or residential care
- ☐ Other (describe): ____________

Referral Details:

ACA scores should be interpreted and reported by qualified child clinicians.

Figure 2.3 continued

Using the ACC and ACA within comprehensive clinical/psychosocial-developmental assessments

This book assumes that clinicians who are using the ACC or ACA have professional training in mental health assessment and clinical formulation, and thus are familiar with the limitations of single sources of assessment data. It is nonetheless important to emphasise that although the ACC and ACA were designed for use as mental health assessment measures, assessments of children's mental health should *never be solely* based on ACC/ACA scores! This point is emphasised again in the following chapter, which provides guidance on how to interpret Assessment Checklist scores.

A comprehensive mental health assessment of children and young people in various types of care might include: a combination of caregiver-reported checklists that cover a wide range of mental health symptoms (e.g. ACC/ACA and CBCL); a teacher-report mental health checklist (e.g. Teacher Report Form or the SDQ); clinical/psychosocial-developmental interviews with the client child, their caregivers, and possibly the child's teacher and other significant adults; observations of the child engaging with their current family and peers (and if appropriate, observations of birth family contact); engaging the child in various psychological assessment activities (such as a story stem task); obtaining information about the child's maltreatment and social care history through interviews with social workers and/or reviewing their casework file; and reviewing earlier mental health and psychosocial-developmental assessment reports.

Mental health screening with the Brief Assessment Checklists

BAC–C and BAC–A scoring instructions

Add together the scores for each of the 20 items to calculate the child's total score. Since each question can be scored 0, 1 or 2, the total score can range from 0 to 40. Write the total score in the box at the bottom right corner of the checklist, together with the date it was completed.

Unanswered items

Where possible, ask caregivers to score any unanswered items. If one or more items remain unanswered, do the following:

1 you may calculate a prorated total score if 15 or more items have been answered, and if you are using the checklist for screening purposes;
2 you should not calculate a total BAC score if less than 15 items have been answered.

How to prorate a total score for the BAC–C or BAC–A

1 Add together the scores for each of 15 or more answered questions to create a *raw* total score.
2 Divide the raw total score by the number of answered questions, and multiply that value by 20. This is the prorated total score. The screening decision should be based on this prorated total score, and not the raw total score.

Example:
A caregiver answers 15/20 questions on the BAC–A
The raw total score for those 15 questions is 4
The prorated total score is 4 divided by 15, multiplied by 20 = 5.3

Screening decision

For both the BAC–C and BAC–A, a total score of 5 or higher (5+) represents the optimal screening cut-point for maximising sensitivity without excessive trade-off in specificity. The proportions of children and adolescents in the Children in Care study who screened positive using a 5+ cut-point, were 67% and 61% respectively.[2] The 5+ cut-point detected 98% of clinical cases defined by ACC and ACA scores, and 92% to 93% of clinical cases defined by CBCL scores. This is achieved at the cost of misidentifying 25% of ACC/ACA non-cases and 35% of CBCL non-cases. Importantly however, the majority of those who were false negative screens had at least one mental health score in the elevated (ACC) or borderline clinical (CBCL) range. For these children and young people, further clinical assessment is warranted.

Notes

1 The ACC, ACC–SF and BAC–C instructions state 'for your child', while the ACA, ACA–SF and BAC–A state 'for this young person'.
2 The proportions who screen positive using 4+, 6+ and 7+ cut-points are 74%, 67% and 58% on the BAC–C, and 65%, 57%, and 52% on the BAC–A.

Part II

Interpreting Assessment Checklist scores

Guidelines and research findings

Chapter 3

Interpreting checklist scores within comprehensive assessments

This chapter provides guidance on how to *interpret* ACC and ACA score profiles within comprehensive clinical/psychosocial-developmental assessments. This guidance assumes that clinicians who use the ACC and ACA have reasonable prior understanding of psychometric theory and administration, and are familiar with the rationale for carrying out multi-method, comprehensive clinical assessments.

A key message from Chapter 2 is further emphasised in the present chapter; that mental health assessments of vulnerable children require extensive enquiry and multiple sources and types of assessment data. Clinical formulations should never be based solely around ACC/ACA score profiles!

Interpretation requires relevant clinical training and specialized knowledge

The extent to which ACC and ACA score profiles are interpretable is governed to a large degree by the clinician's knowledge and understanding of what the scales measure. More generally, those users who have acquired advanced and specialized knowledge of mental ill-health experienced by children with care backgrounds have greater scope for interpreting the meaning of ACC and ACA score profiles, especially in relation to: (a) children's developmental and present contexts; and (b) other available assessment data.

In particular, interpreting the ACC and ACA score profiles of children with more severe difficulties requires some understanding of the nature of complex attachment- and trauma-related symptomatology.

This book attempts to cover some of this knowledge base in Chapters 4 to 7, by describing analyses of ACC scores obtained in the Children in Care study, including complex symptom profiles. Clinicians who wish to interpret ACC and ACA score profiles are thus encouraged to read these chapters closely. Conversely, readers should not anticipate that this book can provide all of the knowledge and guidance they require to interpret ACC and ACA score profiles within a comprehensive mental health assessment.

What do scores in the normative, elevated and clinical ranges suggest?

The ACC and ACA scales include defined *clinical* ranges, and sub-clinical *elevated* ranges (the latter are similar to the CBCL borderline ranges). Whereas the clinical ranges for CBCL scales are defined statistically using uniform T-score cut-points (such that each CBCL disorder is defined as having equal population prevalence), clinical and elevated sub-clinical ranges for the ACC and ACA clinical scales were each separately defined using a combination of criterion-referenced procedures and clinical reasoning. Further details about how these ranges were defined is provided in Chapter 10.

The clinical range indicates scores that are highly predictive of psychiatric impairment.

The elevated range encompasses scores that indicate a moderate likelihood of psychiatric impairment. The elevated range is meant to encompass sub-clinical scores that:

- may warrant further monitoring;
- can have uncertain clinical meaning;
- may be maladaptive for some children;
- would not be considered normative among children at large.

Scores that fall below the elevated range are considered to be *normative*, reflecting a low level of difficulties that do not warrant concern or further monitoring.

For the ACA only, the clinical range is further divided into two severity ranges:

1 scores in the moderate end of the clinical range are identified on the ACA score profile as *clinically indicated*;
2 scores in the severe end of the clinical range are identified on the ACA score profile as *marked clinical*.

Clinical formulation of complex symptomatology

There are big question marks for children in adoptive and alternate care around the coherence and validity of clinical formulations that are based on standard conceptualisations of psychopathology. In 1996, as part of the development of the ACC, I reviewed 110 clinical assessment reports sourced from 50 psychological records of children in care, and other child welfare clients. Most of these reports were written by psychologists and psychiatrists working in specialist public health services, child welfare and alternate care agencies, and private practice. The reports revealed considerable diagnostic disagreement and uncertainty, as well as a tendency to frame complex psychopathology as a series of discrete, co-morbid disorders. From a practice perspective, the accumulation of multiple and conflicting diagnoses provides little clarity or guidance for children's social workers, teachers and carers (Tarren-Sweeney, 2010).

In the following chapter, symptom profile types derived from cluster analyses of ACC and CBCL DSM-oriented scale scores are presented. These analyses identified around 20 per cent of subject children as reportedly having complex and severe symptomatology that is not adequately conceptualised within DSM and ICD classifications of mental disorders, and which reflected an absence of typology. These children experienced more profound developmental adversity, endured greater placement instability and had greater evident need for mental health services than children with less complex disorders.

This presents a particular quandary for clinical practice with children in care; namely, that standard clinical reasoning is likely to produce inaccurate formulation of the mental health difficulties of those children who have greatest need for our professional opinions and interventions. Accurate formulation of clinical phenomena is an essential component of evidence-based psychological practice. It is thus important that clinicians understand the particular limitations of standard classifications of mental disorders as they apply to children with complex symptomatology, and modify their clinical reasoning and formulations to account for this. Rather than diagnosing complex presentations as discrete, overlapping or inter-related co-morbid disorders, I would argue that for many children it is more valid to formulate such complexity around symptom profiles. To this end, I am presently attempting to devise a *symptom profile approach* to clinical formulation of complex presentations, which would take account of the forms, severity and complexity of a child's mental health difficulties. As yet this work isn't sufficiently developed to include in this book, but will be advertised in due course on the Assessment Checklists website (www.childpsych.org.uk).

Some practical steps for interpreting ACC and ACA scores

Step 1: examine reliability indicators

The following *may* indicate unreliable responses (i.e. possible response set biases):

i *Excessively high scores*. Pay close attention to ACC total clinical scores above 80 and ACA total clinical scores above 70. Consider the extent to which these scores agree with other assessment data obtained for the child. If all other assessment data suggest the child's difficulties are less pronounced, then regard such a high ACC or ACA score as having suspect reliability.

ii *Excessively low scores*, when other assessment data suggest the child has mental health difficulties. Pay close attention to ACC and ACA total clinical scores below 3. Very low scores are likely to be reliable if all other assessment data suggests the child has no clinically meaningful mental health difficulties.

iii A *very 'flat' profile* can be a consequence of random scoring, e.g. where a respondent scores the items without reading them. Please note, however, that a substantial proportion of children in care manifest complex attachment- and trauma-related psychopathology, where their ACC/ACA score profiles are characterised more by elevation than shape.

iv *Evidence of a response set bias*. A tendency to score symptoms exclusively as '1' or exclusively as '2' suggests a response set bias.

Step 2: consider pressures for response bias

The next step is to consider score reliability in relation to referral context. Could the referral context lead to a caregiver consciously or unconsciously biasing their responses? Examples include overstating the number and level of difficulties when seeking a clinical service, or when the level of support services provided to a family is linked to the child's level of impairment. Clinicians need to be aware that over-estimation of baseline difficulties due to response biases can lead to incorrect estimations of treatment effectiveness. Once again, the remedy is to consider how well the caregiver-reported ACC/ACA scores concord with assessment data obtained from other sources or using other methods.

Step 3: consider the overall scale of a child's difficulties

i Consider the overall (global) scale of reported mental health difficulties, in terms of the total clinical score population percentile and T score (ACC only) and the severity range (normative/elevated/clinically indicated marked clinical ranges).

ii The ACC and ACA total clinical score provide a reasonable indication of 'global' psychopathology, even if no other standardized measures have been used. They have a very high correlation with the CBCL total problems score.
iii Highlight sub-scale scores in the elevated and clinical ranges.

Step 4: examine the pattern and complexity of a child's difficulties

i To what extent does the score profile point to specific symptom types? Are there distinct areas of concern, or is there a lack of symptom specificity?
ii Is the profile elevated but relatively flat, suggesting complex and severe difficulties?
iii If scores from other assessment checklists are available (SDQ, CBCL, Connors), examine score profiles across combined sub-scales?
iv Compare a child's score profile (i.e. ACC only) with the gender-specific score profiles identified through cluster analysis that are presented in Figure 4.1.

Step 5: carry out a qualitative item analysis

Clinicians should also look more closely at individual item scores and score patterns to see if they communicate additional meaning that is not inferred by the scale scores. Some items may have particular or alternative meaning when considered in light of the context of children's present lives. For example, you might consider whether some items are possibly indicative of a sub-cultural orientation for an adolescent client.

Step 6: explore the child's symptomatology more closely with their caregiver

It is often preferable to ask a child's caregiver to complete the ACC or ACA in the early stages of an assessment, before carrying out a detailed caregiver interview. This helps reduce the scope for response bias arising out of any discussions between the clinician and caregiver. It also provides an opportunity for the clinician to enquire more deeply about the nature, severity and course of mental health difficulties identified in the ACC or ACA responses. Whereas the checklist format yields standardized mental health estimates, caregiver interviews can provide a more detailed picture of the severity and course of a child's difficulties, as well as more qualitative information (such as contextual influences and triggers). It is important to be mindful that checklist score profiles only estimate the severity of mental health difficulties through the number and range of symptoms, and the frequency with which they are manifested, whereas caregiver accounts can describe additional severity parameters, such as the intensity of a child's distress or misbehaviour. Depending on the length of a child's placement, a caregiver interview provides an opportunity to determine the course of his/her difficulties, e.g. do these symptoms appear to be following a long-term developmental course, or have they only been observed in recent times? Do particular symptoms appear to be statically present, or does their expression vary over time?

Step 7: context is everything!

Enquire about the ecological context in which a child is experiencing mental health difficulties, in interviews with the child, their caregivers, teachers, and other significant adults.

i. Do any symptoms appear to be reactive to specific stressors or events?
ii. Do some tend to be manifested more often in specific settings?
iii. Is there evidence that a child's mental health difficulties fluctuate in response to their level of felt security?
iv. What evidence is there of social care systemic pressures on both a child's felt security and mental health?

Some examples of systemic pressures include: the level and type of involvement of a statutory authority in a child's life; perceived impermanence; planned respite care; birth family contact; and restoration plans. For more thoughts on this topic, read Tarren-Sweeney (2010) and Simmonds (2010).

Step 8: avoid interpreting scores in isolation from other assessment data

i An ACC/ACA score profile provides only a single data source, reflecting the observations and opinions of one of a child's caregivers. It should not be solely relied upon to generate formulations;
ii Valid formulations of the mental health and well-being of children in care and those adopted from care, require comprehensive clinical psychosocial-developmental assessments;
iii Comprehensive assessments are dependent on multiple and varied sources of data, as that may include:

- other relevant psychometric data;
- clinician observations of children and families in controlled and naturalistic settings;
- interviews with a range of significant adults, i.e. caregivers, teachers, extended family and in some instances, children's birth parents;
- involving the child in a range of structured and unstructured assessment tasks, including interviews, drawing, social re-enactment through play, attachment measures, etc.;
- access to children's pre-care and in-care mental health, education, developmental and child welfare records.

Chapter 4

Attachment-related difficulties, felt insecurity and symptom complexity

The ACC provides opportunities for researchers to examine more closely the nature, patterns and complexity of mental health symptomatology experienced by children in various forms of alternate care, as well as other high risk groups. This chapter describes CICS investigations into the nature and complexity of attachment- and trauma-related difficulties, including cluster analyses of ACC and CBCL DSM-oriented scale scores.

Attachment-related difficulties of children in care

A high prevalence of social and interpersonal relationship difficulties was found among the CICS sample, both in absolute terms, and relative to other mental health concerns. The findings suggest such difficulties are a hallmark feature of the clinical presentations among a large proportion of children in care. Inhibited and disinhibited forms of attachment disturbance were hypothesised during the development of the ACC, and scales that broadly refer to these phenomena ('non-reciprocal' and 'indiscriminate' interpersonal behaviour) were derived through factor analysis. It is likely that high scores on these scales represent, in most instances, socially determined attachment-related disturbances, since sample scores on these scales were strongly predicted by children's exposure to social adversity, and their age at entry into care (Tarren-Sweeney, 2008). Nonetheless, one should be mindful that social relatedness problems among children in care may in some instances be determined more by brain injury, intellectual disability, autistic spectrum disorders or temperament (Richters and Volkmar, 1994). The author has also observed cases in which non-reciprocal interpersonal behaviour is situation-specific. For example, these difficulties may be apparent in a child's relationship with their foster parents, but not with their birth parents. The emergence of the 'pseudomature' factor had not been anticipated. This pattern of interpersonal behaviour has been described previously (Lieberman and Zeanah, 1995), but is not presently thought of as an attachment-related clinical phenomenon.

Inhibited and disinhibited attachment disorder behaviours were conceptualised as distinct sub-types of DSM-IV-TR Reactive Attachment Disorder (RAD). This distinction is maintained within the DSM-V delineation between RAD (representing the inhibited form) and Disinhibited Social Engagement Disorder (the disinhibited form). It has been suggested these types may not be symptomatically distinct (Minnis and Keck, 2003; Smyke, Dumitrescu and Zeanah, 2002), and an alternative classification of infant mental health disorders (the Diagnostic Classification: 0-3R) includes a mixed pattern of inhibition and disinhibition (Zero to Three, 2005). Among the CICS sample, there was moderate to high correlations of scores on the pseudomature, non-reciprocal, indiscriminate and insecure scales (see Table 8.4). A number of ACC-CBCL symptom profiles derived through cluster analyses (described later in this chapter) include simultaneous high scores on combinations of two to four of those scales. Furthermore, few children were reported with discrete (or pure) forms of social or interpersonal relationship difficulties. Together, this suggests that many children in care present with a complex array of attachment-related difficulties that is more correctly conceptualised as individual profiles of attachment-related difficulties, rather than discrete types of attachment disorder.

Felt insecurity in relation to attachment security and trauma-related anxiety

The meaning of high scores on the insecure scale remains somewhat uncertain, because the scale does not delineate between state and trait insecurity. Insecure and overly conforming behaviours may indicate an insecure attachment style, but equally may represent a child's adaptation to previous losses (including foster placement breakdowns). Furthermore, there are likely to be many and varied systemic pressures affecting the felt security of children in care. The CICS provided several insights into the characteristics and patterns of felt insecurity and emotional difficulties experienced by children in care. Although the ACC 'insecure' and 'anxious–distrustful' scales appear to respectively measure felt security and trauma-related anxiety, they correlated highly with the CBCL 'anxious–depressed' and 'withdrawn–depressed' sub-scales, and with the DSM-oriented 'affective problems' and 'anxiety problems scales' (see Table 8.5). However, all but one of ACC-CBCL symptom profiles derived through cluster analyses (described later in this chapter) were characterised by relatively low DSM-oriented affective problems and anxiety problems, and ACC anxious–distrustful behaviours. This was somewhat unexpected given the extent of social adversity and developmental trauma that children experience before entering care. The present findings point to the possibility that anxiety amongst children in care tends to be more strongly experienced as a component of felt insecurity (i.e. as measured by the ACC insecure scale).

Identification of symptom profile types

Cluster analysis method

Gender-specific cluster analyses were performed across six ACC scales (sexual behaviour, pseudomature interpersonal behaviour, nonreciprocal interpersonal behaviour, indiscriminate interpersonal behaviour, insecure and anxious–distrustful) and five CBCL DSM-oriented scales (affective problems, anxiety problems, attention-deficit/hyperactivity problems, oppositional defiant problems and conduct problems). While the CBCL syndrome scales have stronger empirical validity than the DSM-oriented scales, the latter were selected so that the identified clusters might be better referenced to standard classifications of child mental disorders. Importantly, there is evidence that the DSM-oriented scales effectively delineate between young people with identified discrete DSM-IV-TR disorders (Nakamura *et al.*,2009). The DSM-oriented Somatic Problems scale was excluded because few children in the present study were reported with clinical-level somatic problems. The remaining ACC scales were excluded because of the need to contain the number of variables included in the analyses (the excluded ACC scales measure less common difficulties).

The purpose of conducting the cluster analyses was to identify and delineate between characteristic clinical profiles. Scores of children who were not reported as having clinically meaningful difficulties were therefore excluded from the analyses. The inclusion criteria were having at least one score in the clinical range on any CBCL syndrome, broadband or DSM-oriented scale or on any ACC scale. This yielded scores for 236 children (128 boys, 108 girls) for the cluster analyses.

Cluster analyses were carried out in two stages to overcome some limitations presented by both hierarchical and non-hierarchical analyses (Henry *et al.*, 2005; Steele and Aylward, 2007). Exploratory cluster analysis was first performed using a hierarchical method, after which confirmatory cluster analysis was performed using a non-hierarchical method. Exploratory hierarchical cluster analyses were performed using the Ward's linkage method with Euclidean squared distance measure. It was decided that any clustering solution should exclude clusters containing fewer than five children. Non-hierarchical cluster analysis was performed using the K-Means agglomerative method with Euclidean distance measure, and randomly generated starting centres.

The exploratory analyses indicated 8- and 9-cluster solutions yielded the best number of distinct symptom profiles containing five or more children, for girls and boys respectively. The confirmatory analyses (specifying these numbers of clusters) yielded cluster sizes ranging from 5 to 22 girls and 7 to 24 boys.

Derived symptom profiles

Symptom profile types were drawn for each of the boy and girl symptom clusters, with mean cluster scores placed on a four-range severity scale. For the DSM-oriented scales, the four ranges were defined as: *normative* (T-scores < 63, representing scores that are clearly normative); *elevated* (T-scores = 63–69, representing sub-clinical scores that are less clearly normative, with the upper end encompassing the CBCL borderline clinical range); *clinically indicated* (T-scores = 70–73, the moderate end of the clinical range); and *marked clinical* (T-scores > 73, the severe end of the clinical range). For the ACC scales, existing cut-points delineating between the normative and elevated ranges and between the elevated and clinical ranges were utilised. Given a relative lack of research on the clinical meaning of high ACC scale scores, it was reasoned that assignment of scores to a marked clinical range should be conservative. Consequently, in comparison with the CBCL scales, greater proportions of the ACC score ranges were defined within the clinically indicated range, and lesser proportions within the marked clinical range. The derived symptom profiles are shown in Figure 4.1.

Both the boy and girl symptom profile types are delineated more by elevation than shape. Only a few of the profiles point to discrete, non-complex disorders. Profile 1 describes normative behaviour with elevated, sub-clinical conduct problems. Profile 2 represents an anxious–insecure type for girls, and an anxious–insecure–sexual-problems type for boys, both of which are fairly specific to these symptoms. Boy profile 3 is a relatively simple conduct/oppositional-defiant type. However, the other profile types reveal varying degrees of symptom complexity. Girl profile 3 and boy profile 4 consist of one or two clinical-level scores combined with elevated sub-clinical difficulties across most of the remaining scales. Boy profile 5 and girl profile 5 are more complex externalizing types, characterised by co-occurring interpersonal difficulties (as well as sexual behaviour problems for girls). While both profile 5s are possibly 'accommodated' within present DSM and ICD classifications, profiles 6, 7 and 8 and boy profile 9 all describe complex symptom patterns that are inadequately conceptualised within present nosology.

Complex symptomatology that is inadequately conceptualised within DSM and ICD

The cluster analyses of ACC and CBCL DSM-oriented scale scores revealed that 30 per cent of children were reported with normative difficulties; another 15 per cent had elevated, subclinical checklist scores; and around 35 per cent had relatively non-complex, clinically significant psychopathology that can be conceptualised as discrete mental disorders or comorbidity within standard classification systems.

The remaining 20 per cent of subject children were reported with complex and severe symptomatology that is not adequately conceptualised within DSM and ICD classifications of mental disorders.

The presence of hallmark social and interpersonal relationship difficulties among a large proportion of children in care, which overlays and possibly mediates children's experience of other types of symptoms, adds to symptom complexity. This complexity accounts for some surprising results. Despite a high prevalence of clinical-level DSM-oriented attention-deficit hyperactivity scores among the present sample (Tarren-Sweeney and Hazell, 2006), an ADHD profile type was not located for either gender. Instead, the findings suggest that clinically significant inattention/over-activity is largely manifested as a component of complex symptomatology that includes social impairments. Similarly, a lack of symptom specificity precluded the presence of the CBCL dysregulation profile among the CICS sample.

The psychopathology described by the most complex and elevated symptom profiles mirrors somewhat the diagnostic criteria and clinical presentations of Bessel van der Kolk and colleagues' proposed Developmental Trauma Disorder (DTD) (D'Andrea *et al.*, 2012; van der Kolk, 2005). Notably, the present study sample had almost universal exposure to severe and chronic social adversity and trauma prior to their entry into care. The present findings partially support the rationale for introducing DTD or a similar construct into DSM and ICD classification systems, in that these findings demonstrate that DTD provides a more accurate conceptualization of complex attachment- and trauma-related psychopathology than that provided by existing taxonomies. However, the present findings caution against thinking of Developmental Trauma Disorder, or complex symptomatology in general, as discrete, symptom-specific, clinical phenomena; suggesting instead the need for a *symptom profile approach* to clinical formulation.

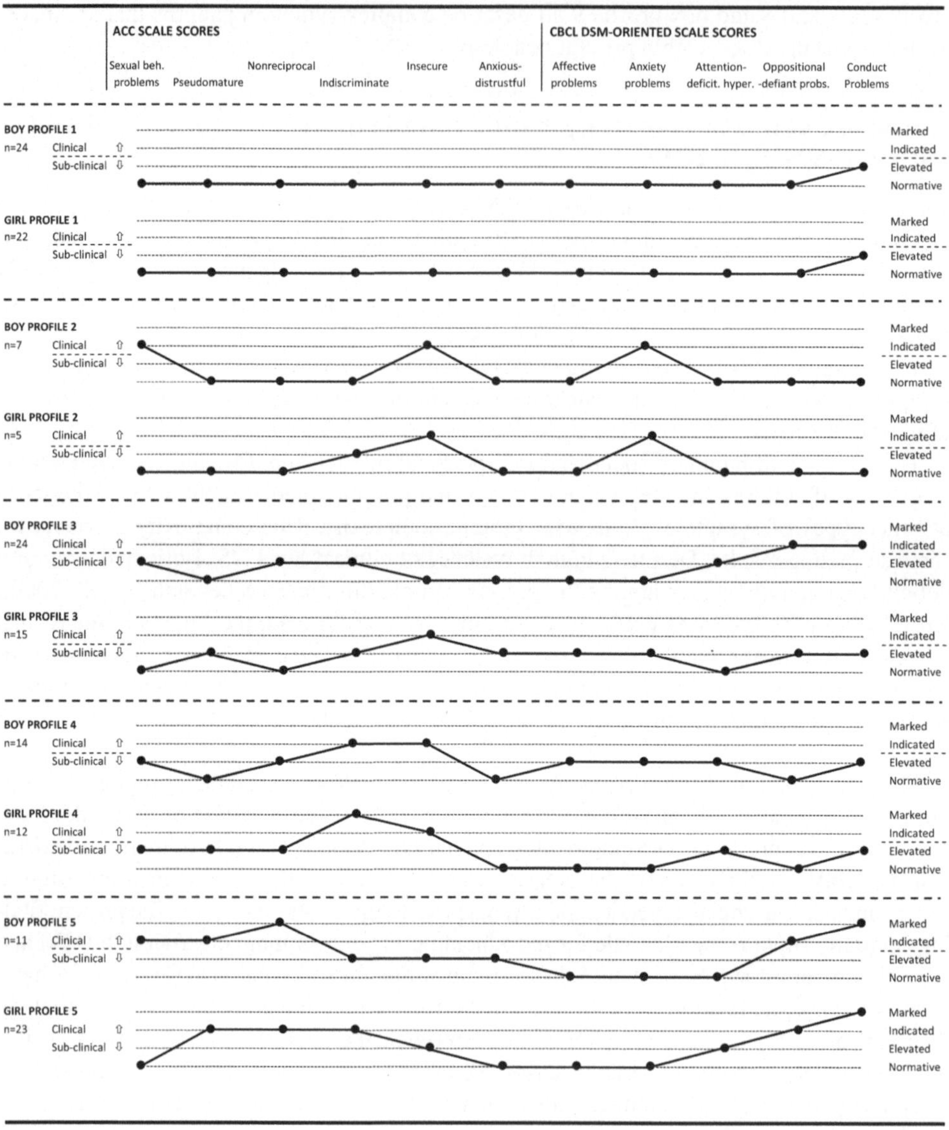

Figure 4.1 Symptom profile types derived from cluster analyses of ACC and CBCL DSM-oriented scale scores

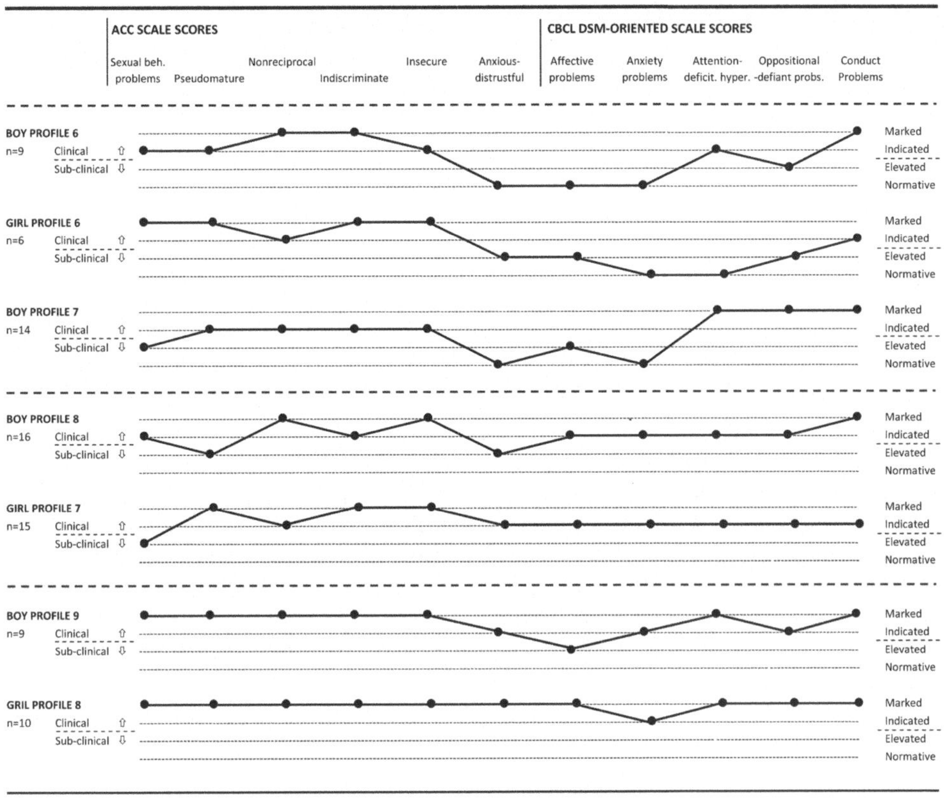

Figure 4.1 continued

No basis for a new taxonomy of complex attachment- and trauma-related disorders

There are some distinct differences between the derived symptom profiles that merit further research, and which suggest new ways of conceptualising complex attachment- and trauma-related disorders. Beyond this however, the profiles do not provide a basis for a taxonomy of complex attachment- and trauma-related disorders. The clusters are differentiated more by profile elevation than profile shape or pattern, suggesting an absence of typology. Furthermore, whilst the present cluster analyses yielded statistically delineated symptom profile types, their clinical distinctness is questionable. Close inspection of children's individual score profiles shows a lack of clear delineation between the derived profile types, and considerable variability between children's symptom profiles. This implies that any taxonomy of complex attachment- and trauma-related disorders is likely to have poor specificity. It may be that the much of the symptomatology identified in the CICS is too complex, and shows too much variability across children's individual profiles, to allow for traditional classification.

Chapter 5

Sexual behaviour problems

While the nature and distribution of SBP among pre-adolescent children is becoming clearer to researchers, the developmental mechanisms that account for it are largely unknown. A recent taskforce defined SBP among pre-adolescent children as sexual behaviour that is developmentally inappropriate (i.e. age-inappropriate) or potentially harmful to the self or others (Chaffin *et al.*, 2008). This includes behaviour of a sexual nature that infringes on the rights of others (such as use of coercion or force), and that which is indicative of emotional distress (Silovsky and Niec, 2002). The task of defining SBP has been made easier by identification of normative child sexual behaviour within age and gender groupings, using standardized measures such as the Child Sexual Behavior Inventory (Friedrich *et al.* 1998; Friedrich and Grambsch, 1992). Among children at large, the frequency of caregiver-reported sexual behaviours peaks at around age 5, after which it steadily declines throughout childhood, before re-emerging in adolescence. Normative sexual behaviour, especially in early childhood, consists mainly of self-stimulating behaviours, exposing private parts, and intrusion of personal boundaries (Friedrich *et al.*, 1998). Conversely, intrusive or coercive sexual behaviour is uncommon among children in general.

The ACC sexual behaviour scale

Why was the ACC designed to measure problematic sexual behaviour? First it was realised that the CBCL's five sexual behaviour items do not adequately describe the range of SBP observed among children in care. A second consideration was a need to restrict the length of the survey questionnaire so as to not overwhelm potential respondents. This ruled against using an additional instrument to measure sexual behaviour, such as the Child Sexual Behavior Inventory (CSBI) (Friedrich, 1997), or the Child Sexual Behavior Checklist (CSBCL) (Johnson, 1993). The results of a US normative study of child sexual behaviour, using the CSBI, helped identify normative behaviours that should be excluded from the ACC (Friedrich *et al.*, 1998). Fifteen nominal SBP items were written for a 132-item research version of the ACC. Following item and factor analyses, nine items were allocated to a SBP sub-scale, one item was assigned to another sub-scale, two items were retained as 'other items', and three items were discarded. Factor loadings and score distributions for the 15 ACC nominal items are listed in Table 5.1, and sexual behaviour scale scores distributions are listed in Table 5.2.

Table 5.1 ACC nominal sexual behaviour items: factor loadings (n=412) and CICS item score distributions (n=347)

	Factor[a] loading	*Item-rest[a] r*	*Mean item score[b]*			*Proportion scoring 0, 1 or 2[b]*					
			Boys n=176	*Girls n=171*	*p < .05*	*Boys*			*Girls*		
						0	1	2	0	1	2
Items assigned to sexual behaviour sub-scale											
describes or imitates sexual behaviour	.68	.70	.14	.21		90%	7%	3%	85%	8%	7%
'flirts' with strangers	.49	.55	.13	.38	< .001	90%	6%	4%	74%	14%	12%
forces or pressures children into sexual acts	.80	.65	.06	.11		94%	5%	1%	92%	5%	3%
kisses with open mouth	.57	.52	.03	.19	< .001	97%	3%	0%	88%	6%	6%
sexual behaviour not appropriate for age	.72	.71	.15	.26		90%	5%	5%	84%	6%	10%
shows sex parts to children (other than siblings)	.51	.46	.13	.10		89%	9%	2%	93%	5%	2%
starts 'rude' conversations, tells jokes about sex	.37	.45	.15	.15		88%	9%	3%	88%	9%	3%
touches or puts mouth on other person's sex parts	.69	.51	.02	.06		99%	0.6%	0.6%	95%	4%	1%
tries to involve others in sexual behaviour	.86	.75	.09	.16		93%	5%	2%	89%	6%	5%
Item assigned to another scale											
hugs men (other than relatives or male caregivers)	.33		.19	.40							
Retained as 'other items'											
masturbates at home in view of others			.13	.14							
masturbates at school, or in public			.05	.06							
Discarded items											
inserts object into anus or vagina			.02	.03							
shows sex parts to adults other than caregivers			.02	.01							
touches or puts mouth on animal's sex parts			.01	.02							

[a] Factor loading on sexual behaviour factor, and item-rest correlation (correlation of the SB item score and the sum of all other items in the SB scale) for 10-factor model, n=412.

[b] Mean sexual behaviour item scores and proportions of CICS baseline sample scoring 0, 1 or 2 on sexual behaviour sub-scale items, n=347

Table 5.2 Distributions of ACC sexual behaviour sub-scale scores (n=347)

	Mean	SD	*Proportion (%) in score range* 0	1–2	3–4	5–6	7+
Boys (n=176)	0.9	2.1	70	18	5	3	4
Girls (n=171)	1.6	3.2	63	16	9	4	8
Total	1.3	2.7	66	17	7	4	6

What accounts for child sexual behaviour problems?

Early studies of sexually offending youth found that coercive sexual behaviour was strongly correlated with sexual and physical abuse, as well as with broader indicators of family dysfunction (Fehrenbach *et al.*, 1986; Kahn and Lafond, 1988). However, the developmental pathways of such youth may differ to that of children and young people with SBP who do not proceed to sexual offending. Importantly then, a number of contemporary studies have identified correlates and independent predictors of SBP among population and treatment samples of youth and pre-adolescent children, without reference to offending status (Adams and McClellan, 1995; Friedrich, 2005; Friedrich *et al.*, 2003; Gray *et al.*, 1999; Letourneau *et al.*, 2004; Silovsky and Niec, 2002).

A strong link between child sexual abuse (CSA) and SBP has been found among diverse groups of children, including maltreated (Cosentino *et al.*, 1995; Friedrich *et al.*, 2001; Friedrich and Grambsch, 1992; Mian *et al.*, 1996; White *et al.*, 1988), forensic (Burton, 2000) and clinic-referred (Adams and McClellan, 1995) populations, as well as among children at large (Friedrich *et al.*, 2003). The specificity of the relationship between SBP and CSA has been a major focus of research, with particular reference to the reliability of SBP as a marker for CSA (Drach, Wientzen, and Ricci, 2001). There is some evidence that CSA influences sexual behaviour and sexual relationships into adulthood (Paolucci *et al.*, 2001). Several reviews have concluded that CSA is specifically harmful to children's mental health, relationship capacity and sexual development (Kendall-Tackett *et al.*, 1993; Putnam, 2003; World Health Organization, 2002). Yet, CSA was found to predict only a moderate proportion of the variance in SBP among a large population sample (Friedrich *et al.*, 2003). Given the secrecy surrounding CSA, it is difficult to obtain valid estimates of children's exposure. If there is a direct and strong relationship between CSA and SBP, then research estimates of the effect size will be diluted by undetected CSA (Friedrich *et al.*, 2005b; Ricci *et al.*, 2005).

Other identified correlates of SBP can be construed under broad categories of child maltreatment, indicators of family dysfunction and parenting difficulties, developmental difficulties and age-inappropriate exposure to sexually explicit behaviour and knowledge. Beyond CSA, the most cited maltreatment correlate of SBP is physical abuse (Friedrich *et al.*, 2003; Gray *et al.*, 1999; Letourneau *et al.*, 2004; Silovsky and Niec, 2002). There is evidence of a relationship between physical abuse and the development of coercive/aggressive sexual offending behaviour (Becker, 1998; Benoit and Kennedy, 1992). However, not all SBP is coercive, and research designs rarely control for potential confounders of physical abuse (including CSA). In a study that did control for several key confounders, physical abuse independently predicted SBP (Friedrich *et al.*, 2003). One other form of maltreatment that has been identified as a correlate of SBP is exposure to (i.e. witnessing) parental violence (Friedrich *et al.*, 2003; Gray *et al.*, 1999; Silovsky and Niec,

2002). The relationship between SBP and physical neglect and emotional deprivation is less certain. A study of the caregiving provided to a small sample of children with SBP found that most children encountered emotional conditions that were likely to engender attachment problems (Pithers *et al.*, 1998). However, the study design failed to control for children's exposure to other social adversity, including known correlates of SBP.

A number of studies have reported associations between SBP and indicators of family dysfunction, poverty, parental stress, parental substance abuse and other social adversity (Friedrich *et al.*, 2003; Silovsky and Niec, 2002). Further research is needed to establish the meaning of these findings, specifically whether such conditions have a proximal influence on SBP, or are markers for other influences. SBP is also associated with early, age-inappropriate exposure to sexual behaviour or knowledge, such as witnessing parental sex and pornography (Friedrich *et al.*, 2003).

The mechanisms accounting for the correlates of SBP have been largely speculative. There is ample evidence that CSA is traumatic (World Health Organization, 2002), and that the severity of children's psychopathology and SBP co-vary (Bonner and Walker, 1999). This suggests the possibility of a trauma or dissociative mechanism leading to SBP. Additionally, much SBP is intrusive and coercive, resulting in sexual infringement against other people. The development of coercive sexual behaviours might thus involve similar biological, learning and attachment mechanisms to that which links child physical abuse to physically coercive behaviour (Cicchetti *et al.*, 2000; Lewis, 1992; Patterson *et al.*, 1989). Friedrich (2007) also speculated about the operation of an attachment mechanism acting as a mediator between trauma and sexual behaviour, noting similarities between behavioural styles employed by children with SBP, and maladaptive behavioural patterns postulated by Crittenden's (1997) dynamic-maturational model of attachment. More might be learned about the mechanisms that account for SBP among children with complex exposure to maltreatment and other adversity, including children in care. Children typically enter care with complex maltreatment histories, including multiple notifications of various types of harm including CSA (Jellinek *et al.*, 1995; Kalland and Sinkkonen, 2001; Klee *et al.*, 1997). Prior to the Children in Care study there was good evidence that children in care manifest a high rate of SBP (Baker *et al.*, 2007; Friedrich *et al.*, 2005a; Smith and Howard, 1994), especially among children and youth in residential care (Farmer and Pollock, 2003).

What was learned about child sexual behaviour problems in the Children in Care study?

About a third of children were reported as manifesting at least some problematic sexual behaviour. Girls had significantly higher mean SBP scores than boys (1.6 versus 0.9, $p = 0.01$). SBP scores were also slightly and positively correlated with children's ages ($r = 0.17$, $p = 0.002$). The rate of concordance for the presence ($n = 39$) versus absence ($n = 13$) of any SBP (i.e. scores above zero) among 52 sibling dyads was 75 per cent (Chi2 = 13.4, $p = 0.0003$). Among 39 concordant pairs, 27 were concordant for absence and 12 were concordant for presence of SBP. The odds ratio for reported SBP among a younger sibling if SBP was reported for their older sibling was 14.7 (95% CI: 2.5 – 147.8). There was also moderate within-pairs rank correlation of continuous SBP scores (Spearman's rho = 0.58, $p<0.0001$).

There was moderate correlation of the sexual behaviour scale with ACC scores measuring various types of interpersonal/attachment difficulties, as well as with the CBCL externalising sub-scales (see Table 5.3). The proportions of children with SBP scores above

Table 5.3 Correlation of ACC sexual behaviour scores with other mental health sub-scale scores

ACC sub-scales	*R*	*CBCL sub-scales*	*R*
Pseudomature	.50	Anxious–depressed	.29
Non-reciprocal	.53	Withdrawn–depressed	.35
Indiscriminate	.51	Somatic complaints	.27
Insecure	.43	Social problems	.39
Anxious–distrustful	.46	Thought problems	.46
Abnormal pain response	.31	Attention problems	.33
Food maintenance	.26	Rule-breaking behaviour	.55
Self-injury	.23	Aggressive behaviour	.41
Suicide discourse	.26		
Negative self-image	.36	Internalising	.36
Low confidence	.31	Externalising	.48
Total ACC score -SBP[a]	.58	Total CBCL score	.49

[a] Total ACC score minus the sexual behaviour score

two (n = 57) having total CBCL and ACC scores in the clinical range were 89% and 93% respectively. The equivalent proportions of the aggregate sample with total scores in the clinical range were 48% (CBCL) and 45% (ACC). Very similar correlations were found within the unique observations sub-sample.

Factors found to be strongly associated with SBP scores included children's age at entry into care, their estimated length of time exposed to maltreatment, the ratio of time in present placement/time in care (a measure of placement stability), several measures of care status and permanency, and confirmed exposure to contact sexual abuse. According to Cohen's criteria (1988), most effect sizes were moderate. Some notable factors not associated with SBP scores were type of care (kinship versus foster care), reported intellectual disability, non-contact sexual abuse and most other forms of abuse and neglect, including physical abuse and witnessing parental violence. Very similar effect sizes were found with the unique observations sub-sample.

The relationship between the timing of sexual abuse exposure and present sexual behaviour was examined, in light of prior suggestions that the association between CSA and SBP is stronger among recently abused children (Putnam, 2003). Among children with a confirmed history of contact sexual abuse (n = 33), there was moderate rank correlation between their SBP score and age when last known abuse occurred (Spearman's rho = 0.49, $p<0.004$), and moderate inverse rank correlation between their SBP score and *time elapsed since that event* (Spearman's rho = -0.59, $p<0.001$).

Independent predictors of ACC sexual behaviour problems

The Children in Care study identified concurrent and retrospectively-measured correlates of SBP from a large number of potential risk factors. Independent predictors of clinically meaningful SBP were identified in a two-step hierarchical logistic regression model. Further to the two-step hierarchical logistic regression model, a three-step analysis was conducted to explore relationships between sexual behaviour and scales that are suggestive of attachment difficulties, while controlling for potential confounders. The results of the hierarchical linear regression analyses are listed in Table 5.4. The model accounted for 20% of the SBP

Table 5.4 Predictors of sexual behaviour problems: two- and three-step hierarchical logistic regression models for aggregate (n=347) and unique observation (n=281) samples[a]

Hierarchical logistic regression model	*Aggregate sample (n=347)*			*Unique observation sample (n=281)*		
	Odds ratio	*95% C.I.*	*P value*	*Odds ratio*	*95% C.I.*	*P value*
STEP 1						
Developmental factors						
Age	1.0	(0.8–1.3)	0.81	0.9	(0.7–1.2)	0.43
Female gender	2.0	(1.0–3.9)	0.04	2.0	(1.0–4.3)	0.06
Reported reading difficulty	1.5	(0.8–2.9)	0.23	1.5	(0.7–3.1)	0.30
Pre-care factors						
Length of exposure to maltreatment[b]	0.9	(0.8–1.1)	0.42	1.0	(0.8–1.2)	0.74
Contact sexual abuse[c]	3.9	(1.6–9.3)	0.002	3.2	(1.2–8.3)	0.02
Non-contact sexual abuse[d]	0.7	(0.1–6.3)	0.78	0.9	(0.1–8.9)	0.96
Verbal assault or threat	0.9	(0.4–1.9)	0.78	0.9	(0.4–2.1)	0.84
Classic emotional abuse[e]	1.2	(0.6–2.4)	0.76	1.1	(0.5–2.5)	0.80
Exposure to domestic violence	0.6	(0.3–1.2)	0.65	0.6	(0.3–1.3)	0.21
Physical abuse	1.0	(0.5–2.1)	0.99	0.9	(0.4–2.1)	0.89
Inadequate supervision	0.7	(0.3–1.4)	0.32	0.7	(0.3–1.5)	0.36
Other physical neglect	1.4	(0.7–2.8)	0.39	1.2	(0.5–2.6)	0.68
Inadequate nurturance[f]	1.2	(0.6–2.4)	0.66	1.4	(0.6–3.1)	0.38
N. temp placements before entry into care	1.1	(0.9–1.3)	0.33	1.0	(0.8–1.2)	0.92
Age at entry into care	1.4	(1.1–1.7)	0.001	1.5	(1.2–1.9)	0.001
Adjusted R squared for Step 1		0.16			0.16	
STEP 2						
In-care factors						
Foster versus kinship care	0.5	(0.2–1.6)	0.24	0.2	(0.1–1.2)	0.08
Time in placement/time in care	0.3	(0.1–1.0)	0.05	0.3	(0.1–0.9)	0.03
Care order expires < age 16	1.0	(0.4–2.5)	0.92	0.7	(0.2–1.9)	0.47
Caregiver uncertain about restoration	2.1	(1.0–4.7)	0.06	3.1	(1.3–7.7)	0.01
N. adverse events in last year	1.2	(0.9–1.6)	0.18	1.1	(0.8–1.6)	0.52
Poor caregiver health	0.9	(0.3–3.4)	0.94	1.5	(0.4–5.8)	0.59
Increase in adjusted R squared (Step 1 to 2)		0.04			0.07	
Adjusted R squared for 2-step model		0.20			0.23	
STEP 3						
ACC interpersonal behaviour sub-scale scores						
Pseudomature	1.0	(0.9–1.2)	0.68	1.0	(0.9-1.2)	0.87
Non-reciprocal	1.2	(1.1–1.4)	< 0.0001	1.3	(1.1–1.4)	< 0.0001
Indiscriminate	1.3	(1.1–1.5)	< 0.0001	1.3	(1.1–1.6)	< 0.0001
Increase in adjusted R squared		0.25			0.24	
Adjusted R squared for 3-step model		0.45			0.47	

[a] Two- and three-step logistic regression models. Outcome variable is a dichotomous transformation of the ACC sexual behaviour score, namely: score 0-2 versus score > 2

[b] Length of time exposed to maltreatment: time from 1st confirmed notification to entry into care

[c] Any form of sexual abuse involving physical contact, including penetrative sexual abuse and non-penetrative genital contact

[d] Excludes children who have also been exposed to contact sexual abuse (i.e. hierarchical exposure)

[e] Emotional abuse other than threats or verbal assaults, e.g. scapegoating

[f] Refers mainly to early developmental neglect, such as resulting in non-organic failure to thrive

dichotomous score variance, with steps 1 and 2 accounting for 16% and 4% of the variance respectively. By contrast, linear regression modelling predicted 31% of the variance of each of the ACC and CBCL total scores (Tarren-Sweeney, 2008). The analysis for the aggregate sample identified four independent predictors of SBP scores above 2, namely older age at entry into care (O.R. = 1.4, p = 0.001), contact sexual abuse (O.R. = 3.9, p = 0.002), female gender (O.R. = 2.0, p = 0.04) and lower ratio of time in present placement/time in care (a measure of placement stability) (O.R. = 0.34, p = 0.05). The exploratory three-step logistic regression, which added the pseudomature, non-reciprocal and indiscriminate ACC sub-scale scores, accounted for an additional 25% per cent of the dichotomous score variance (i.e. 45 per cent in total). This model suggests that the moderate relationships between SBP and non-reciprocal and indiscriminate interpersonal behaviour problems are independent of other variables. As anticipated, most key variables were inter-correlated, confirming the need to account for confounding among children exposed to complex adversity. Only 20 per cent of the SBP dichotomous score variance was accounted for in the two-step regression model, and most associated variables were not independent predictors.

Possible mechanisms for development of sexual behaviour problems among children in care

Gender

In the CICS there were large gender differences in item score distributions, with girls scoring more often than boys on 7 of the 9 SBP sub-scale items. Girls had significantly higher mean SBP scores than boys (1.6 versus 0.9, p = 0.01). The finding that girls in this high-risk pre-adolescent sample had higher SBP scores than boys was intriguing. Friedrich *et al.* (2003) did not find a gender effect in their normative study of pre-adolescent SBP. The CICS result seems consistent with the higher reported incidence of contact sexual abuse among subject girls (McClellan *et al.*, 1997). However, female gender strongly predicted SBP scores, even after controlling for sexual abuse. SBP among high-risk girls might possibly be linked to acculturation and attachment development in the face of severe deprivation and abuse. Boys and girls also presented with different patterns of disturbance in interpersonal behaviour (Tarren-Sweeney and Hazell, 2006). The CICS data suggest that, given similar early adverse experiences, boys in care are more likely to develop emotionally withdrawn, inhibited attachment responses, and abnormal responses to pain, while girls are more likely to develop controlling, pseudomature attachment behaviour and sexual behaviour problems (Tarren-Sweeney and Hazell, 2006). An alternative explanation is that the ACC could be biased towards measurement of SBP that is more commonly manifested by girls, while failing to measure sexual behaviours that are more commonly reported among boys (such as aggressive sexual behaviours).

Cumulative exposure to adversity

In the CICS, age at entry into care was a strong independent pre-care predictor of children's SBP scores, as it was of mental health in general (Tarren-Sweeney, 2008). For chronically deprived and maltreated children, their age at entry into care provides an approximation of their length of exposure to adversity. This does not imply that all children endured chronic maltreatment and deprivation from birth. However, the child protection histories of subject children suggest the vast majority resided in dysfunctional family environments for most of their pre-care lives. It should be remembered that these children represent the most seriously and chronically maltreated children in the state.

Whereas a single harmful event may have life-altering consequences for children at large, the impact of individual events is tempered among children exposed to chronic and multiple adversities. A number of researchers have reported that broad indicators of exposure to maltreatment, family conflict and other psychosocial risk factors account for a greater proportion of the variance in children's mental health, than exposure to specific types or single instances of harm (Fergusson and Lynskey, 1996; Rutter, 1999). The CICS findings suggest this may also be true for SBP. Aside from contact sexual abuse, no specific form of abuse or neglect predicted children's SBP. Indeed, the only other maltreatment-related variable associated with children's SBP continuous scores was the time between their first confirmed notification and their entry into care, which is perhaps a crude indicator of cumulative exposure to adversity. Furthermore, several factors previously identified as correlates of SBP were not associated with SBP scores in the CICS sample, notably physical abuse and witnessing parental violence.

At first glance, the positive correlation between age and SBP scores found in the CICS contradicts prior findings that sexual behaviour is more conspicuous among younger preadolescent children (Bonner and Walker, 1999; Friedrich *et al.*, 2001, 2003). However, the CICS age effect is probably illusory, accounted for by children's age at entry into care. Older children were more likely to have entered care later, with greater cumulative exposure to adversity. Similarly, the moderate recency effect found in the relationship between contact sexual abuse and problematic sexual behaviour was at least partially confounded by children's age at entry into care. Although children who were sexually abused before age 3 showed almost no SBP, they mostly entered care shortly after the abuse occurred.

An alternative explanation for these findings would be afforded by a higher rate of undetected sexual abuse among late arrivers into care. Although the rate of undetected abuse cannot be estimated, the rate of confirmed sexual abuse (12 per cent) was rather low for such a high-risk population. My own clinical experience is that children in care often first disclose pre-care sexual abuse many years after entering care.

Attachment difficulties

Aside from sexual behaviour, SBP has a strong interpersonal dimension, reflecting maladaptive socialization. Children in care are particularly prone to poor socialization and relationship disturbances, in the wake of early attachment difficulties (Fonagy, 2003; Howe and Fearnley, 2003; Minnis *et al.*, 2006; O'Connor and Rutter, 2000). As mentioned earlier in this chapter, Friedrich (2007) theorised that attachment difficulties underlie the development of SBP. Although his attachment-focused intervention was based on this premise, there has been a lack of data to support this theory. Furthermore, the variant of attachment theory that these ideas are based around (the dynamic-maturational model) remains largely untested. However, the CICS findings provide some empirical support for a proximal relationship between attachment and SBP. Children's SBP scores correlated strongly (around $r = .50$) with ACC sub-scales measuring pseudomature, nonreciprocal and indiscriminate interpersonal behaviour. Furthermore, logistic regression modelling suggests these close relationships are not confounded by other factors. Although it remains uncertain as to how closely these scales reflect either attachment insecurity or attachment disorder behaviours, at this point it is useful to consider some possible mechanisms linking attachment difficulties to the development of SBP. It should be emphasised that the following discussion is speculative, referring to generated, rather than tested hypotheses.

The non-reciprocal sub-scale measures an avoidant, disengaged and non-empathic relationship style. It is speculated that high scores on this scale approximate the inhibited form of DSM-IV Reactive Attachment Disorder (American Psychiatric Association, 2000), which possibly represents a severe manifestation of attachment disorganization (Howe, 2003; van Ijzendoorn and Bakermans-Kranenburg, 2003). This scale correlates moderately with CBCL rule-breaking behaviour, as well as SBP. These findings suggest that low empathy in the context of attachment disturbance may contribute to the development of SBP among high-risk children.

The indiscriminate sub-scale measures over-familiarity and absence of discrimination and personal boundaries in social relationships, which parallels a disturbance of non-attachment commonly observed among emotionally deprived children (O'Connor *et al.*, 1999). It is speculated that high scores on this scale approximate the disinhibited form of DSM-IV Reactive Attachment Disorder, as well as the proposed DSM-V Disinhibited Social Engagement Disorder. It is not inconceivable that this type of attachment disturbance could be manifested as sexualised indiscriminate affection. We might also speculate whether, in the absence of meaningful attachments, such children might have difficulty in discriminating between non-sexual and sexualised affection. This might be especially so if they have been sexually abused.

The pseudomature sub-scale measures a pattern of aberrant interpersonal behaviour marked by precocious pseudo-maturity and controlling behaviour, and an element of parent-child role-reversal. It has been suggested that this pattern represents an additional form of attachment disturbance (Lieberman and Zeanah, 1995), or using alternative conceptualization, a maladaptive attachment strategy (e.g. Type A5-6 of the dynamic-maturational model) (Crittenden, 2006). Pseudo-maturity and associated role reversal has been previously linked to SBP (White *et al.*, 1988). Much SBP is problematic because it is highly age-inappropriate. The behaviour is deviant because it is developmentally harmful for the child. Yet, precocious, pseudo-mature children attempt to maintain an adult lifestyle. This might in some instances be precipitated or facilitated by sexual abuse by an adult, or by family conditions in which the child assumes responsibility for the care of their parents and/or siblings (role reversal). The pseudomature profile also entails controlling behaviours, consistent with intrusive SBP. It can thus be hypothesised that precocious pseudo-maturity represents one pathway to SBP among children with attachment difficulties. However, the CICS findings provide only limited support for this hypothesis. The pseudomature sub-scale score did not independently predict SBP, suggesting it was confounded by other variables.

Chapter 6

Abnormal pain response

Over several decades of working with children in care, caregivers have often told me that their foster child shows little or no sign of pain following accidents or injuries. This is not limited to instances when a child is emotionally aroused, such as when they are fighting with another child. These children's responses to injury seem different to that of the stoic child, who shows some initial recognition of pain, but then grits her teeth and suffers in silence. On several occasions I have witnessed such behaviour among children that I am assessing, while colleagues sometimes refer to abnormal pain responses in clinical assessment reports and case presentations of children in care. Yet, such a phenomenon has not been described in the literature. The present chapter describes exploratory findings of abnormal pain response in the Children in Care study, as measured by the ACC. The term Abnormal Pain Response (APR) is used to refer to any observable behaviour or self-reported experience suggestive of abnormal experiences, tolerance or communication of pain.

The diversity of children's pain experiences

Pain arises through interactions of physiologic, genetic and psychosocial mechanisms (Cheng *et al.* 2003). The pain experience is generated within a complex neural network, of which sensory neural inputs are but one component (Melzack, 1999). While neural pain pathways are programmed by genetics and sensory conditions, they are further shaped by subjective interpretation of pain-inducing events, as well as one's emotional state and stress-regulation systems (Melzack, 1999). The experience of pain thus shapes children's subsequent pain experiences (Cheng *et al.*, 2003). For example, neonates exposed to repeated painful interventions undergo neuroplastic alteration of central pain pathways (Woolf and Salter, 2000), resulting in higher sensitivity to pain during childhood and adolescence (Hermann *et al.*, 2006).

Behavioural responses to pain need not equate to felt experience. Pain responses that appear abnormal to caregivers may in some cases reflect very high or low pain tolerance, or failure to effectively communicate felt pain. Children at large show sizeable variation in pain tolerance; that is, the level of pain they are able or willing to tolerate (Demyttenaere *et al.*, 2001). Children with high pain tolerance include those who are characteristically stoic and those who show situation-specific endurance (e.g. in the company of peers, on the sports field or when they know the pain will be brief).

Developmental influences

Aside from studies of children with painful medical conditions and those exposed to painful medical procedures, there have only been a few studies reporting abnormal responses to pain among children. These are mostly restricted to children with specific neurological or developmental impairments. In a study of 145 children with borderline to profound intellectual disability, half of the respondent parents thought that their child experienced pain differently to non-impaired children, with most of these believing their child had less sensitivity to, and higher tolerance for pain (Fanurik *et al*, 1999). Pain insensitivity has also been reported among small case series of children in foster care with foetal alcohol syndrome (Gardner, 2000), and hyperphagic short stature (or psychosocial dwarfism) (Money, 1977; Money *et al.*, 1972). Pain insensitivity is also reportedly characteristic of children with autism (American Psychiatric Association, 2000), with speculation that this is due to excess production of endogenous opioid (Gillberg, 1995). However, it isn't clear whether such children feel pain differently to others, or whether they are just unable to communicate felt pain using recognizable behaviours. A recent study lends support to the latter hypothesis, finding that children with autism experience pain as acutely as do other children, but their parents have difficulty recognizing this pain (Nader *et al.,* 2004). This could be pertinent to children in care, a quarter of who have some degree of intellectual disability (Tarren-Sweeney, 2008).

The influence of early psychological trauma on children's pain experiences has particular relevance to an investigation of APR among children in care. There is some evidence that maltreated children experience more painful somatic complaints (such as recurrent abdominal pain) than other children (Haugaard, 2004). Abnormal pain responses among adult clinical samples have also been linked to retrospectively-reported childhood trauma. Child sexual abuse (CSA) is possibly associated with chronic pain in adulthood, with depression being a likely mediating mechanism (Arnow, 2004). Several studies have identified increased frequency and severity of pain among adult survivors of childhood maltreatment who have post-traumatic stress disorder (PTSD), (Asmundson *et al.*, 2004; Heckman and Westefeld, 2006).

The present review did not locate any reference to reduced pain sensitivity among children who have been maltreated or who experienced other psychological trauma. However, several studies describe associations between self-reported childhood trauma and pain insensitivity among adult clinical groups (Claes *et al.*, 2006). Pain insensitivity has been measured among adult clinical populations that have high prevalence of self-injury, specifically Borderline Personality Disorder (Bohus *et al.*, 2000; Schmahl *et al.*, 2006) and eating disorders (especially bulimia) (Claes *et al.*, 2003). Among both groups, associations have been found between the level of insensitivity to pain from self-injury, and self-reported emotional difficulties, dissociative symptoms and exposure to childhood trauma (Claes *et al.*, 2003; Russ *et al*, 1993).

Development of an abnormal pain response scale

ACC content was derived though a combination of inductive and deductive procedures. Several items referring to APR were identified: from a review of 110 assessment reports sourced from psychological records of 50 children in care and other child welfare clients; and by respondents to a state-wide survey of clinicians who work with children in care. An *abnormal pain response* factor was identified in various rotations of a principal components factor analysis of ACC scores for 412 children in court-ordered care in NSW. Five items were notionally assigned to an APR scale. The strongest loading item was ‘does not show pain if physically hurt’. The weakest loading item, ‘risks physical safety, fearless’, loaded almost as strongly (0.35) on a ‘non-reciprocal interpersonal behaviour’ factor. Since there are several mechanisms that might account for fearless and reckless behaviour, it is possibly more a marker than an expression of APR. Hence it was excluded from the APR scale for conceptual reasons. The four items that constitute the APR scale are listed with factor loadings in Table 6.1. The APR scale displays reasonable internal consistency (Cronbach’s alpha = 0.70) relative to its small item set.

Clinical reasoning was employed to identify clinically significant APR scores within the possible range of 0 to 8. It was reasoned that scores in the range of 0 to 2 do not confirm an abnormal response to pain, since it is feasible that some of the items at times measure behaviours that are not APR. For example, ‘does not cry’ may sometimes measure inhibited attachment behaviour, or even social norms. Conversely, it is reasonable to expect that children with clinically significant APR need not score on each of the four items. For example, not all children with APR will laugh when injured. The distributions of item scores for boys versus girls revealed some interesting findings. On three of the four items, identical proportions of boys and girls scored 2. However, on the same items, one and a half to two times more boys than girls scored 1. It is possible that boys are more likely to suppress their communication of felt pain because of society’s construction of masculinity (i.e. ‘boys don’t cry’). If there was a real gender difference in the experience of pain, then that difference should also be apparent in the proportions of boys and girls scoring 2. It was thus reasoned that elevated ranges for girls and boys be defined as scores of 3–4 and 4 respectively, and the clinical range as scores of 5 and above for both genders. This provides two definitions of APR caseness, namely scores at and above the elevated and clinical cut-points.

Table 6.1 ACC abnormal pain response items: factor loadings and item score distributions

	Factor[a] *loading*	*Item-rest*[a] *r*	*Mean item score*[b]		*Proportion scoring 0, 1 or 2*[b]					
			Boys (n=176)	*Girls* (n=171)	*Boys*			*Girls*		
					0	**1**	**2**	**0**	**1**	**2**
does not cry	.52	.45	.35	.26	73%	19%	8%	81%	11%	8%
does not show pain if physically hurt	.76	.68	.23	.17	82%	13%	5%	88%	7%	5%
laughs when injured or hurt	.56	.38	.24	.15	81%	14%	5%	88%	10%	2%
won’t say when physically hurt	.58	.47	.18	.15	85%	12%	3%	89%	8%	3%

[a] Item loading on APR factor, and item-rest correlation (correlation of the item score and the sum of all other items in the scale) for factor analysis sample (N=412)

[b] Mean item scores and proportions of CICS baseline sample (N=347) scoring 0, 1 or 2 on the abnormal pain response items

Subsequently defined ad hoc measures

Subsequent to conducting the CICS, a number of ad hoc scales of mental health and developmental constructs were formed from CBCL and ACC items (including some items subsequently deleted from the ACC), to allow for exploratory analyses of relationships between these constructs and APR. Clinical reasoning and research literature guided the selection of these constructs, and assignment of items. Ad hoc scales were constructed to measure 'dissociation from reality' (5 items), 'impulsivity/recklessness' (4 items), 'low empathy/cruelty' (5 items), 'self-injury' (6 items), 'trance-amnesic type dissociation' (5 items) and 'inhibited-avoidant attachment spectrum' (7 items). In relation to the latter scale, items were selected to measure a range of socially inhibited, withdrawn and avoidant behaviours that are consistent with inhibited-type reactive attachment disorder, but which also might be observed on an inhibited-avoidant continuum of attachment difficulties (Minde, 2003).

Distributions of APR scores and clinical cases

The distribution of APR scale scores in the CICS baseline survey, as well as proportions scoring in the borderline and clinical ranges, are listed in Table 6.2. Most children scored zero (boys = 59%, girls = 67%). APR scores did not vary by age. Sibling concordance was investigated via within-pairs comparisons of APR for fifty-two sibling dyads, from a nested study of sibling mental health. There was no evidence of sibling concordance of APR caseness (defined as scores in the borderline or clinical ranges). Among 52 sibling dyads, 44 consisted of concordant non-cases; one consisted of concordant cases, while seven were discordant.

Table 6.2 Distribution of abnormal pain response scale scores (n=347)

	Mean	*(SD)*	*Proportion (%) in nominal range*		
			Normal	*Borderline*	*Clinical*
Boys (n=176)	1.0	(1.5)	91	4	5
Girls (n=171)	0.7	(1.5)	92	3	5
Total (n=347)	0.9	(1.5)	91.5	3.5	5

Relationship of APR to other mental health difficulties

Thirty children (8.6 per cent of the sample) were identified as APR cases, defined by APR scores in the borderline or clinical range. These children had a high level of corresponding mental health problems. There was a substantial difference in the mean residual total ACC scores (i.e. the total score minus the APR scale score) of APR cases versus non-cases (59.5 versus 26.1, $p < 0.0001$, Cohen's $d = 1.4$). The equivalent difference in mean total CBCL scores was of similar magnitude (78.5 versus 44.5, $p < 0.0001$, Cohen's $d = 1.1$). Almost all of the APR cases (29/30) manifested residual global mental disorder, as defined by residual ACC total scores (total ACC minus APR score) falling in a residual clinical range (ACC clinical range minus 4 points). Twenty four cases had CBCL total scores in the clinical range.

Among all children with residual global mental disorder (n = 168), mean residual ACC total scores of APR cases (n = 29) and non-cases (n = 139) were 61.0 and 45.3 respectively ($p < 0.001$, Cohen's d = 0.78). This suggests that APR cases represent a particularly impaired group of children with psychological disturbances.

Correlations of APR scores with other ACC and CBCL sub-scale scores are listed in Table 6.3. Correlations between APR scores and the ad hoc indices of mental health constructs are listed hierarchically in Table 6.4. Moderate correlation was found between APR scores and indices of impulsivity/recklessness (r = 0.63) and inhibited-avoidant attachment behaviours (r = 0.51). APR scores were not associated with CBCL item scores for sleep problems, elimination problems or smearing faeces.

Independent predictors of abnormal pain response

A two-step hierarchical regression model of APR caseness was conducted with a view to identifying independent predictors of clinically meaningful APR, while controlling for other clinically significant psychopathology. A categorical control variable was defined by residual ACC scores below versus within the previously defined residual clinical range. Logistic regression was selected because two thirds of subject children scored zero on the APR scale. The first step modelled the extent to which caseness is independently predicted by residual psychopathology and developmental and pre-care study factors. The latter refers to exposure to social adversity and other factors prior to entry into court-ordered care. The second step modelled the extent to which scores are predicted by in-care experiences and events. Factors associated with the outcome measure at $p \leq 0.1$ were included in the model, as well as age, gender, age at entry into care and reported intellectual disability. The results are summarised in Table 6.5. Two factors independently predicted APR caseness, 'residual ACC psychopathology' and 'planned entry to the child's present placement'.

The CICS identified several independent predictors of global mental health, attachment difficulties, sexual behaviour problems and food maintenance behaviours (Tarren-Sweeney, 2008). However, after controlling for residual psychopathology, the only predictor of APR

Table 6.3 Correlation of abnormal pain response scale scores with CBCL and ACC scales

CBCL scales	*Correlation (r)*	*ACC clinical scale*	*Correlation (r)*
Anxious–depressed	.26	Sexual behaviour	.26
Withdrawn–depressed	.36	Pseudomature	.31
Somatic complaints	.22	Non-reciprocal	.42
Social problems	.31	Indiscriminate	.31
Thought problems	.40	Insecure	.42
Attention problems	.35	Anxious–distrustful	.26
Rule-breaking behaviour	.30	Food maintenance	.26
Aggressive behaviour	.29	Self-injury	.35
		Suicide discourse	.07
Total CBCL score	.39	Total ACC clinical score	.52
		ACC self-esteem scale	
		Negative self-image	.21
		Low confidence	.35

Table 6.4 Hierarchy of behavioural indices associated[a] with abnormal pain response scores

	Correlation	*Cronbach's alpha*	*Mean construct score*[b]		
			Cases	*Non-cases*	*D*[c]
A. Impulsivity/recklessness	.63	.72	5.6	2.3	*1.3*
Gets hurt a lot, accident prone (CBCL+ACC)	.26				
Impulsive, acts without thinking (CBCL)	.30				
Risks physical safety/fearless (ACC)	.40				
Runs on to road (deleted ACC item)	.33				
B. Inhibited-avoidant attachment spectrum	.51	.80	6.1	2.1	*1.4*
Avoids eye contact	.32				
Does not show affection	.25				
Hides feelings	.51				
Refuses to talk	.31				
Resists being comforted when hurt	.30				
Secretive	.33				
Withdrawn	.27				
[source = ACC non-reciprocal and insecure scales]					
C. Trance-amnesic type dissociation	.46	.70	4.1	1.8	*1.1*
Daydreams or gets lost in thoughts (CBCL)	.28				
Has blackouts or periods of amnesia (ACC)	.15				
Seems to be in a trance (deleted ACC item)	.30				
Stares blankly (CBCL)	.34				
Very forgetful (ACC)	.28				
D. Low empathy/cruelty	.41	.82	4.8	2.5	*0.9*
Cruelty to animals (CBCL)	.22				
Cruelty, bullying or meanness to others (CBCL)	.25				
Doesn't seem to feel guilty after misbehaving (CBCL)	.25				
Lacks guilt or empathy (ACC)	.26				
Uncaring, shows little concern for others (ACC)	.25				
E. Self-injury	.36	.70	1.9	0.4	*1.1*
Asks to be physically punished	.13				
Bites him/herself	.17				
Causes him/herself to vomit	.24				
Causes injury to him/herself	.29				
Hits head, head-banging	.18				
Rocks back and forth	.21				
[source = ACC self-injury scale]					
F. Dissociation from reality (de-realisation/identity fragmentation)	.34	.58	2.0	0.6	*1.1*
Has an imaginary friend (ACC)	.17				
Hears sounds or voices that are not there (CBCL)	.11				
Lives in a fantasy world (ACC)	.25				
Sees things that aren't there (CBCL)	.32				
Thinks is someone or something else (ACC)	.18				

[a] All APR scale score–item correlations significant at $p < 0.05$
[b] Mean total construct score for APR cases (n=30) versus non-cases (n=317)
[c] Effect size expressed as standardized mean score differences (Cohen's *D*), all differences significant at $p < 0.0001$

Table 6.5 Two-step hierarchical logistic regression model of dichotomous APR status (cases versus non-cases)[a]

Hierarchical logistic regression model	*Odds ratio*	*95% C.I.*	*P value*
Step 1			
Residual psychopathology[b]	21.1	(2.7–166)	0.004
Developmental factors			
Age	0.9	(0.7–1.3)	0.67
Female gender	1.3	(0.5–3.6)	0.61
Reported intellectual disability	1.6	(0.6–4.6)	0.35
Pre-care factors			
Length of exposure to maltreatment[c]	1.1	(0.8–1.6)	0.48
Neglect of basic physical needs	2.2	(0.7–7.4)	0.19
Age at entry into care	0.8	(0.6–1.1)	0.22
Step 1 adjusted R squared = 0.18			
Step 2			
In-care factors			
Planned permanent placement[d]	3.2	(1.0–10.2)	0.05
Time in placement/time in care	2.4	(0.3–18.3)	0.41
N. placements since entering care	1.1	(0.9–1.3)	0.32
Caregiver uncertain about restoration	1.7	(0.6–5.3)	0.34
Increase in adjusted R squared (step 1 to step 2) = 0.04			
Adjusted R squared for overall 2-step model = 0.22			

[a] Outcome variable is a dichotomous transformation of the ACC APR score, namely: 0 = non-cases; 1=cases, where caseness is borderline +/- clinical range

[b] Variable controlling for residual psychopathology is a dichotomous measure of residual ACC total scores (i.e. total ACC scores minus APR scores) falling in a residual clinical range, as defined by ACC total residual scores > 23

[c] Length of time exposed to maltreatment: time from 1st confirmed notification to entry into care

[d] Child entered present placement in a planned way, rather than as a temporary or emergency placement

was 'planned entry to present placement' (as distinct from children entering their present placement as a temporary or emergency arrangement). There is no immediate explanation for this finding. However, it is notable that this factor did not predict other measures of psychopathology (Tarren-Sweeney, 2008).

The absence of other independent effects suggests that, if the presently identified APR is found to be a valid clinical phenomenon, then its determinants were either not measured in the CICS, or they were inadequately or unreliably measured, or they are shared by other mental health problems measured in the study. This raises a question as to whether APR is a discrete clinical phenomenon (as suggested by factor analysis), or a severity marker for mental health difficulties among children exposed to complex social adversity (as suggested by the absence of specific predictors). Correlations between APR scores and residual ACC and CBCL total scores among children scoring in the clinical range on the ACC and CBCL total scores were relatively low, suggesting APR is not a severity marker. Instead, given that half of the aggregate sample presented with global mental disorder (CBCL and ACC total scores in the clinical range), high APR scores appear to represent a specific clinical phenomenon that is not generalised among disturbed children in care, and which is not predicted by exposure to any specific forms of social adversity. This raises another possibility, namely that APR is manifested as a phenotype characterised by co-morbid psychopathology and attachment difficulties, expressed in response to severe psychosocial adversity.

Speculation about the nature and determinants of abnormal pain response

The Children in Care study identified a pattern of caregiver-reported abnormal responses to physical hurt among a large sample of pre-adolescent children in care, which is partially validated by factor analysis. The pattern of APR is suggestive of pain insensitivity or failure to communicate felt pain, or of failure by caregivers to recognise children's pain. While determinants of caregiver-reported APR were not identified in the CICS, the findings point to a number of hypothesised developmental processes, and weigh against several other hypotheses. Moderate correlations between APR scores and ad hoc measures of inhibited-avoidant attachment behaviours, and trance-amnesic type suggest the possibility that either discrete or complex attachment- and trauma-related phenomena bear some relationship to the presently identified APR. However, this lacks substantive support from previous research, and in most instances is contradicted by prior findings.

A recent study found that continuous measures of both ambivalent and controlling/disorganised attachment behaviours among five-year-old children were positively correlated with increased sensitivity to everyday pain events and immunizations (Walsh *et al.*, 2008). Otherwise, the extent to which children with disorganised attachments have altered pain experiences is not known. A number of researchers have proposed conceptual links between early attachment disorganization/organization and dissociative-conversion symptoms. Liotti (2006) has argued that disorganised attachment behaviour, observed predominantly among maltreated children (Cicchetti and Rogosch, 1994), is a dissociative phenomenon. Longitudinal data suggest that infant disorganised attachment predicts later dissociative experiences, independent of subsequent trauma (Lyons-Ruth *et al.*, 2006). Yet few studies have examined dissociation among maltreated children, and none have identified dissociation as a mechanism for APR among traumatised children. Kozlowska (2007) has hypothesised that the freeze response observed among young maltreated children is a precursory mechanism for development of conversion symptoms, including altered perception of pain. Her model proposes that the freeze response manifests within a system of organised self-protective strategies, conceptualised within the Dynamic Maturational model (DMM) of attachment (Crittenden, 2006) as compulsive Type A (3–4, 5–6) attachment organization (Kozlowska, 2007). The CICS found no specific relationships between APR scores and ACC measures of some behaviours postulated to be characteristic of these DMM sub-types, namely over-compliance (ACC item: 'Too compliant [over-conforms]') and precocious pseudo-maturity (ACC 'Pseudomature Interpersonal Behaviour' scale).

It is feasible that physically painful maltreatment of young children causes alterations to neural pain pathways, as is suspected to occur for children exposed to chronic, painful medical conditions (Cheng *et al.*, 2003; Woolf and Salter, 2000). If so, then one might predict that onset of painful abuse in infancy incurs greater neuro-developmental changes than later onset abuse, given the infant brain's greater plasticity (Glaser, 2000). Despite a relatively large aggregate sample, the CICS lacked statistical power to test this hypothesis. However, it is notable that among subjects with global mental disorder, identical proportions (52 per cent) of APR cases and non-cases had a confirmed history of physical abuse.

The CICS findings weigh against two other possible explanations for the reported APR.

First, as noted in the introduction, some literature refers to aberrant communication or experience of pain among children with developmental or cognitive impairments (Nader *et al.*, 2004). This is pertinent to the present study, given that a quarter of subject children were reported as having some level of intellectual disability. But observed APR was not found to be associated with reported intellectual or language impairment among the CICS sample. Second, a hypothesised sensory impairment mechanism seems inconsistent with the finding that clinically significant APR occurred almost exclusively among children with complex psychological disturbances.

The CICS suffered from a number of methodological weaknesses. Predictive modelling was limited by the absence of genetic and pre-natal risk exposure. Similarly, the study lacked measures of infant temperament. Other key variables not measured include indicators of the quality of care provided to children in their present placements, with the exception of confirmed maltreatment in care. Despite the relatively large aggregate sample, the number of APR cases (n = 30) was rather small, limiting statistical power. Hence, some moderate effect sizes were not statistically significant. Subtle influences on APR might yet be revealed among a larger sample of high risk children. Another limitation of the present examination of APR is that it was largely exploratory, conducted without a priori hypotheses (the CICS study hypotheses referred to other mental health parameters). This chapter describes an exploratory investigation of a previously unreported clinical phenomenon, and as such is more concerned with hypothesis generation than hypothesis testing. While there is some evidence that foster parents of children in long-term care are at least as reliable as parents in reporting children's mental health difficulties, the present findings are limited by the absence of other measures of children's pain experience. It is known that parents and alternate caregivers are less able to reliably identify children's felt experiences than readily observable externalizing behaviour problems (Tarren-Sweeney *et al.*, 2004). Hence, validation of the presently formulated APR construct requires additional investigations, including the employment of standardized pain measures with an in-care sample. This could help delineate between children's felt pain, how they communicate such pain and the extent to which caregivers can recognise behavioural cues.

Chapter 7

Eating problems

Previous knowledge of eating problems experienced by children in care

Although little is known about the eating patterns of children in care, there are some indications they are problematic. In a large (n = 300) survey of foster parent experiences of behaviour problems among sexually abused children in foster care, 77 per cent reported that such children display eating problems either sometimes or frequently, and 23 per cent of carers felt 'bothered' by these problems (Thompson *et al.*, 1994). Two studies have described children in foster care who are chronic excessive eaters (hyperphagia), but who are neither obese nor growth impaired (Ayoob *et al.*, 1994; Demb, 1991). The first study identified 13 cases of hyperphagia among children referred for evaluation of developmental disabilities (Ayoob *et al.*, 1994). Whereas 24 per cent of the referred children resided in foster care, all 13 cases were in care. In the second study, 10 reported cases of hyperphagia were located in a file review of 200 clinic-referred children in care (Demb, 1991).

Clinical assessments of children in foster and kinship care also describe patterns of aberrant eating and food-related behaviour, characterised by excessive eating and drinking and food maintenance (hoarding, storing, stealing, etc.), with or without concurrent obesity (Tarren-Sweeney, 2007). Food is not always stored with the intention of being eaten. Indeed, some children hide or store food indefinitely, despite knowing it will spoil. This pattern resembles the behavioural correlates of Hyperphagic Short Stature (HSS), a form of psychosocial growth failure occurring in children older than two years (Skuse *et al.*, 1996). HSS is thought to be determined by acute pathogenic or stressful parental care (Green, W. *et al.*, 1984). It describes children with a normal body-mass index, who display aberrant eating behaviours, especially hyperphagia and polydipsia. An often reported feature of HSS is rapid and spontaneous recovery in alternate care, as evidenced by reversible growth hormone deficiency, 'catch-up' growth and reduction in aberrant eating behaviour (Green, W. *et al.*, 1984; Powell *et al.*, 1967). However, there is also evidence that some children fail to spontaneously recover in care (de Kerdanet *et al.*, 1993). Money (1972) referred to children placed in foster care, where 'severe and at times bizarre forms of behaviour typical of the syndrome would sometimes recur'. Whereas maltreated growth-delayed children typically attain 'catch up' growth in their first year in foster care (Oliván 2003), a sizeable minority show static or declining growth velocity (Taitz and King, 1988; Wyatt *et al.*, 1997).

Clinical assessments also occasionally describe school-aged children in foster or residential care who eat or drink from unhealthy sources (e.g. eat from garbage, drink from a toilet or pet bowl), or engage in pica. The latter is not surprising, given that pica is mostly observed among children and adults with developmental disabilities (Stiegler, 2005), and rates of intellectual and language disability among children in care are well in excess of that found among children at large (Halfon *et al.*, 1995; Klee *et al.*, 1997).

Children in care may also be at risk of more conventional eating problems in adolescence, given their early exposure to maltreatment. Self-reported emotional abuse in childhood (but not other forms of maltreatment) independently predicted unhealthy eating attitudes in a community sample of 236 adult women (Kent *et al.* 1999). Another study found that most adults with Binge Eating Disorder recall some history of child abuse or neglect (Grilo and Masheb, 2001). Notwithstanding some negative findings, there is also reasonable evidence of associations between adult eating problems and child sexual and physical abuse (Molinari, 2001). Retrospective studies of the effects of child maltreatment often fail to account for exposure to multiple risk factors that correlate with abuse, such as emotional deprivation, and loss. Nonetheless, it is plausible that social learning, attachment- and trauma-related mechanisms account for a higher prevalence of eating problems among adolescent and adult survivors of child maltreatment.

Eating problems measured in the Children in Care study

Eating problems measured by the Assessment Checklist for Children

Four ACC items that refer to excessive eating and the acquisition and retention of food, loaded on a food maintenance factor; while three items that describe pica, unhealthy drinking and eating from garbage, loaded on a self-injury factor. A further ACC item 'causes self to vomit', was designed to measure intentional vomiting as self-injury. However, it may also measure bulimic purging, as well as vomiting caused by hyperphagia. The item was scored infrequently, and loaded relatively weakly on the self-injury factor. Item factor loadings on the ACC food maintenance and self-injury scales are listed in Table 7.1. In the factor analysis, the two restrictive eating items did not load on any factor, while the item 'constantly thirsty (always asking for drinks' correlated poorly with excessive eating, and did not load on any factor. The prevalence of the three latter items (which were deleted from the final version of the checklist), were: 'eats too little' (18%), 'fasting or excessive dieting' (2%), and 'constantly thirsty (always asking for drinks)' (31%). The contrast between food maintenance behaviour (including excessive eating) and the more bizarre pica-type behaviour was also apparent in correlations of ACC eating and food-related item scores (see Table 7.2). The findings thus suggest that food maintenance and pica-type behaviours represent different domains of aberrant eating among pre-adolescent children in care.

A pica-type eating problems index was constructed from the three eating items loading on the self-injury factor, namely 'eats non-food' (i.e. pica), 'unhealthy drinking (e.g. from discarded drink bottle, from toilet bowl' and 'eats from garbage'. Nominal clinical and borderline clinical ranges were constructed for both the food maintenance and pica-type problem domains. It was reasoned that a score of 2 or below on the food maintenance scale was not clinically significant (i.e. one behaviour occurring often, or one or two behaviours occurring sometimes). However, it was though that any occurrence of pica-type behaviour is clinically significant among school-aged children. Cases were defined as children with scores above the borderline clinical cut-point on either domain.

The distributions of scores on the food maintenance scale and pica-type index are listed in Table 7.3. There were sizeable proportions of children with scores in the nominal clinical

Table 7.1 Item factor loadings on the ACC food maintenance and self-injury scales (n = 412)

	# items	*Internal consistency*[a] *Boys*	*Girls*	*Loading*[b]	*Item-rest*[c]	*Prevalence (%)*[d]
Scale VIII Food maintenance	4	.78	.82			
eats too much				.65	.62	25
gorges food				.67	.65	23
hides or stores food				.68	.57	14
steals food				.69	.60	18
Scale IX Self-injury	14	.76	.84			
eats from garbage				.63	.49	7
eats things that are not food				.62	.42	8
unhealthy drinking (e.g. from discarded drink bottle, from toilet bowl)				.59	.51	5
asks to be physically punished				.44	.42	4
bites him/herself				.49	.52	9
causes him/herself to vomit				.42	.31	4
causes injury to him/herself				.56	.55	10
cuts or pulls out own hair				.43	.41	8
cuts or rips own clothes				.46	.45	10
hits head, head-banging				.55	.51	10
intentionally harms her/himself with				.64	.38	2
knives/implements				.64	.38	2
intentionally swallows dangerous substance to harm self				.77	.40	1
rocks back and forth				.42	.39	8
throws her/himself against walls, onto floors, etc.				.36	.46	13

[a] Cronbach's alpha: Boys, n = 209; girls, n = 203
[b] Factor loading
[c] Item-rest correlation (correlation of the item score and the sum of all other items in the scale)
[d] Item prevalence (percentage of sample with item score of 1 or 2, n = 412)

ranges. Although there was moderate correlation of continuous scores on the two domains (r = 0.40 for boys, 0.36 for girls), only a quarter of identified cases manifested problems on both domains (21/83). No gender differences in score distributions were detected. The rates of reported obesity among cases exceeded that reported for children with normal scores on both domains (food maintenance: 10% versus 0.4%, P2 = 22.9, p < 0.0001; Pica-type: 7% versus 1%, P2 = 5.7, p = 0.02).

Obesity and overeating measured by the CBCL

Non-obese children (n = 320, 92%) were defined as having a CBCL 'overweight' item score of zero, while obese children (n = 7) were defined by a score of '2' (i.e. overweight = 'very true'). Children scoring '1' (i.e. overweight = 'somewhat true') were considered neither obese nor non-obese (n = 20). Sample item prevalence (i.e. proportions of index children

Table 7.2 Correlation matrix of ACC eating and food-related items (n = 412)

	Gorges food	Hides/stores food	Steals food	Constant thirst	Eats from garbage	Eats non-food	Unhealthy drinking	Eats too little	Fasting or excessive dieting
Food/drink maintenance									
Eats too much	.67	.42	.44	.31	.29	.21	.19	.08	.06
Gorges food		.45	.51	.32	.45	.26	.28	-.06	.06
Hides or stores food			.61	.27	.22	.09	.14	.11	.15
Steals food				.37	.41	.26	.29	.04	.00
Constant thirst/drinking					.22	.23	.23	.13	.03
Pica-type behaviour									
Eats from garbage						.49	.63	.02	.14
Eats non-food (Pica)							.42	.02	.06
Unhealthy drinking								.17	.11
Restrictive eating									
Eats too little									.21

Table 7.3 Distribution of ACC food maintenance and pica-type scores (n = 347)

Scale (max score)		*Mean*	*(SD)*	*Proportion (%) in nominal range* Normal	Borderline	Clinical
Food maintenance scale (8)[a]				0–2	3–4	5+
	Boys	1.2	(1.9)	82	9	9
	Girls	1.1	(2.0)	84	6	10
Pica-type index (6)[b]				0	1	2+
	Boys	0.3	(0.8)	87	7	6
	Girls	0.2	(0.7)	87	9	3

[a] ACC food maintenance scale, contains four items: eats too much, gorges food, hides or stores food, steals food

[b] Nominal ACC pica-type index, contains three items: eats from garbage, eats things that are not food, unhealthy drinking

scoring 1 or 2) on the four CBCL eating items are compared in Table 7.4 with that reported for normative and clinic-referred samples (Achenbach, 1991). Compared to children at large, index children were reported with low prevalence of obesity against high prevalence of over-eating, with the greatest discrepancy being observed among boys.

Table 7.4 Prevalence (%) of CBCL eating problems among study, normative and clinic-referred samples

CBCL item		% very/often true (score = 2) Sample[a]	Norm[b]	Clinic[c]	% ever true (score = 1 or 2) Sample	Norm	Clinic
Doesn't eat well	Boys	6	6	10	28	27	33
	Girls	9	4	10	26	30	36
Eats/drinks things not food	Boys	3	< 0.5	2	7	2	6
	Girls	2	< 0.5	1	9	2	5
Overeating	Boys	11	2	7	22	14	18
	Girls	8	3	10	21	17	23
Overweight	Boys	1	3	3	6	10	8
	Girls	3	3	7	10	12	14

[a] Study sample: 347 children aged 4–11 years (176 boys, 171 girls)
[b] 1991 US normative sample aged 4–11 years (582 boys, 619 girls) (Achenbach, 1991)
[c] 1991 US clinic-referred sample aged 4–11 years (582 boys, 619 girls) (Achenbach, 1991)

The CICS findings

Relationships between the presence of clinically significant scores (caseness) on either problem domain, and continuous and categorical measures of: (a) exposure to potential risk/protective factors; and (b) other mental health problems, are presented in Table 7.5. Groups stratified by food maintenance caseness excluded overweight children. Caseness on either domain was closely associated with reported developmental and learning difficulties (intellectual, speech and reading), with odds ratios of 2.3 to 2.5 for *Food Maintenance* syndrome and 3.2 to 3.9 for pica-type problems (see Table 7.5 for confidence intervals). A risk factor for both aberrant eating patterns was an anticipation or expectation that the index child would be restored to their birth parents' care. Entry into care before age 6 months was protective for food maintenance problems, while residing in kinship care was protective for pica-type behaviour.

Confirmed maltreatment in care (OR = 4.5) and confirmed maltreatment in the child's present placement (OR = 17.4) were exceptional risk factors for food maintenance syndrome, but not for pica-type behaviour. Non-obese food maintenance cases were significantly more likely to have been maltreated in care, than non-obese non-cases (34% versus 13%, P2 = 9.0, p = 0.003). There was no apparent difference in the severity of abuse in care experienced by cases and non-cases. However, there was a startling relationship between the timing of abuse in care events and food maintenance caseness. Most children with food maintenance problems still resided with the carers who had maltreated them (8/11, 73 per cent), whereas most non-cases moved to a new placement (16/19, 84 per cent). Furthermore, the three non-cases who remained in abusive placements experienced less severe maltreatment than equivalent cases.

Sibling concordance of food maintenance caseness was as follows: 34 dyads had nil cases; 17 dyads were discordant; and just one dyad consisted of two cases. For pica-type caseness: 44 dyads had nil cases; five dyads were discordant; and three dyads consisted of

Table 7.5 Univariate relationships between food maintenance and pica-type caseness and exposure to study factors and other psychopathology

	Clinically significant food maintenance[a]					*Clinically significant pica-type behaviour*[b]				
	Cases n = 44	*Non-cases* n = 276				*Cases* n = 45	*Non-cases* n = 302			
Continuous study factors	*Mean*	*Mean*	*d*[c]	*p*[d]		*Mean*	*Mean*	*d*	*p*	
Present age (years)	8.1	7.7	0.28			7.8	7.8			
Age at entry into care (years)	4.0	3.3	0.27			3.8	3.4	0.18		
Time in care (years)	4.2	4.3	0.07			4.0	4.4	0.17		
Number of placements in care	3.6	3.0	0.21			3.3	3.1	0.10		
Length of present placement	2.8	3.4	0.26			2.9	3.4	0.19		
Exposure to maltreatment (years)[e]	2.0	1.6	0.22			1.8	1.7	0.06		
N. adverse events in last year	1.9	1.66	0.20			2.2	1.5	0.53	***	
Carer's age (years)	45.0	46.7	0.18			46.5	46.5			
Categorical study factors										
Developmental factors	*% exposed*		*Odds ratio*	*95% C.I.*	*p*	*% exposed*		*Odds ratio*	*95% C.I.*	*p*
Reported intellectual disability	39%	20%	2.5	1.2–5.1	**	47%	19%	3.8	1.8–7.8	***
Reported speech problem	36%	20%	2.3	1.1–4.8	**	42%	19%	3.2	1.5–6.4	***
Reported reading difficulty	53%	33%	2.3	1.2–4.7	**	65%	32%	3.9	1.9–8.5	***
Pre-care factors										
Reported maternal drug abuse	41%	34%	1.3	0.6–2.6		29%	37%	0.7	0.3–1.4	
Reported maternal alcohol abuse	18%	25%	0.7	0.3–1.6		24%	25%	1.0	0.4–2.1	
Reported maternal psych disorder	18%	19%	1.0	0.4–2.3		9%	20%	0.4	0.1–1.2	
Sexual abuse	9%	13%	0.7	0.2 - 2.0		20%	11%	2.0	0.8–4.6	
Physical abuse	45%	44%	1.1	0.5–2.1		44%	43%	1.1	0.5–2.1	
Classic emotional abuse[f]	36%	21%	2.1	1.0–4.4	*	31%	22%	1.6	0.7–3.3	
Exposure to domestic violence	32%	31%	1.0	0.5–2.2		24%	33%	0.7	0.3–1.4	
Neglect: inadequate supervision	41%	45%	0.9	0.4–1.7		40%	43%	0.9	0.4–1.6	
Neglect of basic physical needs	55%	49%	1.3	0.6–2.5		53%	49%	1.2	0.6–2.4	
Developmental neglect[g]	25%	32%	0.7	0.3–1.5		36%	30%	1.3	0.6–2.6	
Entry into care before age 6 months	2%	13%	0.2	0.0–0.9	*	4%	13%	3.0	0.0–1.3	
In-care factors										
Resides in kinship care	Nil	16%	0.0	0.0–0.5	**	<1%	16%	0.2	0.1–1.0	*
Confirmed maltreatment in care[h]	41%	13%	4.5	1.5–13	***	22%	16%	1.5	0.3–5.3	

Table 7.5 continued

	Clinically significant food maintenance[a]					*Clinically significant pica-type behaviour*[b]				
	Cases n = 44	*Non-cases* n = 276				*Cases* n = 45	*Non-cases* n = 302			
Maltreatment in present placement	27%	2%	17.4	3.2–114	***	11%	6%	2.2	0.2–12	
Care order expires before age 16	22%	14%	1.7	0.7–4.1		17%	15%	1.1	0.4–2.8	
Carer expects restoration	27%	14%	2.3	0.9–5.2	*	34%	18%	2.4	1.1–5.1	**
Carer has poor health	11%	4%	2.8	0.7–9.2	*	9%	5%	1.7	0.4–5.8	
Other psychopathology[i]										
CBCL DSM-oriented scales	*% with disorder*					*% with disorder*				
Affective problems	45%	11%	6.6	3.0–14	***	42%	14%	4.4	2.1–9.1	***
Anxiety problems	36%	10%	5.1	2.3–11	***	29%	12%	3.0	1.3–6.5	**
Somatic problems	18%	6%	3.4	1.2–9.0	**	11%	7%	1.6	0.4–4.6	
Attention-deficit hyperactivity	55%	18%	5.3	2.6–11	***	49%	21%	3.7	1.8–7.4	***
Oppositional–defiant problems	64%	24%	5.6	2.7–12	***	56%	27%	3.3	1.7–6.7	***
Conduct problems	80%	29%	9.7	4.3–24	***	62%	34%	3.2	1.6–6.6	***
Elimination/sleep problems	*% with symptom*					*% with symptom*				
Encopresis	36%	12%	4.4	2.0–9.4	***	36%	13%	3.6	1.7–7.8	***
Smearing/playing with faeces	14%	2%	8.6	2.0–37	***	13%	3%	5.0	1.4–17	***
Day-wetting	34%	14%	3.2	1.5–6.9	***	36%	14%	3.3	1.5–6.9	***
Bed-wetting	30%	28%	1.1	0.5–2.3		38%	26%	1.7	0.8–3.4	
Sleeps less than most children	41%	20%	2.7	1.3–5.6	**	40%	21%	2.5	1.2–5.0	**

[a] Non-obese children (n = 320) stratified by food maintenance caseness (i.e. scores above 2)
[b] Aggregate sample (n = 347) stratified by pica-type caseness (i.e. scores above 0)
[c] Standardized mean score difference (Cohen's *d*), namely the difference in mean scores expressed as a proportion of the score standard deviation for the aggregate sample
[d] * $p \leq 0.05$, ** $p \leq 0.01$, *** $p \leq 0.001$
[e] Length of time exposed to maltreatment: time from 1st confirmed notification to entry into care
[f] Emotional abuse other than threats or verbal assaults. Examples include scapegoating and overt rejection
[g] Refers to reported inadequate nurturance in infancy, including non-organic failure to thrive
[h] Records on maltreatment in care were checked for about half of the study sample: food problems, 22 cases and 142 non-cases; bizarre eating, 14 cases and 150 non-cases
[i] Categorical estimates of psychopathology, namely: CBCL DSM-oriented scale scores in clinical range, and presence of CBCL elimination and sleep problems (i.e. items scored either 1 or 2)

two cases. Within-pairs correlation of food maintenance and pica-type caseness was r = –0.08 and 0.35 respectively.

A predictive model of food maintenance caseness using logistic regression is listed in Table 7.6. In the logistic regression model, abuse in care, and more specifically, abuse in one's present placement, independently predicted food maintenance caseness after controlling for all other significant relationships.

Table 7.6 Predictors of food maintenance syndrome (n = 182)[a]

	Odds ratio	*95% C.I.*	*P value*
Reported intellectual disability	2.5	1.0–6.7	0.06
Sexual abuse	0.6	0.1–2.6	0.50
Physical assault	0.7	0.3–1.9	0.51
Classic emotional abuse [b]	2.3	0.8–6.5	0.11
Any form of neglect	0.6	0.2–1.8	0.42
Age at entry into care	1.1	0.9–1.4	0.20
Kinship care	0.3	0.1–1.7	0.18
Confirmed maltreatment in present placement	21.6	3.7–127	0.001
Poor carer health	2.5	0.6–12	0.23
Care order expires before age 16	1.0	0.3–3.6	0.94
Carer anticipates restoration	1.3	0.7–2.6	0.39

Log Likelihood = - 67 *Pseudo R squared = 0.20*

[a] Logistic regression model of predictors of food maintenance syndrome (caseness defined by scores above 2 on the food maintenance scale), restricted to children for whom abuse in care records had been checked (n = 182)
[b] Emotional abuse other than threats or verbal assaults, e.g. scapegoating

Types and prevalence of eating problems

The present data reveal a distinction between excessive eating and related food maintenance behaviours, and the more bizarre pica-type eating problems. These patterns are also associated with different developmental profiles. Whereas both patterns present with co-occurring psychopathology and developmental disabilities, food maintenance behaviour is more consistently aligned with co-morbid psychiatric disturbances (particularly disruptive behaviour and affective problems), while pica-type behaviour is more closely associated with reported developmental problems (namely intellectual disability, speech problems and reading difficulties). The present findings thus support the validity of two distinct forms of eating disturbance, termed food maintenance syndrome and pica-type cluster.

The prevalence of eating problems in the present sample was much higher than anticipated, with a quarter (24 per cent) of children scoring in the nominal borderline or clinical ranges on one or both domains. While non-obese hyperphagia has been noted previously among children in care, it is surprising that problems of this magnitude have attracted such little research or clinical attention. Aside from systematic measurement bias (discussed at the start of this chapter), it is possible that clinicians have failed to query aberrant eating behaviours among children with normal stature. Importantly, most children with eating problems were reportedly not overweight. Although excessive eating was closely associated with obesity, three quarters of children with food maintenance problems were not obese. There were insufficient overweight children to compare obese and non-obese representations of excessive and bizarre eating.

The significance of the ACC restrictive eating scores is difficult to gauge, since there are no comparative community data. The CBCL item 'doesn't eat well' provides a less accurate measure of restrictive eating, as it also measures poor eating habits. But, the proportions of index boys and girls reported to not eat well, were similar to normative rates (see Table 7.4). Hence, restrictive eating among pre-adolescent children in care is probably unremarkable.

Risk and protective factors

As anticipated, reported intellectual disability, speech problems and reading difficulties (which are highly inter-correlated) were strongly associated with caseness on both domains, and particularly with the pica-type cluster. The prevalence of pica among index children with intellectual disability versus children at large with intellectual disability was identical (15 per cent) (Ali, 2001), suggesting its presence among such children is unrelated to their 'in-care' status. A more interesting finding was that 9 per cent of index children without developmental disabilities displayed pica or pica-like behaviours. The phenomenological meaning of this is not known. Children with developmental disabilities were also highly vulnerable to food maintenance problems, which are not characteristic of children at large with developmental disabilities (aside from Prader-Willi syndrome), and which contrasts the pattern of fussy, selective and restrictive eating displayed by children with autism (Schreck *et al.*, 2004).

Evidence of sibling concordance for pica-type caseness was found in CICS, but not for food maintenance caseness. However, the within-pairs analyses of sibling concordance were hampered by small numbers of cases. A prior case series found a high number of sibling pairs were concordant for HSS (Skuse *et al.*, 1996), leading to speculation of a genetic link. However, this is somewhat unjustified, given that sibling dyads mostly have shared environments, and therefore, shared exposure to acute stressors.

Although various forms of maltreatment have been linked to HSS (Gohlke *et al.*, 1998), only emotional abuse was associated with non-obese food maintenance cases in the CICS (including emotional abuse in care). This is an important finding, as exposure to contact sexual abuse and physical assault predicted other types of psychopathology among index children. A history of early developmental neglect, including reports of psychosocial failure to thrive, bore no relationship to either eating problem domain. The hypothesis that maternal substance use is a determinant of hyperphagia among children in care (Ayoob *et al.*, 1994; Demb, 1991) was not supported in the present findings. Although hyperphagia is a common feature of neo-natal drug withdrawal (Shephard *et al.*, 2002), there are no indications that hyperphagia persists beyond withdrawal.

Relationships between eating problems and other psychopathology

Almost all cases on either domain manifested global mental disturbance, as indicated by ACC and/or CBCL total problem scores in the clinical range. The estimated rates of global disturbance were: 92% (ACC) or 93% (CBCL) among food maintenance cases, and 89% (ACC) or 91% (CBCL) among pica-type cases. Similarly, there were significant relationships between caseness on either eating problem domain, and almost all other aspects of psychopathology measured on the CBCL, as well as elimination problems and poor sleep (see Table 7.5). The notable exception was that bed-wetting wasn't associated with patterns of aberrant eating.

Consistent with prior findings (Gilmour and Skuse, 1999; Gohlke *et al.*, 1998; Powell *et al.*, 1967), patterns of aberrant eating were closely linked to encopresis, smearing faeces and day-wetting, but were unrelated to nocturnal enuresis. The phenomenological meaning of this is unclear. The study did not delineate between intentional and unintentional soiling. Previous studies have referred to intentional or aggressive urination, which is not measured by either checklist, but which is possibly aligned to day-wetting. There is speculation that intentional urination and smearing are responses to recent severe maltreatment (Felman and Nikitas, 1983).

One study of children in care noted a relationship between self-injury and excessive eating (Ayoob *et al.*, 1994), while studies of children with HSS described co-morbidity with self-injury and pain agnosia (Green, W. *et al.*, 1984; Money *et al.*, 1972; Silver and Finkelstein, 1967) It was found in the CICS that the pica-type cluster is closely aligned to self-injurious behaviours, and that excessive eating was moderately correlated with self-injury. However, pain agnosia (measured by the ACC abnormal pain response scale) correlated moderately with girls' food maintenance scores, but not with boys' food maintenance scores, or pica-type scores for either gender.

The CICS also found a very high prevalence of co-morbid conduct problems and aggression among food maintenance cases, and a close relationship between pica-type behaviour and self-injury. Otherwise, it should be noted that children with aberrant eating problems have complex, multifaceted psychopathology, similar to that reported for other disturbed children in care, including attachment disturbance and hyperactivity. Nearly all children with clinically significant eating problems present with global psychiatric disturbance. Finally, children with either type of eating problem were more likely than others to have sleep problems, as measured by the CBCL item 'sleeps less than most children'. It has been speculated that abnormal sleep patterns may interrupt growth hormone activity, which is optimal during sleep (Wolff and Money, 1973).

Acute stress model

A number of findings suggest that food maintenance syndrome among index children was primarily triggered by acute stress. First, food maintenance caseness was not associated with age at entry into care, placement stability or prior exposure to sexual or physical abuse, despite these factors being strongly associated with most other forms of psychopathology (Tarren-Sweeney, 2008). Second, food maintenance behaviour was closely associated with confirmed maltreatment in care. Third, among children known to have been maltreated in care, those displaying food maintenance behaviour were mostly residing in the abusive placements when their behaviour was measured (i.e. abuse was reported after survey questionnaires were completed), whereas most non-cases were in new, non-abusive placements. Indeed this finding was exceptional (odds ratio = 17.4). Furthermore, abuse in care, and abuse in one's present placement independently predicted food maintenance syndrome.

The majority of children don't develop aberrant eating problems in response to acute pathogenic care. Hence, other factors are likely to mediate the development of a food maintenance syndrome. It is proposed that developmental disabilities and co-morbid psychopathology increase a child's vulnerability for engaging in food maintenance behaviour. Co-morbid psychopathology is in turn largely determined by children's exposure to early social adversity, including maltreatment and emotional deprivation (Tarren-Sweeney, 2008). One probable mechanism is that children's psychopathology (especially aggression and attachment disturbances) reduces carers' coping abilities as well as emotional bonding, thus increasing the risk of maltreatment in care. Similarly, there are likely to be bi-directional effects accounting for the association between aberrant eating and maltreatment in care.

Short stature versus decreased growth velocity?

There are as yet no data describing relationships between the eating behaviours of children in care, and their growth velocity or endocrine functioning. If these factors are found to be linked, it is perhaps more likely that non-obese children with food maintenance syndrome manifest decreased linear growth velocity, rather than operationally-defined short stature. If so, then food maintenance syndrome and HSS might be re-conceptualised as hyperphagic growth failure. Some alternative hypotheses are that food maintenance syndrome is: (a) a less severe variant of HSS; and (b) not associated with growth failure (i.e. is unrelated to HSS).

Conclusion and implications for clinicians

The CICS identified two common and distinct patterns of aberrant eating behaviour among pre-adolescent, school-aged children in alternate care, which are unrelated to gender or age, and which have previously attracted little research interest. The first is a pattern of excessive eating and food acquisition, termed food maintenance syndrome. This syndrome appears to be primarily triggered by acute stress, and resembles the behavioural correlates of Hyperphagic Short Stature. The second is a cluster of pica-type eating behaviour that is strongly associated with developmental disabilities and is moderately correlated with self-injury. Both patterns are components of complex and multi-faceted psychopathology. Yet, neither pattern is associated with the primary predictors of co-morbid problems, namely exposure to early maltreatment and deprivation, and older age at entry into care. There is tentative evidence that restrictive eating is unremarkable in this population.

The CICS findings have several implications for clinicians assisting children in care. First, there is a need for assessment of eating and food-related problems in clinical evaluations, and where possible, to track the course of such behaviour (especially across multiple placements). Second, these children should have routine paediatric screening and regular measurement of linear growth velocity, especially if they manifest a pattern of excessive eating and food maintenance behaviour, while having normal body-mass index. Finally, the presence of such behaviour in the absence of obesity should alert clinicians to the possibility that a child is encountering abuse or deprivation in care (especially emotional abuse, such as scapegoating or rejection), or other major stressors. It should be emphasised however, that the presence of such behaviours does not confirm pathogenic foster care. In other words, abuse in care should not be diagnosed from children's eating and food-related behaviour.

Part III

Development and psychometric properties

Chapter 8

Background to the Children in Care study

This chapter describes the study design and methodology for the New South Wales Children in Care study (CICS) baseline survey, within which the Assessment Checklist for Children was developed.

Background to alternate care in NSW

In the decade 1996–2006, the number of children residing in alternate care in NSW rose from about 5,500 to almost 10,000 (82 per cent increase) (Australian Institute of Health and Welfare, 2007). In that period, the rate of NSW children residing in care rose from 3.4 to 6.2 per 1,000 children. The equivalent rate for NSW indigenous children in 2006 was 44.7 per cent! Almost all pre-adolescent children who enter court-ordered care do so following maltreatment (abuse and/or neglect) by their parents, or because of parental inability to protect them from maltreatment. In the early 1990s the state's large residential care facilities were closed as part of a reform of alternate care services. At the time of the present study (2000–3), fewer than 5 per cent of placements were in non-family type settings (Australian Institute of Health and Welfare, 2004). Conversely, kinship care has expanded in NSW to the point where it is now the predominant form of alternate care (56 per cent of all placements) (Australian Institute of Health and Welfare, 2007). There are two distinct kinship care systems in NSW, demarcated by custody (or 'parental responsibility') rights. The Children's Court may assign such rights to kin, with the statutory child welfare agency (currently Community Services) providing backup support. Alternatively, custody may be assigned to Community Services, with kinship carers having similar legal status to foster carers. Until recently, permanency planning in NSW lacked legislative support. Adoption by foster and kinship carers is uncommon for children under 12, given difficulties of gaining parental consent and running contested cases in the state's Supreme Court. However, NSW made some progress in this direction, with introduction of permanency provisions to the Children's Act in 2001.

Study design and timeline

The CICS is a prospective, epidemiological study of the mental health of children in court-ordered foster and kinship care in New South Wales (NSW), Australia, and of associated study factors. The CICS pilot study was carried out in 1997 and the baseline survey was carried out between 2000 and 2003. The final stages of the CICS, consisting of a follow-up survey and a parallel adolescent survey were completed between 2010 and 2012. The CICS baseline survey involved collection of carer-reported mental health estimates of children in care, as well as concurrent and retrospective measures of potential risk and protective factors. Data were collected from a mail-out carer questionnaire, and from the Community Services child welfare and alternate care database (the Client Information System – CIS). Children were not active participants in the survey. Special steps were taken to assure caregivers that the child welfare agency did not know the identity of participants and non-participants.

Sampling procedure

The sampling frame for the CICS cohort was all four to nine year-old children residing in court-ordered foster or kinship care in NSW, under the guardianship of the Minister for Community Services, and for whom casework responsibility rested with Community Services. The sampling frame was differentiated from children residing in temporary care without a court order, and from children with custody orders whose parents retained guardianship rights. The study was initially designed to include the latter group, which would have required the consent of their birth parents. A pilot study indicated that this was not feasible, as birth parents could not be reliably located. The sampling frame excluded children in the care of private fostering agencies, because it was not practical to enter into separate research agreements with each agency. A 100 per cent sampling procedure was employed, with the proviso that carers contact details could be confirmed via either the electoral roll or a telephone listing. This was necessary because piloting had revealed that carer details were not regularly updated on the CIS.

Study sample

Survey questionnaires were mailed to the caregivers of 621 eligible children, for whom contact details could be confirmed. The study sample was 347 children (176 boys, 171 girls), aged 4 to 11 years, providing a 56 per cent response rate. Comparisons of participant and non-participant children found the latter entered care at a younger age, had less exposure to maltreatment, and were more likely to have spent the larger part of their life with their present caregivers. Sixty per cent of children were 6 to 8 years old, with a mean age of 7.8 years.

The gender of participants was evenly distributed (176 boys, 171 girls). Though the sampling frame was defined as children aged 4 to 9 years, delays between drawing up the sampling frame and completion of survey materials saw some children recruited at ages 10 and 11. However, most children (>60%) were 6 to 8 years old, with the mean age being 7.8 years. The proportions of children residing in Sydney, other metropolitan NSW (Wollongong, Central Coast, Newcastle) and regional NSW were 35.5%, 16.5% and 48% respectively. Ethnicity was not reliably measured and hence is not reported. Numbers of children residing in foster and kinship care were 297 (86%) and 50 (14%) respectively. Fewer than six per cent (n = 20) of children entered care without known exposure to maltreatment, with 80 per cent experiencing one or more forms of abuse and 78 per cent experiencing neglect. The median number of confirmed notifications of maltreatment for the sample was 3, the mean time between the first confirmed notification and entry into care was 1.7 years, and the mean age at entry into care was 3.5 years.

Mental health measures

Children's baseline mental health, socialization and self-esteem were estimated from carer-report responses on the CBCL and the ACC. These were incorporated in the mail-out survey questionnaire sent to participant carers. The CBCL measures child problem behaviour across eight empirically-derived clinical sub-scales, with two 'higher order scales approximating spectrums of depressive/anxious symptoms ('internalizing') and disruptive behavioural symptoms ('externalizing') (Achenbach, 1991; Achenbach and Rescorla, 2001). It was selected because of its demonstrated validity and reliability (Doll, 1998), and the availability of comparative data for high-risk populations (Armsden *et al.*, 2000; Heflinger *et al.*, 2000).

Study factors

A large number of potential risk and protective factors were measured retrospectively and concurrently in the baseline survey. Factors pertaining to children's development, education and present status (e.g. type and makeup of present placement, recent life events) were measured from a carer questionnaire. Historical data (e.g. maltreatment history, care history and birth family factors) were measured retrospectively from the CIS. Since historical events were mostly recorded on the CIS shortly after they occurred, these data are thought to be more reliable than those typically obtained in a retrospective design. Essentially, the study sought to measure every factor that might be reliably obtained from the two data sources, and which might have some influence on children's mental health. The accessibility and reliability of study factors were examined in a 1997 pilot study, with some variables being discarded from the main study. A summary of study factors measured in the baseline survey is listed by data source in Table 8.1. Prospective exposure will be measured in the forthcoming follow-up study.

Classification of maltreatment

Maltreatment was coded using a modification of the US National Centre on Child Abuse and Neglect's (NCCAN) Harm Standard (Sedlak and Broadhurst, 1996). The harm standard was modified to account for the operationalisation of maltreatment by the Community Services child protection service. In most instances, NSW codes were readily translated (e.g. 'attempted strangulation' translates to 'physical assault'). However, some were ambiguous. For example, 'other physical abuse' might translate to either 'physical assault' or 'close confinement', while 'exposure to/used for pornography' can refer to quite different events. There was no classification for educational neglect, possibly because school attendance matters are the concern of the state education department. Although 'risk of harm' was not defined as maltreatment in the harm standard, it was grounds for notification in NSW. Hence, risk of sexual abuse (e.g. 'child's behaviour is indicative of sexual abuse') and risk of physical abuse were included in the modified classification. Finally, it was decided that exposure to domestic violence should be included as a separate, non-aggregated category of emotional abuse. In the pilot study, it was noted that caseworkers' coding of child maltreatment events was often ambiguous or incorrect, when referenced to their narrative descriptions of these events. Most events had quite detailed narrative descriptions recorded on the CIS. While these accounts might also be prone to error, they provided an opportunity to improve the

Table 8.1 Study factors measured in the CICS baseline survey

I *Measured from carer-report questionnaire*

Type of care (foster or kinship)
Length of care order
Carer's prior training
Child's placement initially temporary or permanent
Relationship of informant to child
Number of carers
Occupational status of carers
Who lives in the home?
Carer's health
Carer's experience
Carer's prior training
Support of other carers
Carer's perceived training needs
Child's case plan
Expectations about restoration
Recent adverse and positive events for the child
Child's birth family contact
Child's physical health problems
Medications
Reported intellectual disability
History of speech problems and speech therapy
Reading difficulties
Education, special education support, tuition
In-school behavioural support, school disciplinary actions
Child's utilisation of services
Perceived service needs
Provision of casework support
Sibling-related factors:
1 Number of children in foster home
2 Age difference to nearest aged child in placement
3 Sibling in shared placement is study participant

II *Measured from child welfare/alternate care database (CIS)*

Maltreatment history prior to entering care:
1 Forms of reported maltreatment
2 Timing and frequency of maltreatment events
Birth parent factors related to child maltreatment
Maternal age
Reports of maltreatment in care
Child's age at entry into care
Care history (e.g. placement changes, history of temporary care, prior restoration)
Length of care order
Demographic factors (child's age, ethnicity, gender, location)
Time in care
Type of care (foster or kinship)
Child's case plan
Sibling-related factors:
1 Child's birth order
2 Any siblings ever in care
3 Current placement shared with sibling
4 Oldest sibling in shared placement
5 Biological relationship to sibling in shared placement

reliability and validity of the coded classifications. Research assistants were trained to classify maltreatment events from the narrative reports, and to check their interpretations against the initial coding. The reliability of these classifications was checked periodically by the author. The lifetime incidence of various forms of maltreatment among the study sample is listed in Table 8.2.

Table 8.2 Lifetime incidence of maltreatment (confirmed notifications)

	Boys (%) n = 176[a]	*Girls (%)* n = 171
Sexual abuse	10.2	14.6
Non-contact	4.0	6.4
Contact	5.7	7.0
Intercourse	2.8	5.3
Emotional abuse	61.9	62.0
Verbal assault or threat	29.0	29.2
Classic emotional abuse	26.1	20.5
Exposure to domestic violence	27.3	36.3
Physical abuse	49.4	39.8
Physical assault	47.2	39.2
Close confinement	5.1	2.3
Any abuse	**77.3**	**73.1**
Abandonment/refuse custody	20.4	12.9
Inadequate supervision	42.6	42.7
Neglect of basic physical needs	48.9	49.7
Medical neglect	10.2	10.5
Inadequate nurturance (failure to thrive, etc)	34.7	26.3
Any neglect	**81.8**	**73.1**
Any maltreatment (abuse and/or neglect)	**94.9**	**92.4**

[a] No gender differences achieved statistical significance

Mental health predictors

The CICS identified retrospective and concurrent predictors of children's mental health from a large number of potential risk and protective factors. While a large number of potential risk and protective factors were associated with children's mental health, most were confounded. Predictors identified in two-stage hierarchical regression models accounted for 0.31 of the variance of continuous mental health scores. Risk modelling suggests that the risk of developing mental health problems among children in care is largely explained in terms of: (a) the effects of cumulative exposure to adversity; (b) attachment development; and (c) systemic influences on children's felt security (Tarren-Sweeney, 2008).

The principal finding was that entry into care at younger ages protects chronically maltreated children who are in need of care from developing mental health problems. The main implication of this is that psychological ill health can be prevented if child welfare agencies can identify such children at younger ages. The obvious challenges of earlier identification are: (a) avoiding false positive identifications that result in children being improperly removed from their parents; and (b) predicting which parents can attain substantive and lasting improvements in their caregiving within reasonable timeframes. There is need for research on how children who are in need of long-term care can be differentiated from other at-risk children in infancy, and what barriers there are to early entry into care.

Distributions of mental health difficulties

Mean ACC total clinical scores for boys and girls were 29.8 (SD = 22.4) and 29.9 (SD = 26.3). Older children had higher ACC total scores than younger children, although the effect size was fairly small ($r^2 = 0.03, p = 0.003$). Proportions of boys' and girls' ACC total scores in the clinical range were 46.6% and 42.7% respectively, and in the elevated plus clinical ranges were 55.1% and 54.4%. Sample distributions of ACC clinical and low self-esteem scales are described in Table 8.3. These score distributions suggest the following: about a third of the children were reported as manifesting at least some age-inappropriate sexual behaviour; a majority of children have a meaningful social difficulties, most notably in the form of non-reciprocal and indiscriminate interpersonal behaviour; most children have behaviours that are suggestive of felt insecurity (insecure scale); sizeable minorities of children are reported to manifest self-injury, abnormal responses to pain, and food maintenance behaviours; and very few children engage in suicidal talk or behaviour.

Girls were reported with more age-inappropriate sexual behaviour (boys mean = 0.9, girls mean = 1.6, p = 0.01) and pseudomature interpersonal behaviour (boys mean = 2.8, girls mean = 3.8, p = 0.008) than boys, whereas boys were reported with higher non-reciprocal interpersonal behaviour (boys mean = 5.2, girls mean = 3.8, p = 0.005), and more abnormal responses to pain (boys mean = 1.4, girls mean = 0.9, p = 0.01).

Inter-scale correlations of ACC and CBCL scores

Correlations among ACC clinical scale scores for boys and girls are set out in Table 8.4. Children's scores on the pseudomature, non-reciprocal, indiscriminate and insecure interpersonal behaviour scales were closely correlated (r = .56 to .65). These attachment-related problem scales also correlated highly with scores on age-inappropriate sexual behaviour. As expected, scores on the anxious–depressed and insecure scales were also closely related (r = .62), since both scales measure anxiety symptoms. However, there was low to moderate correlation (r = .16 to .45) between the various low prevalence clinical scales.

There were high correlations of CBCL aggressive and rule-breaking raw scale scores (r = .82 for boys and .78 for girls) and among the social problems, attention problems and thought problems sub-scales (r = .66 to .70 for boys and .67 to .75 for girls). Attention problems correlated highly with each of the externalizing sub-scales and with the social problems and thought problems sub-scales (r = .60 to .70 for boys and .66 to .75 for girls), suggesting they serve as markers for a range of problems observed among children in care. Correlations of the withdrawn–depressed and anxious–depressed internalising scales were more moderate, while somatic problems scores correlated relatively poorly with most other scales.

Table 8.3 ACC scale score distributions (n = 347)

ACC SCALES (maximum score)		*Mean*	*(SD)*	*Proportion (%) of scores in range Score range*						
High prevalence scales				**0**	**1–2**	**3–4**	**5–6**	**7–8**	**9–12**	**13+**
Pseudomature (16)	Boys	2.8	(2.9)	24	33	19	13	5	5	1
	Girls	3.8	(4.1)	25	27	15	11	6	10	6
Non-reciprocal (24)	Boys	5.2	(5.0)	19	22	14	12	9	12	12
	Girls	3.8	(4.2)	24	29	14	12	6	12	3
Indiscriminate (16)	Boys	6.4	(3.8)	6	12	18	16	18	15	5
	Girls	6.4	(4.5)	6	19	18	15	9	20	13
Insecure (28)	Boys	4.9	(4.9)	19	19	18	17	8	12	7
	Girls	5.4	(5.4)	15	24	14	17	9	9	12
Anxious–distrustful (20)	Boys	2.1	(2.8)	37	32	15	9	3	1	2
	Girls	2.6	(3.3)	32	33	15	8	4	6	2
Low prevalence scales				**0**	**1–2**	**3–4**	**5–6**	**7+**		
Sexual behaviour (22)	Boys	0.9	(2.1)	70	18	5	3	4		
	Girls	1.6	(3.2)	63	16	9	4	8		
Abnormal pain response (10)	Boys	1.4	(2.0)	49	29	13	5	4		
	Girls	0.9	(1.7)	63	25	5	4	3		
Food maintenance (8)	Boys	1.2	(1.9)	58	24	9	6	3		
	Girls	1.1	(2.0)	64	20	6	5	5		
Self-injury (28)	Boys	1.4	(2.6)	57	25	10	4	4		
	Girls	1.2	(3.0)	67	19	6	3	5		
Suicide discourse (14)	Boys	0.3	(1.1)	88	6	4	1	1		
	Girls	0.2	(1.1)	92	6	1	0	1		
Low self-esteem scales				**0**	**1–2**	**3–4**	**5–6**	**7–8**	**9–12**	**13+**
Negative self-image (18)	Boys	2.5	(3.7)	41	31	9	5	4	7	3
	Girls	2.2	(3.3)	46	24	12	7	5	4	2
Low confidence (16)	Boys	4.6	(3.7)	14	19	20	20	12	12	3
	Girls	3.8	(3.8)	23	27	13	14	9	12	2

Correlations of ACC clinical scale scores with CBCL syndrome, broadband and DSM-oriented raw scale scores are set out in Table 8.5. Excluding the CBCL somatic scales (syndrome and DSM-oriented), the ACC high prevalence scale scores (numbers II to VI) had moderate to high correlation (ranging from .37 to .76) with the various CBCL scores, while the ACC total clinical and CBCL total problem scores were strongly correlated (r = .88). There were low to moderate correlations between CBCL scales and the sexual behaviour, abnormal pain response, food maintenance, self-injury and suicide discourse scales. These correlations are partially deflated because these ACC scales measure relatively low prevalence problems. The non-reciprocal and indiscriminate scales correlated highly with the externalising and social, attention and thought problems sub-scales, as well as with the equivalent DSM-oriented scales (i.e. attention-deficit, oppositional-defiant, and conduct problems).

Table 8.4 Correlation matrices of ACC clinical scale scores for girls (above diagonal, n=171), and boys (below diagonal, n=176) with P values [a]

	Total Clinical	Sexual behaviour	Pseudomature	Non-reciprocal	Indiscriminate	Insecure	Anxious–distrustful	Abnormal pain response	Food maintenance	Self-injury	Suicide discourse
Total Clinical		.70	.77	.83	.83	.83	.75	.62	.59	.59	.43
Sexual behaviour	.61		.53	.62	.56	.45	.47	.35	.31	.25[***]	.37
Pseudomature	.72	.40		.62	.63	.60	.52	.40	.35	.29[***]	.23[**]
Non-reciprocal	.85	.54	.62		.64	.63	.55	.48	.45	.33	.31
Indiscriminate	.76	.45	.48	.56		.65	.49	.43	.40	.43	.23[**]
Insecure	.83	.40	.56	.65	.57		.65	.51	.43	.38	.20[**]
Anxious–distrustful	.69	.45	.52	.51	.39	.58		.37	.46	.43	.39
Abnormal pain response	.56	.34	.34	.46	.35	.40	.27[***]		.44	.47	.27[***]
Food maintenance	.55	.19[**]	.32	.39	.41	.30	.34	.17[*]		.47	.22[**]
Self-injury	.54	.21[**]	.22[**]	.34	.35	.34	.31	.28[***]	.44		.48
Suicide discourse	.39	.13[ns]	.32	.23[**]	.19[**]	.29[***]	.32	.05[ns]	.41	.39	

[a] All P values are less than 0.0001, except where indicated by: *** (P < .001), ** (P < .01), * (P < .05), ns (not significant)

Table 8.5 Correlation matrix of ACC and CBCL scale scores (age 6–11, n = 296) [a]

ACC SCALES	Anxious–depressed	Withdrawn–depressed	Somatic complains	Social problems	Thought problems	Attention problems	Rule-breaking	Aggressive	Affective problems	Anxiety problems	Somatic problems	ADH problems	Oppositional-defiant	Conduct problems	Internalising	Externalising	Total problems
	Syndrome scales								*DSM-oriented scales*						*Broadband*		
I Sexual behaviour	.30	.37	.27	.40	.47	.33	.54	.41	.35	.30	.21	.30	.35	.43	.38	.48	.50
II Pseudomature	.46	.36	.30	.50	.50	.37	.54	.54	.42	.40	.24	.47	.53	.44	.47	.57	.60
III Non-reciprocal	.48	.62	.24	.67	.68	.64	.76	.71	.53	.48	.18	.57	.62	.72	.55	.76	.78
IV Indiscriminate	.44	.39	.28	.70	.61	.64	.59	.62	.48	.47	.22	.63	.56	.56	.46	.64	.71
V Insecure	.69	.68	.41	.66	.65	.54	.47	.50	.63	.62	.35	.46	.42	.42	.74	.51	.70
VI Anxious–distrustful	.66	.51	.51	.50	.60	.38	.46	.50	.65	.70	.39	.41	.43	.42	.70	.51	.65
VII Abnormal pain response	.30	.41	.21	.35	.49	.43	.40	.40	.32	.30	.16	.40	.35	.39	.37	.42	.47
VIII Food maintenance	.28	.31	.30	.45	.50	.36	.53	.44	.45	.29	.22	.36	.40	.51	.35	.50	.53
IX Self-injury	.41	.40	.43	.43	.54	.40	.41	.44	.57	.36	.41	.37	.38	.44	.49	.45	.55
X Suicide discourse	.40	.27	.24	.31	.36	.21***	.34	.36	.47	.33	.15**	.23	.31	.39	.38	.37	.40
Total clinical score	.65	.65	.45	.77	.81	.68	.75	.73	.70	.64	.36	.66	.64	.68	.72	.77	.88

CBCL SCALES

[a] All P values are less than 0.0001, except where indicated by: *** ($P < .001$) or ** ($P < .01$)

Chapter 9

Content development and item analysis

Development and analysis of ACC items

Development of ACC clinical content

Clinical and self-esteem items were developed separately. The ACC's clinical content was derived systematically over several years, using a combination of deductive and inductive strategies. The aim was to identify all clinically significant problems experienced by children in alternate care that are not adequately measured by the CBCL. Deductive, or content-based strategy, is 'based on a priori or theoretical conceptions of the behavioral or personality domain that the instrument is being designed to measure' (Aiken, 1996). In applying a deductive strategy, items are designed to measure pre-determined constructs. An example would be the development of a diagnostic screening interview. By contrast, inductive (or empirical) strategy is applied without presumption of underlying constructs. Instead, clinical content is identified at the level of individual behaviours or symptoms, and syndromes are identified from statistical analysis of large item sets (Aiken, 1996; Burisch, 1984). Research on the mental health of maltreated children has been limited, and little is known about the phenomenology of problems manifested by children in care. Hence, a purely deductive approach would fail to locate some relevant problems. Conversely, it was thought that content derived inductively could be biased because of the relatively small scale of the project (e.g. via selection bias, responder bias or location bias). Hence, a combination of deductive and inductive strategies was employed to maximise the validity and comprehensiveness of the selected content. These strategies are set out below.

Although children and young people in residential care were not included in the CICS, the ACC's content refers to difficulties manifested by them. At the time the ACC was developed, all large residential facilities were disestablished in NSW (as part of a reform of alternate care). Consequently, most children and young people who formally would have been placed in residential care (because of disruptive behaviour and serial placement breakdown) remained in high-needs foster placements. This partly accounts for the high rates of mental health disturbances detected in the CICS foster care cohort (Tarren-Sweeney and Hazell, 2006). Prior to closure of the facilities, many of the clinicians who contributed to the development and review of ACC content (myself included) had worked extensively with children in residential care.

Step 1: review of clinical assessment reports

Clinical assessment reports of children residing in foster, kinship and residential care, as well as those of maltreated children, were perused for references to individual behaviours, and for diagnostic terms. In all, 110 assessment reports were sourced from 50 psychological records of children who either were, or had been in care, or who were child protection clients. The assessments were conducted by psychologists and psychiatrists working in specialist public health services, child welfare services, private fostering agencies and private practice. Twenty-seven items of problem behaviour were identified in this way. The most commonly listed diagnoses were disruptive behaviour disorders and attachment disorders.

Step 2: state-wide survey of clinicians

Forty-seven clinicians (psychiatrists and psychologists) who worked extensively or exclusively with NSW children in care and or maltreated children were asked to: (a) list mental health problems they had encountered among such children, which are not adequately measured by the CBCL; and (b) comment on 27 proposed items. Seventeen clinicians responded to the survey, most providing detailed written or verbal feedback. Responses endorsed each of the proposed items (as being both relevant and maladaptive), and generated an additional 22 items. They consistently emphasised the presence of attachment difficulties among the target children.

Step 3: literature review

A review of literature describing the mental health of maltreated children, and of children in foster, kinship and residential care, was performed. Types of psychopathology that are known to be over-represented among target children were also reviewed (e.g. attachment disorders, dissociation, post-traumatic stress disorder), so as to identify the component symptoms.

Step 4: development of a conceptual framework

There was considerable concordance in the problems identified in the field versus those described in the literature. Exceptions to this were abnormal eating (barely mentioned in the literature) and symptoms of post-traumatic stress disorder (infrequently identified by clinicians or in assessment reports). Both sources highlighted the pervasiveness of attachment difficulties among the target children. From the information collated to this point, a conceptual framework was developed in the form of hypothesised symptom clusters (see Table 9.1). This framework prompted the inclusion of another 60 items.

Step 5: review by foster parents

A 129-item draft instrument was constructed for use in the CICS pilot study. This version was reviewed by a focus group of fifteen experienced foster parents. The group endorsed the ACC's readability and item validity, and they thought the user instructions were clear. They were also asked whether foster parents might be offended or distressed by any content, notably the sexual behaviour and self-injury items. They argued that, in the context of a clinical assessment or research, foster parents would typically feel affirmed or relieved when reading such content, since it describes real problems that they have to contend with. The group proposed three additional items and revisions to five items.

Table 9.1 Hypothesised symptom clusters for 132-item ACC (research version)

Symptom clusters	*No. of items*
Abnormal sexual behaviour	15
Self-injury, risk-taking and suicidal behaviour	20
Self-injury (12)	
Risk-taking (3)	
Suicide (5)	
Anxiety responses to trauma	12
Dissociative responses to trauma	6
Other maladaptive responses to physical abuse	9
Food/eating problems	9
Attachment difficulties (insecure or disordered attachment)	32
Inhibited, avoidant interpersonal behaviour (13)	
Disinhibited, over-familiar interpersonal behaviour (11)	
Insecure, anxious attachment behaviour (8)	
Peer relationship difficulties	14
Total clinical items [a]	112
Self-esteem items	20

[a] 5 items were listed under two clusters

Step 6: review by clinicians

A 132-item research version of the ACC was constructed for the CICS baseline survey. This version was reviewed by a group of ten experienced child and family psychologists, who worked primarily with children in foster and kinship care and with maltreated children. Many of the reviewers had also worked with children in residential care and three were respondents in the clinician survey. They also endorsed the items' readability and validity, as well as the user instructions. No additional items were proposed.

Development of ACC low self-esteem content

Items measuring low self-esteem were developed separately from clinical content, using a different procedure. Twenty carer-report items were designed to measure low self-esteem constructs derived from the Coopersmith Self-esteem Inventory – School Form (CSEI) (Coopersmith, 1981). The CSEI is a valid and reliable child self-report instrument, designed to 'measure evaluative attitudes towards the self in social, academic, family, and personal areas of experience' (Coopersmith, 1981) Of 58 items, 26 purport to measure general self-esteem, that is, descriptors of self-image and self-confidence that are not specific to a single setting (such as school or home). An analysis of the meaning of the general items suggests they measure: low versus high self-worth; negative versus positive self-image; adjustment to change; self-confidence; and perceived competence, dependability, decisiveness and persistence. Twenty carer-report items were designed to measure these constructs in the ACC.

ACC item analysis

Item and factor analyses were performed on ACC scores for 412 children in long-term care in NSW, obtained via three sources: the CICS baseline survey (n = 347) (Tarren-Sweeney and Hazell, 2006); the CICS pilot study (n = 33); and clinic referrals (n = 32). The latter scores were obtained in clinical assessments conducted by the author. The children ranged in age from 4 to 11 years, but more than 60 per cent were 6 to 8 years old. Gender was evenly distributed (209 boys, 203 girls).

A nominal total clinical score was generated from the sum of clinical item scores, and item-total correlations were calculated. All item-total correlations were positive, with 83% exceeding $r = .30$, and 27% exceeding $r = .50$. Five low prevalence items correlated less than $r = .20$. The procedure was repeated for low self-esteem items.

Thirty-two items had a gender ratio of item mean scores greater than 1.5 (boy > girl = 16 items; girl > boy = 16 items). Four items had item-age correlations between .20 and .30, and 29 items had item-age correlations between .10 and .20, most of which were positive (i.e. older children scored higher). However, these age effects were largely accounted for by children's age at entry into care, which was a confounder. The confounding also suppressed negative correlations.

Item prevalence, defined as the proportion of the sample scoring either 1 or 2, ranged from 0.8 per cent (attempts suicide) to 74 per cent (easily influenced by other children). The prevalences of items retained in the 120-item ACC are listed in Appendix 9. Six items had greater than 50 per cent prevalence. While these problems may thus be normative for children in care, they are maladaptive (each loaded on a factor measuring indiscriminate interpersonal behaviour), and are unlikely to be normative among children at large. Hence they were not discarded. Seventeen items had less than 5 per cent prevalence (referred to as low prevalence items), including three sexual behaviour items with less than 3 per cent prevalence. The latter three items were excluded from subsequent analyses and deleted from the checklist, because their inclusion did not increase the detection of children with sexual behaviour problems (as indicated by a nominal sexual behaviour score). The remaining 129 items were retained for factor analyses.

Development and analysis of ACA items

Development of ACA clinical content

Rather than devising content from scratch, the central strategy for selecting and developing item content for the ACA was to refine and build on the content development carried out for the ACC a decade previously.

Step 1: reviewing age-sensitive/age-appropriate ACC items

The initial step was to identify two sets of age-related items from the original pool of 132 ACC items, using both age-item correlations and clinical-developmental reasoning. First, several items were identified as behaviours that are largely manifested among younger children, and which are developmentally-based (such as pica-related behaviours and masturbation in view of others). Second, several items were identified as being maladaptive during early and middle childhood, but likely to be increasingly normative at ages 15 to 17 (e.g. some of the non-coercive sexual behaviours; cutting or ripping one's clothes). Further to this, two items measuring inattention were removed because 'inattention' is adequately measured by the CBCL. Thirteen items were thus removed from the ACC 132-item pool.

Step 2: state-wide survey of clinicians

Approximately forty psychologists employed by the psychological service of the NSW statutory child welfare agency, who carry out clinical assessments of young people in care, were invited to propose any:

- individual problematic behaviours, emotional states, traits or manners of relating to other people, that are particularly observed among adolescents in care aged 12 to 17 years, and which are not adequately measured by the ACC or CBCL;
- mental health disorders, syndromes or constructs that are particularly manifested by adolescents in care, and which are not presently measured by the ACC or CBCL.

Eight clinicians responded to the survey. Several respondents proposed that adolescents in care present with trauma-related PTSD and dissociative symptoms that are not measured by the ACC. Others emphasised the need to obtain more comprehensive measurement of emotional and behavioural dysregulation.

Step 3: literature review

A review was carried out of literature describing the mental health of maltreated young people, and of adolescents in foster, kinship and residential care, updating a review carried out a decade earlier during development of the ACC.

Step 4: development of a conceptual framework

The steps carried out to this point supported the retention of content contained in the ACC's clinical scales, as well as retention of the two low self-esteem scales, with some modifications to the item pool and item wording. From the collated information, a conceptual framework was developed in the form of hypothesised symptom clusters additional to the ACC's 10 clinical scales. The conceptual framework is summarised in Table 9.2, centring on trauma and dysregulation symptoms. A number of items measuring dissociation were included in the 132-item research version of the ACC, but only a weak dissociation factor was identified at that time. It was thought that the dissociation items written for the ACC may not adequately measure the forms of dissociation manifested by children and young people in care. Further work was done to construct improved dissociation items to pilot in the CICS follow-up and adolescent surveys. Whereas clinicians and the literature did not identify restrictive eating symptoms as being characteristically observed among this population, the present research presented an opportunity to examine the utility and relevance of measuring eating disorder symptoms among young people in care.

Step 5: modification of items for an adolescent population

Fifteen ACC items were modified so as to have greater validity for an adolescent population. The modified ACA items are listed alongside the original ACC items, together with the reasoning for each modification, in Table 9.3.

Table 9.2 ACA hypothesised symptom clusters additional to the ACC's 10 clinical factors

Symptom clusters	*No. of existing ACC items*	*No. of new items*
Trauma-related dissociation symptoms	4	6
PTSD/trauma-related anxiety symptoms	10	4
Emotional dysregulation symptoms	3	9
Disconnection/sense of belonging	0	2
Eating disorder symptoms	4	7

Table 9.3 Modifications to ACC items included in the ACA

ACC item	*Modified ACA item*	*Reason for modification*
Causes herself to vomit	Causes herself to vomit, *after eating (or uses laxatives)*	Younger children vomit during tantrums
Distressed by traumatic memories	Distressed *or troubled* by traumatic memories	Denotes other ways of experiencing negative effects
Easily influenced by other children	Easily influenced by other *young people*	
Fears you will reject her	Fears you *(or other adults)* will reject her	Adolescents have expanded social network and supports
Forces or pressures other children into sexual acts	Forces or pressures other *youth or* children into sexual acts	
Has nightmares	Nightmares *about specific events or people*	More specific to trauma
Has blackouts or periods of amnesia	Has periods of amnesia	'Blackouts' not sufficiently specific to mental ill-health *(e.g. has no memory of what has happened in the last hour)*
Prefers to be with adults, rather than children	Prefers to be with adults, rather than *peers*	
Prefers to mix with older children	Prefers to mix with older *youths*	
Shows sex parts to others	Inappropriately shows genitals to others (in person, or by video or photo)	Rules out appropriate situations; genitals less ambiguous than sex parts; caregivers reporting common transmission of photos by phone and internet
Startles easily	Startles easily *('jumpy')*	Increase comprehension of the item's meaning
Starts rude conversations, tells jokes about sex	Seems overly preoccupied with sex (e.g. crude sexual talk, inappropriate sexual comments)	The child version is increasingly normative in later adolescence
Thinks other children are better than her	Thinks other *young people* are better than her	
Touches or puts mouth on other person's sex parts	Touches or puts mouth on other person's *genitals or breasts*	'Genitals' less ambiguous than sex parts
Wary or vigilant	Wary or vigilant *(over-alert to danger)*	Increase comprehension of the item's meaning

Step 6: proposed new items reviewed by foster parent

A list of proposed new items was reviewed by two groups of foster parents, who were attending research focus groups as part of a study of caregiver perceptions of children and young people's reactions to birth family contact. They were asked to review the readability and validity of the list of proposed new ACA items after the focus groups were completed. Their feedback prompted changes to the wording of three of the items.

Step 7: inclusion of a draft instrument in the CICS follow-up and adolescent surveys

A draft version of the ACA containing 136 items (118 clinical items, 18 low self-esteem items) was completed by foster and kinship caregiver respondents in the CICS follow-up and adolescent surveys. The draft instrument contained 111 existing or revised items from the 132-item research version of the ACC, and 25 newly developed items.

ACA item analysis

Item and factor analyses were performed on ACA scores for 372 young people in long-term alternate care, obtained from three sources: the CICS follow-up survey (n = 85); the CICS adolescent survey (n = 147); and de-identified ACC scores for 142 young people residing in treatment foster care (TFC), provided by a TFC programme in Ontario, Canada. The young people ranged in age from 11 to 18 years, with a mean age of 14.8 years. There was uneven distribution of young people across the age ranges, with fewer numbers in the oldest and youngest age groups (see Table 9.4). The mean age of young people in the three samples outlined above was 15.6, 15.2 and 14.0 years respectively. Gender was also unevenly distributed (54 per cent boys and 46 per cent girls). Eighty-three per cent of young people resided with foster parents, 13 per cent with kin and 4 per cent with adoptive parents. Their mean age at entry into care was 6.2 years and mean time in care (including post-care adoption) was 6.2 years. A total of 78 per cent of young people had clinic referred status, as defined by one or more of the following criteria: (1) residing in treatment foster care; (2) prescribed psychometric medication; (3) caregiver receiving behavioural support or other carer intervention or young person receiving individual or group psychotherapy or counselling; and (4) caregiver actively seeking referral to a mental health service.

Table 9.4 Age distributions of ACA development sample by source and gender

Age	*Total n*		*Study source*		*Gender*	
		CICS follow-up	*CICS adol. survey*	*Canadian TFC*	*Boys*	*Girls*
11	17	1	2	14	11	6
12	37	0	3	34	21	16
13	67	15	28	24	31	36
14	94	23	45	26	52	42
15	56	8	28	20	35	21
16	47	11	18	18	23	24
17	46	24	16	6	25	21
18	8	3	5	0	3	5
Total	372	85	147	142	201	171

A nominal total clinical score was generated from the sum of clinical item scores, and item-total correlations were calculated for the CICS samples (n = 230). All but one of the item-total correlations were positive (the exception was excessive dieting or fasting), with 84% exceeding $r = 0.30$, and 40% exceeding $r = 0.50$. Eight items correlated less than $r = 0.20$. The procedure was repeated for low self-esteem items. The lowest low self-esteem item-total correlation was .44, with all others exceeding $r = 0.50$.

Excluding items that have an aggregate mean score less than 0.2, there were 19 items for which the gender ratio of item mean scores exceeded 1.5 (boy > girl = 11 items; girl > boy = 8 items). Sixteen items had an item-age correlation between .10 and .20 (9 positive and 7 negative), and there was one item-age correlation higher than .20 (uses drugs or alcohol other than prescribed medications, $r = .31$). The latter correlation possibly reflects the increasingly normative use of alcohol in late adolescence. The analyses revealed considerably less age variation in item scores across the 11 to 18 year age-span, than was found across the 4 to 11 year age-span during the development of the ACC, possibly because the present data appear to be less confounded by age at entry into care.

Clinical item prevalence, defined as the proportion of the sample scoring either 1 or 2, ranged from 0.8 per cent to 69 per cent. Seven items had greater than 50 per cent prevalence, such that they might be considered to be characteristic difficulties of young people in care. Five of these were considered to be sufficiently maladaptive to retain for further analysis, while attention-seeking behaviour, and easily influenced by other young people were not retained. Another seven items had very low prevalence and were not retained for factor analysis, including several that refer to restrictive eating. An initial exploratory factor analysis included these items but did not locate a restrictive eating factor. Consequently, a total of 9 clinical items were discarded prior to factor analysis.

BAC–C and BAC–A item selection

The Brief Assessment checklists were purposely designed to contain no more than 20 problem items, with a view to matching the number of problem items contained in the SDQ. This is because the SDQ's widespread use and acceptability for mental health screening for children is due in large part to its brevity. Items were selected on their ability to discriminate between normal and clinical range scores on the ACC and CBCL. Items were initially selected for further analysis based on high correlations with the ACC/ACA/CBCL total scores, as well as the strength of their factor loadings on the ACC/ACA sub-scales. Higher prevalence items tended to have greater discriminatory ability, i.e. to be both sensitive and specific. Low prevalence items however, tended to be clinically specific (i.e. were mostly scored by children with clinical-level difficulties across a range of symptom scales), but lacked sensitivity (i.e. many children with clinical-level difficulties did not score on these items). This generated a pool of the most promising items.

From this pool, various item combinations were then examined collectively (i.e. using their total scores) on their ability to discriminate between normal and clinical range scores on the various ACC and ACA low prevalence sub-scales (since several of these sub-scales had not contributed any items to the pool). Because high scores on the low prevalence scales almost always occur alongside other mental health difficulties, the item pools tended to be quite accurate in screening for low prevalence difficulties. However, item selection required some trade-offs between items that could discriminate across multiple syndromes, and items that increase screening accuracy for a single sub-scale.

BAC–C and BAC–A mean item scores, estimated item population prevalence (estimated per cent scoring 1 or 2), and item correlations with BAC–C/BAC–A and ACC/ACA total scores, are listed in Table 9.5. BAC–A mean item scores are unweighted (i.e. these are the sample means), while the population item prevalences are weighted estimates (CICS sample prevalence multiplied by 1.2). BAC–C sample item (and estimated population) prevalence ranged from 14% to 68%, and the estimated population prevalence of BAC–A items ranged from 8% to 68%.

Table 9.5 Brief Assessment Checklists (BAC-C and BAC-A) item characteristics

Brief Assessment Checklist for Children (BAC-C)

Item		*Item mean score* *Girls*	*Boys*	*Prevalence %*[a]	*Item–ACC correlation*[b]	*Item–BAC-C correlation*[c]
1	Can't concentrate, short attention span	.84	1.16	66	.53	.52
2	Craves affection	1.06	.90	64	.60	.65
3	Distressed or troubled by traumatic memories	.40	.40	28	.53	.57
4	Does not show pain if physically hurt	.16	.23	15	.40	.39
5	Eats too much	.37	.35	25	.43	.39
6	Fears you will reject her/him	.42	.38	31	.54	.59
7	Hides feelings	.22	.19	37	.64	.65
8	Is convinced that friends will reject her/him	.29	.22	20	.61	.61
9	Lacks guilt or empathy	.53	.63	39	.61	.63
10	Prefers to be with adults, rather than children	.54	.34	32	.53	.55
11	Relates to strangers 'as if they were family'	.73	.69	47	.56	.63
12	Seems insecure	.53	.56	44	.62	.66
13	Sexual behaviour not appropriate for her/his age	.27	.17	14	.55	.55
14	Startles easily ('jumpy')	.49	.38	33	.58	.58
15	Suspicious	.24	.34	22	.61	.61
16	Too dramatic (false emotions)	.61	.41	35	.61	.65
17	Too friendly with strangers	1.02	1.00	68	.49	.55
18	Too jealous	.57	.47	40	.59	.63
19	Treats you as though you were the child, and she/he was the parent	.40	.29	26	.47	.50
20	Uncaring (shows little concern for others)	.29	.53	31	.54	.56

Table 9.5 continued

Brief Assessment Checklist for Adolescents (BAC-A)

Item		*Item mean score (unweighted)*		*Prevalence %*[d] *(weighted)*	*Item–ACA correlation*[e]	*Item–BAC–A correlation*[f]
		Girls	*Boys*			
1	Appears dazed, 'spaced out' (like in a trance)	.34	.25	24	.50	.47
2	Constantly seeking excitement or 'thrills'	.32	.34	30	.49	.51
3	Craves affection	.80	.57	46	.54	.57
4	Does not share with friends	.30	.43	29	.48	.51
5	Does not show affection	.42	.52	37	.33	.41
6	Feels victimised or misunderstood	.28	.46	37	.60	.60
7	Gorges food	.31	.50	28	.60	.56
8	Hides feelings	.79	.80	56	.47	.53
9	Impulsive (acts rashly, without thinking)	.68	.95	68	.67	.75
10	Intense reaction to criticism	.58	.65	41	.63	.67
11	Lacks guilt or empathy	.62	.76	50	.69	.74
12	Relates to strangers 'as if they were family'	.36	.42	30	.56	.60
13	Resists being comforted when hurt	.31	.39	30	.38	.42
14	Sexual behaviour not appropriate for her/his age	.19	.14	8	.51	.48
15	Shows intense and inappropriate anger	.42	.63	47	.70	.74
16	Sudden or extreme mood changes	.42	.35	34	.57	.63
17	Too friendly with strangers	.61	.52	50	.48	.57
18	Too jealous	.40	.42	26	.63	.62
19	Tries too hard to please other young people	.53	.47	40	.54	.56
20	Withdrawn	.39	.44	28	.39	.43

[a] Item prevalence = percentage of children with item score of 1 or 2
[b] Correlation of the item score and the ACC total clinical score
[c] Correlation of the item score and the BAC-C total score
[d] Weighted item prevalence = percentage of CICS study participants with item score of 1 or 2, multiplied by 1.2 (i.e. estimated population prevalence)
[e] Correlation of the item score and the ACA total clinical score
[f] Correlation of the item score and the BAC-A total score

Chapter 10

Empirically-derived ACC and ACA scales

The clinical and low self-esteem scales of the ACC and ACA were derived empirically through factor analysis, rather than through deductive reasoning. This chapter describes the factor analyses carried out on ACC and ACA item scores, and the subsequent construction of clinical and low self-esteem scales.

Factor analysis of ACC clinical items

Factor analyses were performed on ACC scores obtained for 412 children in long-term care in NSW (the ACC development sample described in Chapters 8 and 9). Two preliminary analyses were conducted to locate items that load weakly on various models, with a view to maximising the subject to item (STI) ratio. In these analyses, a ten-factor model yielded the most stable and meaningful factors, while an eleven-factor model yielded a weak dissociation from reality factor. Items were withheld from the main analysis if they loaded less than .35 on any of the ten factors, and if their exclusion did not notably alter the factor structure of the retained items. Sixteen items did not load sufficiently (less than .35) on any factor, and were withheld from the main analysis. Five low prevalence items were also withheld from the main analysis.

Eighty-eight items were included in the main factor analysis, providing a STI ratio of 4.7. The sample size was insufficient to perform separate analyses for each gender. Twelve factors were retained after performing a scree plot test, each of which had an eigenvalue greater than 1.5. Oblique (promax) rotations were then performed on models of six to twelve factors. Again, the rotated ten-factor model yielded the most precise and clinically meaningful factors. Larger models produced additional, meaningless factors, while smaller models merged distinct constructs.

Two supplementary analyses were performed. A factor analysis of 92 items was conducted to estimate factor loadings for seven low prevalence sexual behaviour and self-injury items, which had been excluded from the main analysis. An exploratory analysis was also conducted on a pool of 81 items, to examine the factor structure obtained with a STI ratio greater than 5. Increasing the STI ratio did not alter the factor structure. The ten factors describe the following problems:

1 age-inappropriate sexual behaviour;
2 precocious, pseudomature interpersonal behaviour, including role-reversal;
3 emotionally inhibited, non-empathic, and controlling interpersonal behaviour;
4 indiscriminate, disinhibited interpersonal behaviour;

5 insecure, withdrawn and overly conforming interpersonal behaviour;
6 anxious, distrustful behaviour;
7 abnormal responses to pain;
8 food maintenance behaviour;
9 self-injurious and related behaviours;
10 suicidal behaviour and discourse.

The number of subjects in the present sample (n = 412) was sufficient to extract a stable factorial model, though the STI ratio was somewhat low at 4.7. Various rules of thumb have been used to determine an adequate sample size for exploratory factor analysis, including minimum sample sizes of 100 and 200 subjects, and having a minimum STI ratio of 4 or 5 (Bryant and Yarnold, 1995; Floyd and Widaman, 1995). It has been argued that such rules of thumb are arbitrary and that the stability of a factor analysis is more dependent on how strongly the items load on the factors (Floyd and Widaman, 1995; Guadagnoli and Velicer, 1988). In the present analyses, items generally loaded well on the various factors, and the factor structure appears to be stable. The structure did not vary in a proxy factor analysis performed on a reduced item set (with an STI ratio of 5.1).

Factor analysis of ACC low self-esteem items

A preliminary factor analysis examined the factor structure of the combined pool of low self-esteem and clinical items. Eighteen of the twenty low self-esteem items loaded predominantly on two self-esteem factors, in a twelve-factor model, while the other two items loaded on clinical factors. The latter two items were not retained for further analysis, and were deleted from the checklist. A principal components factor analysis with oblique rotations was then performed on the 18 retained low self-esteem items. This yielded a coherent and meaningful two-factor model of low self-esteem. The two factors were quite distinct, with all but one item loading > .60 on one factor, and < .20 on the other factor. These factors represent constructs of negative self-image and low confidence.

Constructing the ACC scales

Clinical and low self-esteem scales were derived from items loading above pre-determined values on the respective ten- and two-factor models. Items were not shared across scales. Initial requirements were that: (a) the correlation between prospective items and all other items in a notional scale (item – rest correlation) should exceed $r = .30$; and (b) an item's presence should not lower the internal consistency of a scale. Items were then assigned to the relevant scale if they loaded ≥ 0.30 on a single factor (n = 81), while items loading ≥ .35 on two factors were assigned to the scale with the highest factor loading (n = 9). There were a few exceptions to this. The item fears he/she might be molested was assigned to the anxious–distrustful scale, despite loading somewhat higher on *the sexual behaviour* factor. The item low self-esteem was not assigned to either of the self-esteem scales. Finally, four items loading on the indiscriminate interpersonal behaviour factor were not assigned to the scale, because they refer to inattention more than interpersonal behaviour. It is known that inattention is a correlate of indiscriminate attachment among children in care (Green, J., 2003; Kreppner *et al.*, 2001). Yet, it was thought that including inattention in this scale would make clinical interpretation difficult for future users.

In all, fourteen items included in this research version of the ACC were subsequently deleted, and ten were retained as other items (i.e. contributing to total scores, but not assigned to scales). Two new items were written to measure sexual behaviour that is more likely to occur in adolescence. The final version of the ACC thus contains 102 clinical items and 18 low self-esteem items. The scales are listed with their constituent items in Appendix 9. The clinical scales are numbered I to X in the order that best reflects inter-scale correlations.

Defining ACC clinical and elevated ranges

The ACC and ACA scales include defined clinical ranges, which indicate scores that are highly predictive of psychiatric impairment, and sub-clinical elevated ranges, which are designed to indicate a moderate likelihood of psychiatric impairment. Whereas the clinical ranges for CBCL scales are defined statistically using uniform T-score cut-points (such that each CBCL disorder is defined as having equal population prevalence), clinical and elevated sub-clinical ranges for the ACC and ACA clinical scales were each separately defined using a combination of criterion-referenced procedures and clinical reasoning.

Total clinical score

Relationships between ACC total score distributions and various indicators of psychiatric impairment (n = 347) were examined for the CICS baseline cohort (n = 347), with a view to identify clinically significant scores. The indicators were: CBCL total problems scores in the clinical range; CBCL total problems scores in the borderline plus clinical ranges; child reported to have a psychiatric diagnosis; child reported to have received counselling or psychotherapy in the previous year; carer received professional advice on managing child's behaviour or emotions; and child presently prescribed psychotropic medication. Sensitivity and specificity were plotted for each criterion in Receiver Operating Characteristics (ROC) analyses, using STATA (Statacorp, 2003). An instrument's screening accuracy is measured by the area under the ROC curve, referred to as the AUC, which is expressed as a proportion. An instrument that predicts no better than chance will have an AUC value in the vicinity of 0.5, while a 'perfect' screening instrument has an AUC of 1.0. Unless an instrument has a score cut-point that is 100 per cent accurate (i.e. incurs no false positive or false negative results), then every screening cut-point involves a trade-off between sensitivity (the proportion of clinical cases who are positively screened, i.e. score at or above the screening cut-point) and specificity (the proportion of non-cases who are negatively screened, i.e. score below the screening cut-point).

Optimal cut-points for each analysis were identified by balancing two objectives: (1) that the cut-point maximises the number of children correctly identified; and (2) that the cut-point has roughly equal sensitivity and specificity. The results of these analyses (listed in Table 10.1) suggest there are no substantive gender differences in clinically significant scores, meaning the same clinical cut-points can be applied to both genders. Two cut-points were selected to identify children with clinically significant mental health problems. First, ACC total scores of 27 and above constitute a clinical range that is highly predictive of psychiatric impairment. Second, ACC scores in the range of 21 to 26 constitute a sub-clinical elevated range, indicating a moderate likelihood of psychiatric impairment. Although neither cut-point incurred an unreasonable compromise between specificity and sensitivity, the

Table 10.1 Receiver Operating Characteristics (ROC) of ACC total score as screen for various clinical outcomes

	Boys (n = 176)				Girls (n = 171)			
	Optimal score	% Correct[a]	AUC[b]	95% C.I.[c]	Optimal score	% Correct	AUC	95% C.I.[c]
CBCL clinical range								
Total problems clinical range [d]	25	88%	.95	.92–.98	23	89%	.95	.91–.98
Total problems borderline [e]	21	85%	.93	.89–.96	22	88%	.94	.90–.97
Any scale in clinical range [f]	22	86%	.93	.89–.96	22	88%	.94	.91–.98
Clinical service use								
Reported diagnosis [g]	25	69%	.76	.68–.83	27	73%	.76	.67–.84
Counselling/psychotherapy [h]	21	67%	.71	.63–.79	25	75%	.79	.72–.86
Professional advice to carer [i]	23	61%	.63	.55–.71	22	63%	.64	.55–.72
Counselling + advice [j]	27	58%	.63	.55–.72	27	67%	.72	.63–.81
Psychotropic medication [k]	29	60%	.62	.52–.72	32	65%	.71	.58–.85

[a] Percent of scores that correctly classify criteria
[b] Area under the curve (AUC)
[c] 95% confidence interval of AUC
[d] CBCL total problems score in the clinical range (yes, n = 167; no, n = 180)
[e] CBCL total problems score in the borderline + clinical range (yes, n = 195; no, n = 152)
[f] Any CBCL scale score (broadband or sub-scale) in the clinical range (yes, n = 191; no, n = 156)
[g] Reported as having a prior diagnosis of an emotional, behavioural or psychiatric disorder (yes, n = 131; no, n = 209)
[h] Received counselling or psychotherapy in previous year (yes, n = 152; no, n = 191)
[i] Carer received professional advice re. management of child's behaviour or emotions (yes, n = 158; no, n = 189)
[j] Received counselling or psychotherapy and carer received professional advice (yes, n = 107; no, n = 236)
[k] Child presently prescribed psychotropic medication (yes, n = 57; no, n = 290)

clinical range is highly specific (resulting in few false positives) and the borderline plus clinical range is highly sensitive (few false negatives). For example, for predicting CBCL total problems scores in the clinical range, the sensitivity and specificity of the ACC clinical cut-point (score = 27) were 83% and 91% respectively, while the sensitivity and specificity of the elevated range cut-point (score = 21) were 91% and 79%.

Sub-scale scores

Clinical and elevated ranges for nine of the ten ACC sub-scales (clinical ranges were not defined for the suicide discourse sub-scale) were defined using a combination of criterion-referenced analyses and clinical reasoning. The sensitivity and specificity of sub-scale scores were referenced against each of the following criteria in Receiver Operating Characteristics (ROC) analyses: CBCL total problems scores in the clinical range; CBCL total problems scores in the borderline plus clinical ranges; child reported to have a psychiatric diagnosis; child reported to have received counselling or psychotherapy in the previous year; carer received professional advice on managing child's behaviour or emotions; and child presently prescribed psychotropic medication. Clinical reasoning was also employed to consider the extent to which various score ranges reflected normative, versus concerning, versus clinically meaningful manifestations of mental health difficulties. Two cut-points were selected to identify children with 'possible' and 'probable' clinically-meaningful mental health problems. Scores above the higher cut-points constitute clinical ranges that are highly predictive of psychiatric impairment (highly specific), while scores above the lower cut-point ranging up to and including the high cut-point constitute sub-clinical elevated ranges that retain high sensitivity for detecting psychiatric impairment.

Suicide discourse

Clinical and elevated ranges were not defined for the suicide discourse scale, for several reasons. The items contributing to this scale had very low prevalence, and were scored exclusively by children with moderate to severe global psychopathology. Second, clinicians understand that we do not have the means to accurately predict suicide risk. My general view is that any score on the suicide discourse scale warrants close follow-up and concern. It would thus be both nonsensical and irresponsible to attempt to define sub-clinical suicide discourse.

Development of the 44-item short form of the ACC

The first step in developing a short form version of the ACC was to limit the scope of what it measures, by excluding the items contained within a number of the ACC scales. The following scales/items were excluded:

1 low self-esteem (18 items);
2 suicide discourse, except 'threatens to injure him/herself' (6 items);
3 the Pica index (3 items);
4 all 'other items' i.e. those not contributing to a clinical scale (10 items).

This left a pool of 83 items that were candidates for the short form version.

Principal components factor analyses were then performed on 83, 33 and 44 items. First, analyses were performed on 82 retained items, using 8, 9 and 10 factor oblique (promax) rotations. Items that loaded strongest on the various factors were then retained for a smaller pool with a view to retaining between 4 and 6 items per short form scale. All items from the abnormal pain response (n = 4) and food maintenance (n = 4) scales were automatically retained. Factor analyses on various size pools indicated that the insecure factor is somewhat unstable, reflecting some overlap with the indiscriminate and anxious–distrustful factors. This is most probably because some of the items have multiple meanings, i.e. they are not specific symptoms for individual constructs. For example, a child might be 'clingy' because they have an insecure relationship style, or because they are fearful for their personal safety and looking for reassurance, or because they have an attachment disorder. The item 'craves affection' might also be indicative of an indiscriminate attachment disorder, or of an insecure relationship. The insecure factor is also possibly unstable because it combines relationship insecurity with over-compliance.

A 33-item analysis was conducted without the anxiety and insecurity items, yielding a stable 7-factor short-form scale. However, this was at the cost of not measuring insecurity or trauma-related anxiety. A final 44-item analysis produced a stable 9-factor model, closely replicating the factor structure of the long-form ACC. A stable 'insecure' factor was identified after removing items that measure over-compliance. The model accounted for 57 per cent of the score variance. This exceeds that of most published checklists for children, as well as that of the ACC long-form 10-factor model (49 per cent). The reason such a large proportion of the variance is accounted for by this short-form model is that it only contains the highest loading items from the long-form version. The structure and psychometric properties of the nine short-form clinical scales (factor loadings, item-rest correlations, item prevalence and internal reliability) are listed in Appendix 10.

Defining ACC–SF clinical and elevated ranges

Total clinical score

Clinical and elevated ranges for the ACC–SF total score were identified using a similar procedure to that used to determine clinical ranges for the ACC total score. Relationships between ACC–SF total score distributions and categorical measures of clinical status were examined for the CICS baseline cohort (n = 347), with a view to identifying clinically significant scores. The clinical indicators were: CBCL total problems scores in the clinical range; CBCL total problems scores in the borderline plus clinical ranges; and any CBCL sub-scale score in the clinical range. Sensitivity and specificity were plotted for each criterion in Receiver Operating Characteristics (ROC) analyses. Optimal cut-points for each analysis were identified by balancing two objectives: (1) that the cut-point maximises the number of children correctly identified; and (2) that the cut-point has roughly equal sensitivity and specificity. The results of these analyses (listed in Table 10.2) suggest there are no substantive gender differences in clinically significant scores, meaning the same clinical cut-points can be applied to both genders. Two cut-points were selected to identify children with clinically significant mental health problems. First, ACC–SF total scores of 14 and above constitute a clinical range that is highly predictive of psychiatric impairment. Second, ACC–SF scores in the range of 10 to 13 constitute a sub-clinical elevated range, indicating a moderate likelihood of psychiatric impairment. Although neither cut-point incurred an unreasonable compromise between specificity and sensitivity, the clinical range is highly specific (resulting in few false positives), and the elevated range is highly sensitive (few false negatives). For example, for predicting CBCL total problems scores in the clinical range, the sensitivity and specificity of the ACC–SF clinical cut-point (score = 14) were 81% and 93% respectively, while the sensitivity and specificity of the elevated cut-point (score = 10) were 92% and 76%.

Sub-scale scores

Elevated and clinical ranges for the ACC–SF sub-scales were selected so as to attain maximum concordance with the equivalent ACC sub-scale elevated and clinical ranges. This was done by plotting the sensitivity and specificity of children's ACC–SF sub-scale scores for predicting elevated and clinical score ranges on the respective long-form scales.

Factor analysis of ACA clinical items

Factor analyses were performed on ACA scores obtained for 372 young people in long-term alternate care (the ACA development sample described in Chapter 9). A series of principal components factor analyses were carried out using oblique (promax) rotations. The analyses were hampered by a relatively low sample size for the number of items under examination. To work around this limitation, a number of exploratory factor analyses were first carried out

Table 10.2 Receiver Operating Characteristics (ROC) of ACC Short-Form versus Long-Form total clinical scores as screen for clinical status

CBCL clinical range	*Short-Form total score (44 items)* Optimal score	% Correct[a]	AUC[b]	95% C.I[c]	*Long-Form total score (102 items)* Optimal score	% Correct	AUC	95% C.I.
Boys (n=176)								
Total problems clinical range[d]	14	87	.93	.90–.97	25	88	.95	.92–.98
Total problems borderline[e]	11	85	.91	.87–.95	21	85	.93	.89–.96
Any scale in clinical range[f]	11	85	.92	.88–.96	22	86	.93	.89–.96
Girls (n=171)								
Total problems clinical range[d]	14	87	.93	.90–.97	23	89	.95	.91–.98
Total problems borderline[e]	11	85	.91	.87–.95	22	88	.94	.90–.97
Any scale in clinical range[f]	11	85	.92	.88–.96	22	88	.94	.91–.98

[a] Percent of scores that correctly classify criteria
[b] Area under the curve (AUC)
[c] 95% confidence interval of AUC
[d] CBCL total problems score in the clinical range (yes, n = 167; no, n = 180)
[e] CBCL total problems score in the borderline + clinical range (yes, n = 195; no, n = 152)
[f] Any CBCL scale score (broadband or sub-scale) in the clinical range (yes, n = 191; no, n = 156)

to: (1) identify those factors that remain robust when selecting different sets of items; and (2) identify those items that do not load on any clinically meaningful factors through various rotations. Those items that performed weakly were progressively removed from the analyses, with a view to maximizing the subject to item (STI) ratio. Ten factors were initially retained after performing a scree plot test, each of which had an eigenvalue greater than 1.5. Rotations were then performed on models of 5 to 10 factors. The various analyses suggested a 7-factor model yielded the most stable and meaningful factors, while an 8-factor model yielded several additional weak factors, depending on which items were retained for analysis. Within the 7-factor model, two factors described very discrete constructs (food maintenance behaviour and sexual behaviour problems). These factors remained robust regardless of which items were included in the analyses. This made it possible to carry out separate exploratory factor analyses of those items loading on the other five factors, again with a view to increasing the STI ratio. The exploratory analyses identified a set of items that reliably loaded .40 or higher on at least one factor.

Two main factor analyses were then carried out. The first identified loadings on the food maintenance and sexual behaviour factors in a 7-factor model using a pool of 72 items, with an STI ratio of 3.2. The Kaiser-Meyer-Olkin (KMO) measure of sampling adequacy for these 72 items was .83 overall, confirming that the item pool was appropriate for factor analysis. This model accounted for 51 per cent of the score variance. The second identified loadings for the remaining five factors using a pool of 58 items (which excluded the food maintenance and sexual behaviour items), providing an STI ratio of 3.9, and with a KMO value of .85. This 5-factor model accounted for 47 per cent of the score variance.

Factor analysis of ACA low self-esteem items

A preliminary factor analysis examined the factor structure of a combined pool of low self-esteem items and the 59 clinical items that loaded on the 5-factor model described above. All of the low self-esteem items loaded on two low self-esteem factors within a 7-factor model, while none of the clinical items loaded on the self-esteem factors. This suggests that the low self-esteem and clinical items are both conceptually and statistically distinct. A principal components factor analysis with oblique rotations was then performed on the 18 low self-esteem items. This yielded the same two-factor model of low self-esteem identified among younger children during the development of the ACC, representing constructs of negative self-image and low confidence.

Constructing the ACA scales

Clinical and low self-esteem scales were derived from items with factor loadings above .40 on the relevant 7-factor and 5-factor clinical models, and the 2-factor low self-esteem model. Surprisingly, no item loaded above .40 on more than one factor. An additional criterion was that an item's presence should not lower the internal consistency of a scale. Seventy-two items met criteria for inclusion with a clinical scale. Fifteen items that were considered clinically important but did not meet criteria for inclusion were retained as other items. One such item (does not show pain if physically hurt) loaded .44 on a dissociation factor, but its presence would have lowered that scale's internal consistency. All of the low self-esteem items met inclusion criteria. The final version of the ACA thus contains 105 items (87 clinical items and 18 low self-esteem items). All of the low self-esteem items and 66 of the 87 clinical items are shared with the ACC. Four of the ACA clinical scales have equivalents on the ACC, while the remaining three describe constructs that are not measured by the ACC. The ACA scales are listed with their constituent items in Appendix 11.

Defining ACA clinical and elevated ranges

The ACC and ACA scales include defined clinical ranges, which indicate scores that are highly predictive of psychiatric impairment, and sub-clinical elevated ranges, which are designed to indicate a moderate likelihood of psychiatric impairment.

Total clinical score

Relationships between ACA total score distributions and various indicators of mental health impairment were examined across the three study samples, with a view to identify clinically significant scores. The indicators were: having CBCL total problems scores in the clinical range, and 'borderline plus clinical' ranges (CICS); having a reported psychiatric diagnosis (CICS); having prescribed psychopharmacologic medication(s) (CICS); and having ACC total scores in the clinical and 'elevated plus clinical' ranges (Canadian TFC sample). Sensitivity and specificity were plotted for each criterion in ROC analyses. An instrument's screening accuracy is measured by the area under the ROC curve, referred to as the AUC, which is expressed as a proportion. An instrument that predicts no better than chance will have an AUC value in the vicinity of 0.5, while a 'perfect' screening instrument has an AUC of 1.0. Unless an instrument has a score cut-point that is 100 per cent accurate (i.e. incurs no false positive or false negative results), then every screening cut-point involves a trade-off between sensitivity (the proportion of clinical cases who are positively screened, i.e. score at or above the screening cut-point) and specificity (the proportion of non-cases who are negatively screened, i.e. score below the screening cut-point).

Optimal cut-points for each analysis were identified by balancing two objectives: (1) that the cut-point maximises the number of young people correctly identified; and (2) that the cut-point has roughly equal sensitivity and specificity. The results of these analyses (listed in Table 10.3) suggest there are likely to be only slight gender differences in clinically meaningful scores, such that the same clinical cut-points can be applied to both genders. Two cut-points were selected to identify young people with clinically meaningful or likely mental health problems. First, ACA total scores of 24 and above constitute a clinical range that is highly predictive of psychiatric impairment. Second, ACA scores in the range of 17 to 23 constitute a sub-clinical elevated range, indicating possible psychiatric impairment and a need for further mental health assessment, or periodic monitoring. Although neither cut-point incurs an unreasonable compromise between specificity and sensitivity, the clinical range is very specific (suggesting few false positives), and the elevated plus clinical range is very sensitive (few false negatives). For example, when predicting CBCL total problems scores in the clinical range, the sensitivity and specificity of the ACA clinical cut-point were 82% and 91% respectively, while those for the elevated range cut-point were 94% and 78%.

Table 10.3 Receiver Operating Characteristics (ROC) of ACA total score as screen for various clinical outcomes

	BOYS				*GIRLS*			
	Optimal score	*% Correct*[a]	*AUC*[b]	*95% C.I*[c]	*Optimal score*	*% Correct*	*AUC*	*95% C.I.*
CBCL clinical ranges (CICS, n=230)[d]								
Total problems clinical range	26	90%	.95	.91–.98	23–26	89%	.96	.93–.99
Total problems borderline + clinical	19	90%	.96	.93–.99	14–18	87%	.95	.91–.98
Any CBCL scale in clinical range	18	91%	.97	.94–.99	12–14	85%	.93	.89–.98
ACC clinical ranges (TFC, n=142)[e]								
ACC clinical range	25	93%	.98	.96–1.00	24	100%	1.00	1.00–1.00
ACC elevated + clinical range	21	99%	1.00	.99–1.00	18	100%	1.00	1.00–1.00
Clinical service use (CICS, n=230)								
Reported diagnosis[f]	19	74%	.77	.69–.86	19	82%	.87	.80–.94
Psychopharmacologic medication[g]	22	77%	.79	.70–.87	23	76%	.88	.81–.95

[a] Percent of scores that correctly classify criteria
[b] Area under the curve (AUC)
[c] 95% confidence interval of AUC
[d] CBCL total problems scores in the clinical range (yes=87, no=143), borderline + clinical range (yes=112, no=118), and having any CBCL scale score (broadband or sub-scale) in the clinical range (yes=113, no=117), Australian CICS sample
[e] ACC total problems score in the clinical range (yes=117, no=25), and elevated + clinical range (yes=117, no=25), Canadian TFC sample
[f] Reported as having a prior diagnosis of an emotional, behavioural or psychiatric disorder (yes = 93; no = 137), Australian CICS sample
[g] Child presently prescribed psychopharmacologic medication (yes = 51; no = 179), Australian CICS sample

Sub-scale scores

Clinical and elevated ranges for ACA sub-scales (clinical ranges were not defined for the suicide discourse sub-scale) were defined using a similar combination of criterion-referenced analyses and clinical reasoning to that described for the ACC sub-scales.

Development of the 37-item short form of the ACA

The first step in developing a short form version of the ACA was to limit the scope of what it measures, by excluding the items contained within a number of the ACA scales. The following scales/items were excluded:

1 low self-esteem (18 items);
2 suicide discourse, except 'threatens to injure him/herself' (6 items);
3 all 'other items', i.e. those not contributing to a clinical scale (15 items).

This left a pool of 66 items that were candidates for the short form version.

Principal components factor analyses were then performed on 66, 40 and 37 items. First, analyses were performed on 66 retained items, using 5, 6 and 7 factor oblique (promax) rotations. Items that loaded strongest on the various factors were then retained for a smaller pool with a view to retaining between 5 and 8 items per scale.

A final 37-item analysis produced a stable 6-factor model, closely replicating the factor structure of the long-form ACA. The short-form 'social instability' factor has a stronger emphasis on attachment-related social difficulties and less emphasis on behavioural dysregulation, than the equivalent long-form factor, and hence the label for the short-term scale does not refer to behavioural dysregulation. The model accounted for 57 per cent of the score variance. This exceeds that of most published checklists for children, as well as that of the ACA long-form 7-factor model (51 per cent). The reason such a large proportion of the variance is accounted for by this short-form model is that it only contains the highest loading items from the long-form version. The structure and psychometric properties of the nine short-form clinical scales (factor loadings, item-rest correlations, item prevalence and internal reliability) are listed in Appendix 12.

Defining ACA–SF clinical and elevated ranges

Total clinical score

Clinical and elevated ranges for the ACA–SF total score were identified using a similar procedure to that used to determine clinical ranges for the ACA total score. Relationships between ACA–SF total score distributions and categorical measures of clinical status were examined for the CICS follow-up and adolescent survey samples (n = 230), with a view to identifying clinically significant scores. The clinical indicators were: CBCL total problems scores in the clinical range; CBCL total problems scores in the borderline plus clinical ranges; and any CBCL sub-scale score in the clinical range. Sensitivity and specificity were plotted for each criterion in Receiver Operating Characteristics (ROC) analyses. Optimal cut-points for each analysis were identified by balancing two objectives: (1) that the cut-point maximises the number of young people correctly identified; and (2) that the cut-point has roughly equal sensitivity and specificity. The results of these analyses (listed in Table 10.4) suggest there are

Table 10.4 Receiver Operating Characteristics (ROC) of ACA Short-Form versus Long-Form total clinical scores as screen for clinical status

	Short-Form total score (37 items)				*Long-Form total score (87 items)*			
CBCL clinical range	*Optimal score*	*% Correct*[a]	*AUC*[b]	*95% C.I*[c]	*Optimal score*	*% Correct*	*AUC*	*95% C.I.*
Boys (n=125)								
Total problems clinical range[d]	13	88%	.94	.91–.98	26	90%	.95	.91–.98
Total problems borderline[e]	10	85%	.94	.91–.98	19	90%	.96	.93–.99
Any scale in clinical range[f]	13	90%	.96	.93–.99	18	91%	.97	.94–.99
Girls (n=105)								
Total problems clinical range[d]	10	88%	.95	.91–.99	23–26	89%	.96	.93–.99
Total problems borderline[e]	8–9	85%	.93	.89–.98	14–18	87%	.95	.91–.98
Any scale in clinical range[f]	9	84%	.92	.86–.97	12–14	85%	.93	.89–.98

[a] Per cent of scores that correctly classify criteria
[b] Area under the curve (AUC)
[c] 95% confidence interval of AUC
[d] CBCL total problems score in the clinical range (yes, n = 87; no, n = 143)
[e] CBCL total problems score in the borderline + clinical range (yes, n = 112; no, n = 118)
[f] Any CBCL scale score (broadband or sub-scale) in the clinical range (yes, n = 113; no, n = 117)

no substantive gender differences in clinically significant scores, meaning the same clinical cut-points can be applied to both genders. Two cut-points were selected to identify young people with clinically significant mental health problems. First, ACA–SF total scores of 12 and above constitute a clinical range that is highly predictive of psychiatric impairment. Second, ACA–SF scores in the range of 9 to 11 constitute a sub-clinical elevated range, indicating a moderate likelihood of psychiatric impairment. Although neither cut-point incurred an unreasonable compromise between specificity and sensitivity, the clinical range is highly specific (resulting in few false positives), and the elevated plus clinical range is highly sensitive (few false negatives). For example, for predicting CBCL total problems scores in the clinical range, the sensitivity and specificity of the ACA–SF clinical cut-point (score = 12) were 82% and 92% respectively, while the sensitivity and specificity of the elevated cut-point (score = 8) were 93% and 76%.

Clinical sub-scale scores

Elevated and clinical ranges for the ACA–SF sub-scales were selected so as to attain maximum concordance with the equivalent ACA sub-scale elevated and clinical ranges. This was done by plotting the sensitivity and specificity of children's ACA–SF sub-scale scores for predicting elevated and clinical score ranges on the respective long-form scales.

Chapter 11

Validation of the ACC and ACA measures

Relationships between the clinical sub-scales

Relationships between the ACC clinical scales

Inter-correlations of ACC clinical scale scores for the development sample (n = 412) are presented in Table 11.1, while gender-specific inter-correlations of ACC clinical scale scores for the CICS baseline sample are listed in Chapter 8 (Table 8.4). As anticipated, scores on the interpersonal behaviour scales were moderately correlated, while scores on the lower prevalence scales (abnormal pain response, food maintenance, self-injury, and suicide discourse) correlated less with other scales. Correlations of clinical scale scores and the total clinical score ranged from r = .38 to .83. A principal components factor analysis conducted on the 10 clinical scale scores indicates the instrument has no higher-order factor structure (such as internalizing versus externalizing factors).

Relationships between ACA clinical scales

Inter-correlations of ACA clinical scale scores for the CICS follow-up and adolescent samples (n = 230) are also presented in Table 11.1. The clinical scales are numbered I to VII in the order that best reflects inter-scale correlations and symptom prevalence, i.e. adjacent scales are more closely related in terms of both correlation and the commonality of the difficulties being measured. A principal components factor analysis conducted on the seven clinical scale scores indicates the instrument has no higher-order factor structure (such as internalising versus externalising factors).

Validity of the ACC and ACA

Content validity

ACC content validity

The ACC's content was derived systematically over several years, with a view to identifying clinically significant behaviour manifested by 4 to 16 year-old children in foster, residential and kinship care that is not adequately measured by the CBCL. The instrument's content is both comprehensive and valid. It was derived using a combination of inductive and deductive strategies, including the development of a conceptual framework. The validity of the content was reviewed by experienced clinicians and foster parents, prior to inclusion in the CICS baseline survey. Content was also subjected to item and factor analyses, resulting in

Table 11.1 Correlation matrices of ACC (n = 412) and ACA (n = 230) clinical scales

ACC scales	Total clinical	Sexual behaviour	Pseudomature	Non-reciprocal	Indiscriminate	Insecure	Anxious–Distrustful	Abnormal pain response	Food maintenance	Self-injury
Sexual behaviour	.64									
Pseudomature	.74	.49								
Non-reciprocal	.82	.50	.57							
Indiscriminate	.79	.50	.57	.56						
Insecure	.83	.40	.58	.63	.61					
Anxious–distrustful	.70	.43	.50	.49	.43	.60				
Abnormal pain response	.58	.31	.34	.49	.36	.43	.31			
Food maintenance	.57	.24	.35	.43	.41	.38	.39	.29		
Self-injury	.57	.23	.25	.36	.38	.35	.36	.39	.44	
Suicide discourse	.38	.23	.25	.25	.20	.24	.33	.15	.28	.40

ACA scales	Total clinical score	Non-reciprocal	Social instability/ behavioural dysregulation	Emotional dysregulation/ distorted social cognition	Dissociation/ trauma symptoms	Food maintenance	Sexual behaviour
Non-reciprocal	.69						
Social instability/behavioural dysregulation	.88	.51					
Emotional dysregulation distorted social cognition	.83	.46	.66				
Dissociation/trauma symptoms	.65	.35	.41	.53			
Food maintenance	.66	.42	.50	.43	.47		
Sexual behaviour	.54	.25	.47	.29	.44	.36	
Suicide discourse	.40	.09	.22	.44	.29	.20	.40

deletion of some items. Item content can therefore be considered valid for 4 to 16 year-olds in various forms of alternate care, including residential care.

ACA content validity

The ACC's content was derived systematically over several years, with a view to identify clinically significant behaviour manifested by 4 to 16 year-old children in foster, residential and kinship care that is not adequately measured by the CBCL (Tarren-Sweeney, 2007). Further to this, a systematic process was pursued to identify additional adolescent-specific mental health difficulties manifested by young people in care, using a similar combination of inductive and deductive strategies, including the development of a conceptual framework. The validity of the content was reviewed by experienced clinicians and foster parents, prior to inclusion in the CICS follow-up and adolescent surveys. Content was also subjected to item and factor analyses, resulting in deletion of some items. Item content can therefore be considered valid for 12 to 17 year-olds in various forms of alternate care.

Construct validity

ACC construct validity

The construct validity of the ACC is strongly supported by estimates of factorial and concurrent validity, obtained in the pilot and baseline surveys of the CICS. The clinical scales were empirically derived from factor analyses. Various analyses revealed a stable factor structure, with most items loading strongly on a single factor. The proportion of the clinical item score variance explained by the 10-factor model (88 items, 49% per cent) is comparable to that reported for other carer-report checklists (Achenbach, 1991; Conners *et al.*, 1998; Dekker *et al.*, 2002; Goodman, 2001). Moreover, each scale appears conceptually coherent, i.e. the factors appear to be clinically meaningful, with few items being out of place. Most of the scales approximate syndromes described in the literature.

To possess construct validity, an instrument should correlate highly with measures of similar or allied constructs, and inversely with measures of opposing constructs (Aiken, 1996). The ACC and CBCL measure constructs that in many instances are phenomenologically-related (e.g. indiscriminate attachment problems with inattention; inhibited attachment problems with aggressive behaviour). It is thus anticipated that a child in care who demonstrates high scores on one instrument would likely have elevated scores on the other. The instrument's validity is supported by high correlations of ACC and CBCL total clinical scores (boys: $r = .89$; girls: $r = .90$) in the CICS baseline survey. This also suggests the ACC total clinical score is a valid measure of global psychopathology for children in care. Concurrent validity is further demonstrated by strong associations between ACC clinical scale scores and the CBCL total problems score. In a linear regression, the 10 clinical scale scores accounted for 80 per cent of the CBCL total score variance (adjusted R squared), with seven scales being independent predictors. Consistent with prior findings of an inverse relationship between children's social competence and problem behaviour (Achenbach and Rescorla, 2001), all boys' and girls' ACC scale scores were negatively correlated with CBCL social competence scores in the baseline survey.

ACA construct validity

The ACA's construct validity is supported by estimates of factorial and concurrent validity. The clinical scales were empirically derived through factor analysis. Various analyses revealed a stable factor structure, identifying a large pool of items that load strongly and exclusively on a single factor. The proportions of the clinical item score variance explained by the 7-factor model (75 items, 51 per cent) is comparable to that reported for the 10-factor ACC (Tarren-Sweeney, 2007), as well as for other carer-report checklists (Achenbach, 1991; Conners *et al.*, 1998; Dekker *et al.*, 2002; Goodman, 2001).

To possess construct validity, an instrument should correlate highly with measures of similar or allied constructs, and inversely with measures of opposing constructs (Aiken,

1996). While the ACA was designed to measure mental health difficulties experienced by adolescents in care that are not adequately measured by the CBCL, the total scores for both instruments should ideally provide estimations of global psychopathology, and thus should be strongly correlated. The ACA's validity is thus supported by high correlations of ACA and CBCL total clinical scores (boys: r = .90; girls: r = .88) for the combined CICS follow-up and adolescent survey samples (n = 230). Concurrent validity is further demonstrated by strong associations between ACA clinical scale scores and the CBCL total problems score. In a linear regression, the seven clinical scale scores accounted for 80 per cent of the CBCL total score variance (adjusted R squared), with five scales being independent predictors.

The Assessment Checklist for Children – Plus (ACC+) is a partially developed, 29-item carer-report checklist of behaviours suggesting adaptive, pro-social functioning and well-being. The items are scaled with a view to detecting small improvements in mental health among children and young people in care who have mental health disorders, i.e. to be more sensitive to therapeutic change than problem measures such as the ACC, CBCL or SDQ. Among the Canadian TFC sample (n = 142), ACC+ scores were moderately inversely correlated (r = -.56) with a nominal ACA total clinical score calculated from the 66/87 ACA items that overlap with the ACC instrument.

Criterion-referenced validity

ACC criterion-referenced validity: sensitivity to risk

The ACC appears to be sensitive to children's complex exposure to multiple risk factors, with clear evidence of dose-response relationships. In predictive modelling of baseline data (n = 347), developmental, pre-care and in-care risk factors predicted a high proportion of the variance in children's attachment problems (adjusted R squared = .29), as measured by a composite of the ACC pseudomature, non-reciprocal and indiscriminate scale scores. The same factors predicted between 15 per cent and 29 per cent of the variance of scores on each of the four interpersonal behaviour scales, the sexual behaviour scale and the anxious–distrustful scale. These factors also accounted for identical proportions of the variance of ACC and CBCL total scores (adjusted R squared = .31).

ACC criterion-referenced validity: referral/diagnostic status

An important measure of a clinical instrument's validity is its ability to differentiate between referred and non-referred children (Achenbach, 1991; Achenbach and Rescorla, 2001). The CICS surveyed several indicators of clinical service use, namely: children's engagement in counselling or psychotherapy in the previous year; psychotropic medication use; and provision of clinical advice to carers (such as behaviour management). However, these indicators don't neatly equate to referral status, since children in care often receive clinical services for reasons other than treatment of mental health problems (such as sexual assault counselling). There were also sizeable numbers of children and carers who had unsuccessfully sought access to clinical services. Hence in this sample, children's diagnostic status may represent a better mental health criterion than their referral status. Nonetheless, there were substantial differences in ACC scale scores stratified by referral, medication and diagnostic status. Group effect sizes, listed in Table 11.2, indicate that the ACC adequately differentiates between referred and non-referred children in care.

Table 11.2 Effect sizes (*d*)[a] of reported diagnostic status and clinical service use on ACC scale scores

	Reported diagnosis[b] (*n = 131*)	*Counselling/ psychotherapy*[c] (*n = 152*)	*Behaviour advice*[d] (*n = 158*)	*Psychotropic medication*[e] (*n = 57*)
Sexual behaviour	.42	.52	.24	.34
Pseudomature	.53	.73	.23	.18
Non-reciprocal	.83	.77	.34	.57
Indiscriminate	.68	.59	.28	.28
Insecure	.52	.76	.31	.32
Anxious–distrustful	.43	.53	.35	.25
Abnormal pain response	.62	.40	.30	.57
Food maintenance	.58	.44	.25	.30
Self-injury	.60	.45	.34	.24
Suicide discourse	.45	.44	.41	.03
Total clinical	.83	.84	.42	.49

[a] Effect size reported as standardized difference between mean scores (Cohen's *d*), i.e. the difference between group mean scores expressed as a proportion of the standard deviation of scores for the aggregate CICS sample
[b] Reported as having a prior diagnosis of an emotional, behavioural or psychiatric disorder
[c] Received counselling or psychotherapy in previous year
[d] Carer received professional advice re. management of child's behaviour or emotions
[e] Child presently prescribed psychotropic medication

ACA criterion-referenced validity: 'diagnosis/treatment/referral'

An important measure of a clinical instrument's validity is its ability to differentiate between referred and non-referred young people (Achenbach, 1991; Achenbach and Rescorla, 2001). The CICS follow-up and adolescent surveys surveyed several indicators of clinical service use or demand for services, namely: having a reported psychiatric diagnosis; being prescribed psychotropic medication; young people's engagement in counselling or psychotherapy in the previous year, and/or provision of clinical advice to carers (such as behaviour management); as well as unsuccessful attempts by caregivers to obtain such services. While these indicators don't neatly equate to referral status (since young people in care often receive preventative clinical services following abuse without regard to their mental health status), there were mostly substantial differences in ACA scale scores stratified by referral, medication and diagnostic status. Effect sizes (listed in Table 11.3) ranged from $d = .45$ to 1.12 for clinical scales measuring relatively common difficulties, and from $d = .14$ to .72 for the lower prevalence sexual behaviour problems and suicide discourse scales.

Predictive validity

The extent to which clinical range ACC and CBCL total problem scores in the CICS baseline survey (n = 347) independently predicted subsequent placement stability over an 8- to 9-year period (while controlling for a range of likely confounding variables), were compared in separate linear regression models. It was found that ACC total clinical scores in the clinical range (beta = .15, p = .008) more strongly predicted placement instability (defined by number of subsequent placement changes) than did CBCL total problem scores in the

Table 11.3 Effect sizes (*d*)[a] of reported diagnostic status and clinical service use on ACA scale scores

	Australian sample (n=230)			*Australian and Canadian samples n=372*
ACA scales	*Reported diagnosis*[b]	*Psychotropic medication*[c]	*Psychotherapy/ behavioural advice*[d]	*Clinic-referred*[e]
Non-reciprocal	.74	.67	.67	
Nominal non-reciprocal score (9/10 items shared with ACC)				.89
Social instability/beh. dysregulation	.73	.78	.67	
Nominal social instability./beh. dysreg. score (17/21 items shared with ACC)				.94
Emotional dysreg./dist. soc. cog.	.84	1.12	.75	
Dissociation/trauma symptoms	.67	.98	.43	
Nominal dissoc./trauma symp. score (4/7 items shared with ACC)				.45
Food maintenance	.68	.68	.57	
Nominal food maintenance score (4/7 items shared with ACC)				.70
Sexual behaviour problems	.27	.23	.14	.39
Suicide discourse	.46	.72	.28	.26
ACA total clinical score (87 items)	.95	1.06	.82	
Nominal ACA total clinical score (66 items shared with the ACC)				1.10

[a] Effect size reported as standardized difference between mean scores (Cohen's *d*), i.e. the difference between group mean scores expressed as a proportion of the standard deviation of scores for the aggregate CICS sample

[b] Reported diagnosis of an emotional, behavioural or psychiatric disorder: yes=137; no=93

[c] Young person presently prescribed psychotropic medication: yes=51; no=179

[d] Received psychotherapy or counselling in previous year, or caregiver received professional advice or training for management of young person's difficulties: yes=143; no=87

[e] CICS clinic-referred young people, plus the Canadian Treatment Foster Care sample 'Clinic-referred' defined as having a reported diagnosis, and/or prescribed psychopharmacologic medication, and/or receiving psychological treatment or behavioural support including TFC, or active attempt to obtain a mental health service: yes=291; no=81

clinical range (beta = .12, p = .03), while controlling for: children's age; age at entry into care; gender; intellectual disability; foster versus kinship care; length of pre-care exposure to maltreatment; number of pre-baseline placement changes; carer health problems at baseline; carer anticipates subsequent restoration; care order expires before age 16; and baseline placement commenced as temporary versus permanent placement. Two of the control variables also independently predicted post-baseline placement instability in both the ACC and CBCL regression models: age at entry into care, and number of pre-baseline placement changes.

Reliability of the ACC and ACA

Internal reliability

ACC internal reliability

Using scores obtained in the CICS baseline survey (n = 347), split-half reliability coefficients for the total clinical and low self-esteem composite scales were calculated from correlations of nominal split-half forms. These were each constructed from half of the available items (items were consecutively allocated to the two forms). The split-half reliability coefficients for the total clinical and low self-esteem composite scales were r = .93 (boys = .93, girls = .94) and r = .85 (boys = .85, girls = .86) respectively.

The internal consistency of the ACC scales was estimated using Cronbach's alpha (see Table 12.4). Cronbach's alpha was .96 for the total clinical score, and ranged from 0.70 to 0.86 for the clinical scales. This is comparable to that of the CBCL (Achenbach and Rescorla, 2001) and the Conners Parent Rating Scale (Conners *et al.*, 1998), and exceeds that of the SDQ (Goodman, 2001). Together these findings suggest the ACC scales have strong internal reliability.

ACA internal reliability

Internal consistency was high, with Cronbach's alpha ranging from .76 to .90 for the clinical and low self-esteem sub-scales (see Table 11.4), and alpha = .96 for the total clinical score and .92 for the composite low self-esteem score. This is comparable to that of the CBCL (Achenbach and Rescorla, 2001) and the Conners Parent Rating Scale (Conners *et al.*, 1998), while it exceeds that of the SDQ (Goodman, 2001). Split-half reliability coefficients for the total clinical and low self-esteem composite scales were calculated from correlations of nominal split-half forms. These were each constructed from half of the available items (items were consecutively allocated to the two forms). The split-half reliability coefficients for the total clinical and low self-esteem composite scales were r = .93 (boys = .94, girls = .92) and r = .88 (boys = .89, girls = .88) respectively.

External reliability

When considering the reliability of a carer-report psychometric measure, we need to delineate between extrinsic and intrinsic reliability. Intrinsic reliability is that which is directly attributable to the instrument's design and statistical properties. For example, an item can be poorly written because it has ambiguous or multiple meanings, such that caregivers interpret the item's meaning in different ways. In this case, the item detracts from the instrument's overall intrinsic reliability. Extrinsic reliability refers to that which is attributable to the general psychometric method, and/or the extent to which a particular construct can be reported on. The Assessment Checklist measures have extrinsic reliability that is attributable to them being caregiver report checklists. There are strengths and limitations with a caregiver-report method that affect the reliability of all caregiver-report measures. This includes situation-specific biases, such as the tendency of parents and other caregivers to overstate their child's difficulties when they are seeking a clinical service for their child. The reliability of foster parent reports of children's problems remains somewhat uncertain, although there is evidence that in respect of children in long-term care, foster parents are at least as

Table 11.4 Internal reliability coefficients for ACC and ACA development samples

ACC clinical scales		*N. Items*	*Reliability coefficients (Cronbach's α)* Aggregate n=412	*Boys* n=208	*Girls* n=203
I	Sexual behaviour[a]	9	.85	.85	.86
II	Pseudomature	8	.82	.75	.86
III	Non-reciprocal	12	.86	.87	.84
IV	Indiscriminate	8	.81	.77	.85
V	Insecure	14	.85	.84	.86
VI	Anxious–distrustful	10	.78	.77	.78
VII	Abnormal pain response	5	.70	.70	.69
VIII	Food maintenance	4	.80	.78	.82
IX	Self-injury	14	.81	.76	.84
X	Suicide discourse	7	.81	.77	.85
	Total clinical score[b]	102	.96	.95	.96
ACC low self-esteem scales					
I	Negative self-image	9	.89	.90	.88
II	Low confidence	8	.83	.82	.85
	Total low self-esteem[c]	18	.91	.91	.90
ACA clinical scales		*N. Items*	*Aggregate* n=230[d]	*Boys* n=125	*Girls* n=105
I	Non-reciprocal	10	.83	.81	.85
II	Social instability/behavioural dysregulation	21	.92	.91	.92
III	Emotional dysregulation/distorted social cog	14	.90	.90	.89
IV	Dissociation/trauma symptoms	7	.76	.83	.65
V	Food maintenance	7	.87	.87	.87
VI	Sexual behaviour	14	.85	.86	.87
VII	Suicide discourse	7	.88	.90	.83
	Total clinical score[e]	87	.96	.96	.95
ACA low self-esteem scales			n=372[f]	n=201	n=171
I	Negative self-image	9	.91	.90	.91
II	Low confidence	8	.83	.82	.84
	Total low self-esteem[c]	18	.92	.92	.92

[a] The sexual behaviour scale consists of 11 items (9 existing items plus two new items)
[b] Sum of the ten scale scores plus nine 'other items'
[c] Sum of the two scale scores plus one 'other item'
[d] Clinical scale reliability coefficients calculated for the combined CICS follow-up and adolescent samples, n=230
[e] Sum of the seven scale scores plus fifteen 'other items'
[f] Low self-esteem scale reliability coefficients calculated for the combined CICS and Canadian TFC samples, n=372

reliable as parents (Tarren-Sweeney *et al.*, 2004). There is further discussion about gauging the reliability of individual ACC scores in Chapter 3.

Important measures of external reliability of the ACC and ACA measures (test-retest and inter-rater reliability) have not yet been carried out, but are planned for forthcoming validation studies. Given the CICS obtained ACC/ACA and CBCL scores completed simultaneously by the same informant, some measure of external reliability can be gained from examining intra-rater correlation of scores on ACC and CBCL (1991 version) items that are highly similar, as well as for ACA and CBCL (2001 version) items that are similar. Intra-rater ACC-CBCL score correlations for six sets of similar items ranged from .70 to .83, while intra-rater ACA-CBCL score correlations for 8 sets of comparable items ranged from .62 to .85 (see Table 11.5).

Table 11.5 Intra-rater correlations of corresponding ACC-CBCL and ACA-CBCL item scores

ACC item	*CBCL item (1991 version)*	*Intra-rater correlation*
5. Can't concentrate, short attention span	8. Can't concentrate, can't pay attention for long	.81
20. Eats things that are not food	28. Eats or drinks things that are not food	.74
21. Eats too much	53. Overeating	.80
28. Feels worthless or inferior	35. Feels worthless or inferior	.70
35. Has nightmares	47. Nightmares	.83
62. Suspicious	89. Suspicious	.74
ACA item	*CBCL item (2001 version)*	
20. Eats too much	53. Overeating	.85
25. Feels worthless or inferior	35. Feels worthless or inferior	.70
32. Impulsive (acts rashly, without thinking)	41. Impulsive or acts without thinking	.80
39. Nightmares about specific events or people	47. Nightmares	.67
43. Prefers to mix with older youths	63. Prefers being with older kids	.74
44. Refuses to talk	65. Refuses to talk	.62
98. Sudden or extreme mood changes	87. Sudden changes in mood or feelings	.65
55. Suspicious	89. Suspicious	.73

Psychometric properties of the ACC and ACA short-form scales

The internal reliability of the ACC short-form total score (44 items) was alpha = 0.92 (n = 347), while the internal reliability of the six short-form scales ranged from 0.67 to 0.84. ACC–SF inter-scale correlations are listed in Table 11.6, and the structure and psychometric properties of the nine short-form clinical scales (factor loadings, item-rest correlations, item prevalence and internal reliability) are listed in Appendix 10.

The internal reliability of the ACA short-form total score (37 items) was alpha = 0.91 (n = 230), while the internal reliability of the six short-form scales ranged from 0.73 to 0.87. Inter-scale correlations are listed in Table 11.6, and the structure and psychometric properties of the six short-form clinical scales (factor loadings, item-rest correlations, item prevalence and internal reliability) are listed in Appendix 12.

Table 11.6 Correlation matrices of ACC (n=412) and ACA (n=230) Short-Form scales

ACC short-form scales	Total short-form	Sexual behaviour	Pseudomature	Non-reciprocal	Indiscriminate	Insecure	Anxious–distrustful	Abnormal pain response	Food maintenance
Sexual behaviour	.57								
Pseudomature	.68	.32							
Non-reciprocal	.76	.41	.42						
Indiscriminate	.73	.40	.41	.50					
Insecure	.70	.32	.41	.39	.42				
Anxious–distrustful	.64	.28	.43	.39	.25	.52			
Abnormal pain response	.53	.24	.34	.37	.28	.26	.23		
Food maintenance	.61	.20	.27	.40	.38	.33	.37	.27	
Self-injury	.45	.16	.15	.28	.29	.28	.27	.26	.34

ACA short-form scales	Total short-form	Non-reciprocal	Social instability	Emotional dysregulation/distorted social cognition	Dissociation/trauma sym.	Food maintenance
Non-reciprocal	.61					
Social instability	.80	.33				
Emotional dysregulation/distorted social cognition	.74	.35	.47			
Dissociation/trauma sym.	.67	.30	.32	.55		
Food maintenance	.69	.30	.44	.37	.44	
Sexual behaviour	.57	.18	.43	.28	.42	.36

Chapter 12

BAC psychometric properties and screening accuracy

Psychometric properties of the Brief Assessment Checklists

Mean (standard deviation) BAC–C total difficulties scores for the aggregate 4–11 year-old sample (n= 347), boys (n = 176), and girls (n = 171) were 10.0 (8.0), 9.9 (7.6) and 10.2 (8.4) respectively, suggesting the score distributions did not vary by gender. Mean (standard deviation) BAC–A total difficulties scores for the aggregate 11–18 year-old sample (n = 230), boys (n = 125), and girls (n = 105) were 8.5 (7.6), 9.0 (7.7) and 7.8 (7.4) respectively, suggesting a slight gender variation in the adolescent score distributions. Consistent with previously reported age analyses of ACC (Tarren-Sweeney, 2007) and ACA scores (Tarren-Sweeney, 2013a): (1) older children scored slightly higher on the BAC–C than younger children (age–total score correlation = 0.16), with this age effect being confounded by children's age at entry into care (older children were more likely to have entered care at older ages, and with greater exposure to pre-care maltreatment); and (2) no age effect was located among BAC–A scores (age–total score correlation = – 0.02).

The internal consistency (Cronbach's alpha) of BAC–C and BAC–A scores were 0.89 and 0.87 respectively. The internal consistency of the derived parent-report BPM total score in the CICS child and adolescent samples was 0.88 (17 items) and 0.91 (19 items) respectively, which is similar to that previously reported for a large US normative sample (n = 3200, a = 0.92) (Achenbach *et al.*, 2011). BAC–C/A internal consistencies are thus somewhat comparable to that of the parent-report BPM (described in Chapter 1), while they compare favourably to a large number of published estimates of the internal consistency of the SDQ parent-report total difficulties scale (weighted mean SDQ total difficulties alpha = 0.80, range = 0.53–0.84) (Stone *et al.*, 2010).

Very high correlations were found between BAC–C and ACC total scores (r = 0.96) and BAC–A and ACA total scores (r = 0.94). Similarly high correlations were found between BPM scores (generated from sample CBCL scores) and CBCL scores for the child (r = 0.93) and adolescent (r = 0.94) samples. Correlations of BAC–C and BAC–A total scores with the CBCL total problem score were 0.82 and 0.88 respectively. By contrast, a weighted mean correlation of parent-report SDQ total difficulties scores with CBCL total problems scores for 4 to 12 year-olds, estimated across several studies, was 0.76 (range = 0.70 to 0.87) (Stone *et al.*, 2010), while the correlation of parent-report BESS (described in Chapter 1) scores with CBCL total problems scores in a recent survey of primary-school children (n = 99) was 0.63 (Dowdy *et al.*, 2012). The present findings suggest the BAC–C/A total scores approximate the CBCL total problem score (a measure of global psychopathology) at least as well as the SDQ total difficulties score, but not as well as the BPM (which is derived from the

CBCL). The results also suggest the BAC–C/A total difficulties scores provide comparable estimation of global psychopathology to that suggested by CBCL, ACC and ACA total scores.

Correlations of BAC–C and BAC–A total scores with relevant ACC and ACA clinical scales and with CBCL syndrome, DSM-oriented and BPM scales are listed in Table 12.1. BAC–C/A total scores had moderate to high correlation (0.67 to 0.88) with the ACC and ACA scales that measure commonly experienced difficulties, and moderate correlation (0.27 to 0.63) with scales measuring lower prevalence difficulties. There were mostly moderate to high correlations of BAC–C/A total scores with CBCL syndrome and DSM-oriented scale scores. The notable exceptions were quite low correlations with the two CBCL somatic scales. This is largely accounted for by a relatively low prevalence (compared to other symptoms) of reported somatic problems among children and adolescents in the CICS, and low correlations of CBCL somatic complaints/problems scores with other CBCL scale scores (Tarren-Sweeney and Hazell, 2006).

Table 12.1 Correlations of BAC-C and BAC-A total scores with ACC, ACA and CBCL scale scores

	BAC-C	*BAC-A*		*BAC-C*	*BAC-A*
ACC and ACA scales					
CBCL scales					
Total clinical	.96	.94	Total problems	.82	.88
Sexual behaviour	.63	.46	Anxious–depressed	.61	.65
Non-reciprocal	.79	.73	Withdrawn–depressed	.57	.61
Food maintenance	.51	.55	Somatic complaints	.41	.38
Suicide discourse	.32	.27	Social problems	.71	.75
Low self-esteem	.75	.68	Thought problems	.73	.71
ACC-only scales			Attention problems	.66	.69
Pseudomature	.76		Rule-breaking behaviour	.70	.72
Indiscriminate	.79		Aggressive behaviour	.69	.83
Insecure	.82				
Anxious–distrustful	.67		DSM affective problems	.62	.58
Abnormal pain response	.53		DSM anxiety problems	.58	.61
Self-injury	.44		DSM somatic problems	.34	.29
ACA-only scales			DSM attention deficit/hyp.	.64	.72
Social–behavioural dysregulation		.88	DSM oppositional defiant	.61	.71
Dissociation/trauma symptoms		.51	DSM conduct problems	.63	.78
Dysregulated emotion/distorted social cognition		.80	Brief Problem Monitor (BPM)	.74	.83

Screening accuracy of the Brief Assessment Checklists

A series of Receiver Operating Characteristics (ROC) analyses were carried out to identify the screening accuracy of the BAC–C/A instruments, as well as optimal screening cut-points, in relation to various clinical case identification criteria. An instrument's screening accuracy is measured by the area under the ROC curve (AUC), which is expressed as a proportion. An instrument that predicts no better than chance will have an AUC value in the vicinity of 0.5, while a 'perfect' screening instrument has an AUC of 1.0. Unless an instrument has a score cut-point that is 100 per cent accurate (i.e. incurs no false positive or false negative results), then every screening cut-point involves a trade-off between sensitivity (the proportion of clinical cases who are positively screened, i.e. score at or above the screening cut-point) and specificity (the proportion of non-cases who are negatively screened, i.e. score below the screening cut-point). Selecting optimal cut-points therefore requires subjective judgement about the relative benefits and costs of incorrectly identifying clinical cases versus non-cases.

The screening accuracies of the BAC–C and BAC–A for identifying clinical caseness as defined by CBCL and ACC clinical range scores, are set out in Tables 12.2 and 12.3 respectively. The tables list AUCs and sensitivity and specificity of selected cut-points, as well as specificity restricted to children without elevated/borderline range scores (i.e. using a more conservative definition of non-caseness). Both instruments were *highly accurate* in screening for clinical and 'elevated or clinical' range ACC and ACA scores, with AUCs ranging from 0.96 to 0.99. They were also *moderately accurate* in screening for CBCL clinical and 'borderline or clinical' range scores, with AUCs ranging from 0.89 to 0.92 for the BAC–C and 0.93 to 0.94 for the BAC–A. Their screening accuracy for identifying CBCL total scores in the clinical range (AUC = 0.92 and 0.94) compares favourably with the accuracy of parent-report SDQ total difficulties scores in predicting clinical range CBCL total scores (AUC = 0.85), in a health screening study of 7–12 year-old Dutch children (n = 711) (Mathilde R. Crone, personal communication, 1 Nov. 2012; see also Crone *et al.*, 2008).

The comparative screening accuracy of the BPM total score for identifying child and adolescent ACC/ACA/CBCL clinical scores is also listed in Tables 12.2 and 12.3. Among children, the BPM was slightly more accurate than the BAC–C in screening for CBCL clinical range scores, while the BAC–C was notably more accurate than the BPM in screening for ACC clinical range scores. The BAC–C was about as accurate as the BPM in identifying if a child had any ACC or CBCL clinical range score (AUCs = 0.94 and 0.93 respectively). Among adolescents, the BPM had comparable accuracy to the BAC–A in screening for CBCL clinical range scores, while the BAC–A was considerably more accurate than the BPM in screening for ACA clinical range scores. The BAC–A was also more accurate than the BPM in identifying if a young person had any ACA or CBCL clinical range score (AUCs = 0.95 and 0.91 respectively).

The screening accuracies of the BAC–C, BAC–A, CBCL, BPM, ACC and ACA total difficulties scores for identifying caregiver-reported clinical referral status (reported use of mental health services within last year or actively seeking a mental health service; reported mental health diagnosis; and reported psychiatric/behavioural medication) are compared in Table 12.4. It should be noted that the reported diagnoses and behavioural medication data for the child and adolescent samples were strongly weighted towards Attention-deficit/Hyperactivity Disorder (ADHD), but that few participants presented with 'pure' ADHD symptomatology (Tarren-Sweeney, 2013b). While these reference criteria provide only proxy estimations of clinical caseness, the findings suggest the Brief Assessment Checklists are likely to be as good at identifying children's clinical referral status, as the much lengthier CBCL, ACC and ACA checklists.

Optimal screening cut-points

In most instances the goal of mental health screening is simply to find as many children as possible who are experiencing clinically meaningful mental health difficulties, using a

Table 12.2 BAC-C screening accuracy (sensitivity, specificity and area under the ROC curve) for identifying ACC and CBCL clinical range scores (n=347, ages 4 to 11)

Caseness criteria: ACC/CBCL scores in clinical range	*Estimated[a] population prevalence*	*Area under[b] ROC curve (95% CI)*	*BAC-C[c] screening cut-point*	*Sensitivity % (estimated no. of cases correctly identified per 1000 children)*	*Specificity % (estimated no. of non-cases correctly identified per 1000 children)*	*Specificity for elevated/ borderline range (estimated no. of non-cases correctly identified per 1000 children)*	*BPM[d] AUC*
ACC total score in clinical range	44.7%	0.99 (0.98–1.00)	4+	100% (447/447)	46.4% (257/553)	56.7% (257/453)	0.90
			5+	100% (447/447)	59.4% (328/553)	72.0% (326/453)	
			6+	100% (447/447)	68.2% (377/553)	81.5% (369/453)	
			7+	100% (447/447)	75.0% (415/553)	87.9% (398/453)	
ACC total score in elevated *or* clinical range	54.7%	0.98 (0.97–0.99)	4+	100% (547/547)	56.7% (257/453)		0.89
			5+	99.5% (544/547)	72.0% (326/453)		
			6+	98.4% (538/547)	81.5% (369/453)		
			7+	96.8% (529/547)	87.9% (398/453)		
Any ACC total or sub-scale score in clinical range	57.6%	0.97 (0.96–0.99)	4+	98.5% (567/576)	58.5% (248/424)	84.5% (204/242)	0.88
			5+	97.5% (562/576)	74.2% (315/424)	95.2% (230/242)	
			6+	96.0% (553/576)	83.7% (355/424)	96.4% (233/242)	
			7+	94.0% (541/576)	89.8% (381/424)	97.6% (236/242)	
CBCL total problem score in clinical range	46.4%	0.92 (0.89–0.95)	4+	98.1% (455/464)	46.2% (248/536)	53.9% (222/412)	0.96
			5+	96.9% (450/464)	58.6% (314/536)	66.4% (274/412)	
			6+	93.8% (435/464)	65.1% (349/536)	73.4% (302/412)	
			7+	93.2% (432/464)	71.5% (383/536)	80.4% (331/412)	
CBCL total problem score in borderline *or* clinical range	58.8%	0.91 (0.88–0.94)	4+	94.1% (553/588)	53.9% (222/412)		0.98
			5+	90.7% (533/588)	66.4% (274/412)		
			6+	87.3% (513/588)	73.4% (302/412)		
			7+	85.8% (505/588)	80.4% (331/412)		

Any CBCL syndrome or total problem score in clinical range	57.1%	0.89 (0.86–0.93)	4+	93.9% (536/571)	51.7% (222/429)	67.4% (190/282)	0.94
			5+	91.4% (522/571)	65.1% (279/429)	75.5% (213/282)	
			6+	87.9% (502/571)	71.8% (308/429)	82.7% (233/282)	
			7+	86.4% (493/571)	78.5% (337/429)	86.7% (244/282)	

[a] Proportion of children in the study sample with scores in the ACC/CBCL clinical, elevated and borderline ranges. The CICS baseline study sample provides a reasonable estimation of the distribution of mental health difficulties across the whole care population (foster, kinship, residential and adopted from care)

[b] Screening accuracy measured as area under the Receiver Operating Characteristics (ROC) curve (AUC).

[c] Proportion of children who are positive screens for each cut-point: 4+ = 74%; 5+ = 67%; 6+ = 62%; 7+ = 58%

[d] Comparative AUC value for the BPM (CBCL short form, 17 items)

Table 12.3 BAC–A screening accuracy (sensitivity, specificity and area under the ROC curve) for identifying ACA and CBCL clinical range scores (n=230, ages 12 to 18)

Caseness criteria: ACA/ CBCL scores in clinical range	*Study prevalence (estimated population prevalence)*[a]	*Area under*[b] *ROC curve (95% CI)*	*BAC-A*[c] *screening cut-point*	*Sensitivity % (estimated no. of cases correctly identified per 1000 children)*	*Specificity % (estimated no. of non-cases correctly identified per 1000 children)*	*Specificity for elevated/borderline range (estimated no. of non-cases correctly identified per 1000 children)*	*BPM*[d] *AUC*
ACA total score in clinical range	36.5% (44.7%)	0.99 (0.99–1.00)	4+	100% (447/447)	55.5% (307/553)	65.9% (291/442)	0.91
			5+	100% (447/447)	61.6% (341/553)	73.2% (324/442)	
			6+	100% (447/447)	67.1% (371/553)	78.9% (349/442)	
			7+	98.8% (442/447)	75.3% (416/553)	87.8% (387/442)	
ACA total score in elevated *or* clinical range	46.5% (55.8%)	0.99 (0.99–1.00)	4+	100% (558/558)	73.2% (324/442)		0.91
			5+	100% (558/558)	73.2% (324/442)		
			6+	99.1% (553/558)	78.9% (349/442)		
			7+	97.2% (542/558)	87.8% (387/442)		
Any ACA total or sub-scale score in clinical range	49.0% (58.8%)	0.96 (0.94–0.98)	4+	98.2% (577/588)	67.5% (278/412)	86.6% (197/228)	0.89
			5+	98.2% (577/588)	75.2% (310/412)	91.5% (209/228)	
			6+	93.8% (552/588)	77.8% (321/412)	95.1% (217/228)	
			7+	87.6% (515/588)	82.9% (342/412)	95.1% (217/228)	
CBCL total problem score in clinical range	37.8% (45.4%)	0.94 (0.91–0.97)	4+	98.9% (449/454)	55.9% (305/546)	66.1% (275/416)	0.91
			5+	96.6% (439/454)	60.8% (332/546)	70.0% (291/416)	
			6+	95.4% (433/454)	65.7% (359/546)	74.6% (310/416)	
			7+	94.3% (422/454)	74.1% (406/546)	83.1% (346/416)	
CBCL total problem score in borderline *or* clinical range	48.7% (58.4%)	0.94 (0.90–0.96)	4+	97.3% (568/584)	66.1% (275/416)		0.91
			5+	93.8% (548/584)	70.0% (291/416)		
			6+	91.1% (532/584)	74.6% (310/416)		
			7+	88.4% (516/584)	83.1% (346/416)		

Any CBCL syndrome or total problem score in clinical range	44.8% (53.8%)	0.93 (0.90–0.96)	4+	96.1% (517/538)	60.6% (280/462)	72.3% (210/290)	0.94
			5+	93.2% (501/538)	65.4% (302/462)	76.6% (222/290)	
			6+	91.3% (491/538)	70.1% (324/462)	79.8% (231/290)	
			7+	89.3% (480/538)	78.8% (364/462)	85.1% (247/290)	

[a] Proportion of adolescents in the CICS with scores in the ACC/CBCL clinical, elevated and borderline ranges. The CICS follow-up and adolescent study samples under-represent the distribution of mental health difficulties of young people in the care system. Population prevalence rates were estimated by multiplying study prevalence rates by 1.2

[b] Screening accuracy measured as Area under the Receiver Operating Characteristics (ROC) curve (AUC)

[c] Proportion of children who are positive screens for each cut-point: 4+ = 65%; 5+ = 61%; 6+ = 57%; 7+ = 52%

[d] Comparative AUC value for the BPM (CBCL short form, 19 items)

Table 12.4 Screening accuracy (area under the ROC curve) for identifying caregiver–reported mental health service use and diagnoses: comparison of BAC–C, BAC–A, BPM, ACC, ACA and CBCL total scores

	Area Under the ROC Curve (95% CI)		
	Reported mental health service use [a]	*Reported diagnosis*[b]	*Reported medication*[c]
Child sample (N=347, age 4–11)			
BAC–C (20 items)	0.74 (0.69–0.80)	0.73 (0.67–0.78)	0.63 (0.55–0.71)
BPM (17 items)	0.75 (0.70–0.81)	0.78 (0.73–0.83)	0.71 (0.63–0.78)
ACC (102 items)	0.75 (0.70–0.81)	0.75 (0.69–0.80)	0.65 (0.57–0.73)
CBCL (120 items)	0.78 (0.73–0.83)	0.78 (0.73–0.83)	0.69 (0.62–0.76)
Adolescent sample (N=230, age 12–18)			
BAC–A (20 items)	0.79 (0.73–0.85)	0.77 (0.72–0.84)	0.79 (0.72–0.85)
BPM (19 items)	0.79 (0.73–0.85)	0.78 (0.72–0.84)	0.83 (0.78–0.89)
ACA (87 items)	0.82 (0.76–0.88)	0.81 (0.75–0.86)	0.80 (0.74–0.87)
CBCL (120 items)	0.81 (0.75–0.87)	0.80 (0.74–0.86)	0.82 (0.76–0.89)

[a] Caregiver-reported use of mental health services within last year *or* was actively seeking a mental health service

[b] Caregiver report of child's mental health diagnosis

[c] Caregiver-report psychiatric/behavioural medication

relatively brief and non-intrusive assessment procedure. In this context, screening is only effective when it correctly identifies the vast majority of clinical cases, and conversely, is counterproductive and harmful when it fails to detect sizeable proportions of clinical cases. Therefore, when screening is the first stage of a two- or multi-stage assessment process, sensitivity is more important than specificity (except where there are seriously adverse social or emotional consequences for false positive screening, e.g. for a life-threatening illness). There are several reasons why this is particularly true for the BAC–C/A target populations. First, there are more serious implications for children with mental health problems remaining undetected in the care system, than for children without clinical level difficulties being referred for further assessment. Second, while false positive screens can be reassigned as non-cases when they are referred for the next stage of assessment, false negative screens are more likely to remain undetected. Finally, because children in care have such high prevalence of clinical level mental health difficulties (above 50 per cent), loss of specificity within this population translates as fewer false positive screens and a higher positive predictive value (the proportion of positive screens that are true cases), than occurs with mental health screening of children and young people at large.

The ROC analyses set out in Tables 12.2 and 12.3 provide the necessary information for selecting optimal screening cut-points. The most useful available reference criteria for establishing a child's need for further, comprehensive assessment are: (1) having *any* ACC/ACA sub-scale or total score in the clinical range; and (2) having any CBCL syndrome or total score in the clinical range, since these criteria cast the widest net for clinical caseness as measured by these two instruments. For both the BAC–C and BAC–A, a score of 5 or higher (5+) represents the optimal screening cut-point for maximising sensitivity without excessive trade-off in specificity. The study sample proportions of children and adolescents who screen positive using a 5+ cut-point, are 67% and 61% respectively.[1] The 5+ cut-point detected 98%

of clinical cases defined by ACC and ACA scores, and 92% to 93% of clinical cases defined by CBCL scores. This is achieved at the cost of misidentifying 25% of ACC/ACA non-cases and 35% of CBCL non-cases. Importantly however, the majority of those who were false negative screens had at least one mental health score in the elevated (ACC) or borderline clinical (CBCL) range. For these children and young people, further clinical assessment is warranted.

Note

1 The proportions who screen positive using 4+, 6+ and 7+ cut-points are 74%, 67% and 58% on the BAC–C, and 65%, 57%, and 52% on the BAC–A.

Chapter 13

Checklists under development

There is scope and need for further development of specialized mental health assessment measures for children exposed to chronic and severe social adversity, especially those placed into alternate care or adoption following maltreatment.

A structural limitation of the Assessment Checklists relative to the other screening measures is the lack of teacher- and self-report versions. In regards to the BAC–C/A, a lack of multi-informant data is less critical for screening purposes than it is for comprehensive assessment. Teacher versions of the ACC, ACA and BAC have not yet been developed because these instruments measure a range of difficulties that are unlikely to be reliably observed and reported on by teachers. Consequently, considerable new work needs to be carried out to develop valid and useful teacher-report versions of the Assessment Checklists. Adolescent self-report versions of the ACA and BAC–A have not been developed because some of its items are likely to be very emotionally confronting for young people (may cause some people undue distress), and also may not be reliably measured through self-report. However, there is scope to develop a self-report shortened version of the Assessment Checklist for Adolescents, consisting of those items that young people are most able to reflect on, and which are least emotionally confronting. Planning for the development of teacher-report and adolescent self-report measures is underway at the time of this book's publication.

This final chapter describes two caregiver-report checklists that are presently 'under development' for use as pilot research measures, and which eventually may be developed into validated clinical assessment and treatment monitoring measures.

Assessment Checklist for Children – Plus (ACC+) (for ages 4 to 17 years)

The Assessment Checklist for Children – Plus (ACC+) is a partially developed, 29-item carer-report checklist of behaviours suggesting adaptive, pro-social functioning and well-being. This instrument is being designed to detect early signs of therapeutic recovery through the emergence of behaviour that is contrary to the clinical constructs measured by the ACC and ACA; what might be termed a 'green shoots' measure. It is speculated that early signs of recovery might be more reliably identified from the appearance of such green shoots, than from changes in symptom scores on problem measures such as the ACC, CBCL or SDQ. A child who is typically callous, withdrawn and resists affection from his caregiver is likely to continue to manifest these attachment-related difficulties for some time after the first green shoots begin to emerge (such as a spontaneous, unsolicited hug), and may continue to score highly on problem scales long after his caregiver recognises qualitative changes to the child's attachment-related behaviours.

The ACC+ items have been deliberately scaled to be sensitive to small improvement from a low base for very disturbed children and young people, e.g. from 'never' being kind or helpful, to 'rarely' being kind or helpful, to 'sometimes' being kind or helpful, represents small but significant progress. Here is an example: let's say a child scores 2 on the item 'affectionless' (i.e. it is mostly true that he is affectionless). This loads onto the non-reciprocal scale, suggesting avoidant, inhibited attachment problems. Yet, on the strengths checklist, he might simultaneously be described as 'sometimes' seeking comfort or hugs, or 'sometimes' being affectionate to family or caregivers. These are not incompatible responses. Yet, they paint a slightly different picture than a symptom checklist does on its own.

Further development of the ACC+ can proceed once pilot data have been obtained to allow for item analysis and validation procedures. Once it is fully developed, it will be available for use in research and clinical settings without user restrictions. A pilot version of the ACC+ is shown as Figure 13.1.

Assessment Checklist for Preschoolers – Short Form ACP–SF (for ages 2.5 to 4 years)

The other measure presently under development is a short form caregiver-report checklist designed to measure the mental health difficulties of children in alternate care and adoption, in the second half of their first five years of life (that is, from age 30 to 60 months), which is presently named the Assessment Checklist for Preschoolers – Short Form (ACP–SF). Two pilot versions (containing 37 and 29 items) were developed in 2010 and 2011 for inclusion in population studies in Australia and the UK. This was in response to a lack of a suitable survey measure of attachment- and trauma-related mental health difficulties experienced by children in care in this age range, and realising that the ACC is not suitable for children younger than four years. This measure will be developed further once sufficient research data have been obtained. Beyond that, long form (ACP) and screening (BAC–P) versions will be developed further down the track after the ACP–SF has been piloted in population studies.

Item development strategy

Initially, each ACC–SF item was considered in terms of relevance for preschool-aged children based on the developer's clinical experience and judgement. Some items that are maladaptive at older ages are more developmentally appropriate for preschool-aged children, e.g. does not share with friends. Other items measure behaviours that become increasingly implausible at younger ages, such as forces or pressures children into sexual acts.

The next step examined the age distributions for each ACC–SF item score, with a view to identify items that were more frequently scored among four- and five-year-olds in the CICS baseline sample, as well as items that were less frequently scored by these ages. This helped to differentiate between mental health difficulties that are more versus less characteristic of younger children. These two steps identified which of the ACC–SF items should be retained for the pilot ACP–SF measure, and which (if any) of these may require some modification. Beyond this, there was a further need to consider what mental health difficulties manifested by preschool-aged children in care are not measured by the ACC–SF or ACC. The ACC items were derived systematically over several years using a combination of deductive and

ACC+ **Assessment Checklist for Children (Plus)** **GIRLS FORM**

Supplementary Strengths Checklist

Child's name:
Child's age:
Your name:
Your relationship to the child: (e.g. mother, father, aunt, foster mother, grandfather)

For each statement, circle the number that best describes your child in the last four to six months

	0 = Never	1 = Rarely	2 = Sometimes	3 = Mostly
Acts her age (not too grown up, or immature)	0	1	2	3
Age-appropriate interest in romance and sex (e.g. 9 year-old boy thinks girls are 'yuk')	0	1	2	3
Comfortable with being looked after by adults (e.g. not excessively independent, doesn't try to 'parent' her caregivers, lets adults care for her younger siblings)	0	1	2	3
Copes well with frustrating circumstances	0	1	2	3
Cries when hurt	0	1	2	3
Embarrassed by sexual talk or sexual themes on television (e.g. looks away)	0	1	2	3
Engages in imaginative play	0	1	2	3
Enjoys talking with family or friends	0	1	2	3
Expresses her feelings	0	1	2	3
Genuinely sorry if she hurts someone's feelings	0	1	2	3
Has a regular appetite	0	1	2	3
Is affectionate towards family or caregivers	0	1	2	3
Is close to you and/or another adult caregiver (seems attached)	0	1	2	3
Is kind or helpful to others	0	1	2	3
Keeps friends (maintains friendships)	0	1	2	3
Misses people when they're away (e.g. if you're away a few days, family living elsewhere)	0	1	2	3
Relaxed about food (not preoccupied with supply of food)	0	1	2	3
Relaxed at bedtime	0	1	2	3
Says when her feelings are hurt	0	1	2	3
Says when she is hurt or experiencing pain	0	1	2	3
Seeks comfort or hugs from family or carers	0	1	2	3
Seems carefree (without concerns or worries)	0	1	2	3
Seems secure	0	1	2	3
Sensible with strangers (appropriately wary, not overfamiliar)	0	1	2	3
Shows concern for others	0	1	2	3
Stands up for herself	0	1	2	3
Tolerates others receiving attention or praise	0	1	2	3
Trusts the people she feels closest to (e.g. family or friends)	0	1	2	3

Is becoming closer to you and/or another adult caregiver (circle yes or no)	Yes	No

Figure 13.1 Assessment Checklist for Children Plus (ACC+): girls' record form

inductive strategies. However, these strategies were only directed towards identifying difficulties manifested by 4 to 17 year-olds, they did not consider how mental ill-health is expressed or experienced by two- and three-year-olds.

Readers may recall that the ACC and ACA were designed to measure those mental health difficulties that are characteristic of children and young people in care and which are not adequately measured by standard mental health survey instruments such as the CBCL and SDQ. Consequently, the ACC and ACA were not designed to measure common mental health problems such as conduct problems, oppositional-defiance, overactivity/inattention, general anxiety problems and depression. Rather the ACC and ACA measure a range of difficulties that are largely attachment- and/or trauma-related. Similarly, the ACP–SF is being designed to exclude measurement of these common mental health difficulties. Thus the final steps in developing items for the pilot ACP-SF were to consider: (a) how various types of attachment- and trauma-related mental health difficulties that are identified among school-aged children could be manifested at younger ages; and (b) the developmental course of attachment- and trauma-related difficulties among children exposed to chronic and severe adversity from an early age.

The 37-item pilot version of the ACP–SF contains 28 items sourced from the ACC (27/28 from the ACC–SF), and 9 new items. Table 13.1 groups the pilot ACP–SF items sourced from the ACC under their respective ACC clinical scales, while one or more notional constructs are listed alongside each of the new items. The table also describes modifications to three of the ACC items to render them more suitable for very young children.

Table 13.1 Assessment Checklist for Preschoolers–Short Form (ACP–SF): 37 pilot items

	Factor loading[a]	*Prevalence (%)*[b]
Items retained from ACC-SF scales		
I *Sexual Behaviour*		
describes or imitates sexual behaviour	.71	12
touches or puts mouth on other person's sex parts	.65	4
tries to involve others in sexual behaviour	.87	9
other sexual behaviour not appropriate for age (describe)[c]	.72	14
II *Pseudomature*		
talks and/or behaves like an adult[d]	.86	32
too independent	.63	27
treats you as though you were the child, and he/she was the parent	.65	26
III *Non-reciprocal*		
avoids eye contact	.57	38
does not show affection	.78	23
uncaring (shows little concern for others)	.71	31
IV *Indiscriminate*		
relates to strangers 'as if they were family'	.79	47
too friendly with strangers	.76	68

Table 13.1 continued

	Factor loading[a]	Prevalence (%)[b]
V *Insecure*		
clingy	.50	52
seems insecure	.62	44
worries something bad will happen to you	.71	38
VI *Anxious–distrustful*		
distrusts adults	.44	27
seems fearful of being harmed[e]	.68	17
wary or vigilant	.48	19
VII *Abnormal pain response*		
does not cry	.49	24
does not show pain if physically hurt	.82	15
won't say when physically hurt	.78	14
VIII *Food maintenance*		
eats too much	.76	25
gorges food	.73	23
hides or stores food	.80	14
IX *Self-injury*		
bites him/herself	.81	9
causes injury to him/herself (describe)	.73	10
hits head, head-banging	.48	10
Item retained from the ACC (long form)		
rocks back and forth (describe)	.48	10

New items written for the pilot ACP–SF	*Notional construct(s) measured by item*
body stiffens when cuddled or hugged	Non-reciprocal/anxious–distrustful
child's affection seems false	Non-reciprocal/indiscriminate
does not seek comfort when hurt or upset	Non-reciprocal/abnormal pain response
does not smile or laugh	Absence of positive affect/non-reciprocal/depression
does not use imagination when playing	Deprivation effect/absence of positive affect/attachment disturbance
freezes for a moment (remains absolutely still)	Anxious–distrustful/dissociation
resists being cuddled or hugged	Non-reciprocal
stares blankly	Dissociation
wanders off without checking back	Indiscriminate

[a] Item factor loading on scale in 44-item (short form), n=412, ages 4–11 years)
[b] Item prevalence (percentage of sample with item score of 1 or 2, n = 347, ages 4–11 years)
[c] The word 'other' is added to the equivalent older child item, and the item is placed directly after the last sexual behaviour item, so that it explicitly measures sexual behaviour not covered by the preceding items
[d] The equivalent item for older children is 'precocious, talks and/or behaves like an adult'
[e] The item begins with 'seems' rather than 'is fearful of being harmed', because caregivers will be less certain of this for younger children

Appendix 1

Assessment Checklist for Children (ACC)

Girls' record form

ACC Assessment Checklist for Children

GIRLS FORM

PART 1

Here are some statements that describe children's behaviour and feelings.
For each statement, please circle the number that best describes your child in the **last 4 to 6 months**.

→ circle **0** if the statement is **not true** for your child in the last 4 to 6 months.
→ circle **1** if the statement is **partly true** for your child in the last 4 to 6 months.
→ circle **2** if the statement is **mostly true** for your child in the last 4 to 6 months.

Please do not check your answers with your child, as they may cause distress or embarrassment.

0	1	2	1.	Adjusts slowly to changes
0	1	2	2.	Attention-seeking behaviour
0	1	2	3.	Avoids eye contact, except if in 'trouble'
0	1	2	4.	Believes she is no good at anything
0	1	2	5.	Can't concentrate, short attention span
0	1	2	6.	Changes friends quickly
0	1	2	7.	Clingy
0	1	2	8.	Complains of not being likeable
0	1	2	9.	Craves affection
0	1	2	10.	Dislikes herself
0	1	2	11.	Distrusts adults
0	1	2	12.	Does not cry
0	1	2	13.	Does not share with friends
0	1	2	14.	Does not show affection
0	1	2	15.	Does not speak up for herself
0	1	2	16.	Easily discouraged at home
0	1	2	17.	Easily discouraged at school
0	1	2	18.	Easily influenced by other children
0	1	2	19.	Eats from garbage
0	1	2	20.	Eats things that are not food
0	1	2	21.	Eats too much
0	1	2	22.	Fearful of men in general
0	1	2	23.	Fearful or nervous at bedtime
0	1	2	24.	Fears she might be molested
0	1	2	25.	Fears she might do something bad
0	1	2	26.	Fears you will reject her
0	1	2	27.	Feels ashamed
0	1	2	28.	Feels worthless or inferior
0	1	2	29.	Finds it hard to make decisions
0	1	2	30.	Gets hurt a lot, "accident prone"
0	1	2	31.	Gives up too easily
0	1	2	32.	Gorges food
0	1	2	33.	Has a low opinion of herself
0	1	2	34.	Has an imaginary friend
0	1	2	35.	Has nightmares
0	1	2	36.	Hides feelings
0	1	2	37.	Hides or stores food
0	1	2	38.	Hugs men, other than relative or male carer
0	1	2	39.	Is convinced that friends will reject her
0	1	2	40.	Is fearful of being harmed
0	1	2	41.	Lacks confidence
0	1	2	42.	Lacks guilt or empathy
0	1	2	43.	Laughs when injured or hurt
0	1	2	44.	Lives in a fantasy world
0	1	2	45.	Low self-esteem
0	1	2	46.	Manipulates or 'uses' friends
0	1	2	47.	Play includes violent or frightening themes
0	1	2	48.	Possessive, can't share friends
0	1	2	49.	Precocious (talks or behaves like an adult)
0	1	2	50.	Prefers to be with adults, rather than children
0	1	2	51.	Prefers to mix with older children
0	1	2	52.	Refuses to talk
0	1	2	53.	Relates to strangers 'as if they were family'
0	1	2	54.	Resists being comforted when hurt
0	1	2	55.	Risks physical safety, fearless
0	1	2	56.	Says friends are against her
0	1	2	57.	Says she is "bad", or "no good"
0	1	2	58.	Secretive
0	1	2	59.	Seems insecure
0	1	2	60.	Startles easily
0	1	2	61.	Steals food
0	1	2	62.	Suspicious
0	1	2	63.	Thinks she is someone or something else
0	1	2	64.	Thinks other children are better than her
0	1	2	65.	Too compliant (over-conforms)
0	1	2	66.	Too dramatic (false emotions)
0	1	2	67.	Too friendly with strangers
0	1	2	68.	Too independent
0	1	2	69.	Too jealous
0	1	2	70.	Treats you as though you were the child, and she was the parent
0	1	2	71.	Tries too hard to please other children
0	1	2	72.	Tries too hard to please you
0	1	2	73.	Turns friends against each other
0	1	2	74.	Uncaring (shows little concern for others)
0	1	2	75.	Very forgetful
0	1	2	76.	Wants to be treated like a baby, or a toddler
0	1	2	77.	Wary or vigilant
0	1	2	78.	Withdrawn
0	1	2	79.	Won't attempt new activities
0	1	2	80.	Won't communicate with other children
0	1	2	81.	Worries that something bad will happen to you

Please turn over to complete part 2

ACC **Assessment Checklist for Children** **GIRLS FORM**

PART 2 Please note that the instructions are different on this page.

On this page only

→ circle **0** if the behaviour **did not occur** in the last 4 to 6 months.
→ circle **1** if the behaviour **occurred once** in the last 4 to 6 months.
→ circle **2** if the behaviour **occurred more than once** in the last 4 to 6 months.

0 1 2 82. Asks to be physically punished
0 1 2 83. Attempts suicide
0 1 2 84. Bites herself
0 1 2 85. Causes herself to vomit
0 1 2 86. Causes injury to herself (describe):______________________
____
0 1 2 87. Cuts or pulls out her hair (describe):______________________
0 1 2 88. Cuts or rips her clothes (describe):______________________
____
0 1 2 89. Describes how she would kill herself
0 1 2 90. Describes or imitates sexual behaviour
0 1 2 91. Distressed by traumatic memories
0 1 2 92. Does not show pain if physically hurt
0 1 2 93. Extreme reaction to losing a friend, or being excluded by other children (describe):______________________
____
0 1 2 94. 'Flirts' with strangers
0 1 2 95. Forces or pressures children into sexual acts
0 1 2 96. Has blackouts or periods of amnesia
0 1 2 97. Has panic attacks (when?)______________________
0 1 2 98. Hits head, head-banging
0 1 2 99. Intentionally harms herself with knives or implements (describe):______________________
____
0 1 2 100. Intentionally swallows dangerous substance to harm herself (e.g. medication, poison) (describe):______________________
0 1 2 101. Kisses with open mouth
0 1 2 102. Masturbates at home in view of others
0 1 2 103. Masturbates at school, or in public
0 1 2 104. Picks at sores or injuries
0 1 2 105. Requests to be harmed
0 1 2 106. Rocks back and forth (describe):______________________
0 1 2 107. Says her life is not worth living
0 1 2 108. Sexual behaviour not appropriate for her age (describe):______________________
____
0 1 2 109. Sexual intercourse with another young person
0 1 2 110. Sexual relations with an adult (describe):______________________
____
0 1 2 111. Shows sex parts to children (other than siblings)
0 1 2 112. Starts rude conversations, tells jokes about sex
0 1 2 113. Talks about suicide
0 1 2 114. Threatens to injure herself
0 1 2 115. Threatens to kill herself
0 1 2 116. Throws herself against walls, onto floors, etc (describe):______________________
____
0 1 2 117. Touches or puts mouth on other person's sex parts
0 1 2 118. Tries to involve others in sexual behaviour (describe):______________________
____
0 1 2 119. Unhealthy drinking (e.g. from discarded drink bottle, from toilet bowl) (describe):______________________
0 1 2 120. Won't say when physically hurt

Please make sure you have answered each question on both sides of the page

ID:
Child's name:
Child's age:
Your name:
Your relationship to the child: (e.g. mother, father, aunt, foster mother, grandfather)

Appendix 2

Assessment Checklist for Children – Short Form (ACC–SF)

Boys' record form

ACC-SF Assessment Checklist for Children – Short Form

BOYS FORM

PART 1

Here are some statements that describe children's behaviour and feelings.
For each statement, please circle the number that best describes your child in the **last 4 to 6 months**.

→ circle **0** if the statement is **not true** for your child in the last 4 to 6 months.
→ circle **1** if the statement is **partly true** for your child in the last 4 to 6 months.
→ circle **2** if the statement is **mostly true** for your child in the last 4 to 6 months.

Please do not check your answers with your child, as they may cause distress or embarrassment.

0	1	2	1.	Attention-seeking behaviour
0	1	2	2.	Avoids eye contact, except if in 'trouble'
0	1	2	3.	Changes friends quickly
0	1	2	4.	Clingy
0	1	2	5.	Distrusts adults
0	1	2	6.	Does not cry
0	1	2	7.	Does not share with friends
0	1	2	8.	Does not show affection
0	1	2	9.	Eats too much
0	1	2	10.	Fearful of men in general
0	1	2	11.	Fearful or nervous at bedtime
0	1	2	12.	Fears you will reject him
0	1	2	13.	Gorges food
0	1	2	14.	Hides or stores food
0	1	2	15.	Hugs men, other than relative or male carer
0	1	2	16.	Is convinced that friends will reject him
0	1	2	17.	Is fearful of being harmed
0	1	2	18.	Lacks guilt or empathy
0	1	2	19.	Laughs when injured or hurt
0	1	2	20.	Manipulates or 'uses' friends
0	1	2	21.	Precocious (talks or behaves like an adult)
0	1	2	22.	Prefers to be with adults, rather than children
0	1	2	23.	Prefers to mix with older children
0	1	2	24.	Relates to strangers 'as if they were family'
0	1	2	25.	Seems insecure
0	1	2	26.	Steals food
0	1	2	27.	Too friendly with strangers
0	1	2	28.	Too independent
0	1	2	29.	Treats you as though you were the child, and he was the parent
0	1	2	30.	Uncaring (shows little concern for others)
0	1	2	31.	Wary or vigilant
0	1	2	32.	Worries that something bad will happen to <u>you</u>

PART 2

For each statement, please circle the number that best describes your child in the **last 4 to 6 months**

→ circle **0** if the behaviour **did not occur** in the last 4 to 6 months.
→ circle **1** if the behaviour **occurred once** in the last 4 to 6 months.
→ circle **2** if the behaviour **occurred more than once** in the last 4 to 6 months.

0	1	2	33.	Bites himself
0	1	2	34.	Causes injury to himself (describe):__________________
0	1	2	35.	Describes or imitates sexual behaviour
0	1	2	36.	Does not show pain if physically hurt
0	1	2	37.	Forces or pressures children into sexual acts
0	1	2	38.	Has panic attacks (when?)__________________
0	1	2	39.	Hits head, head-banging
0	1	2	40.	Sexual behaviour not appropriate for his age (describe):__________________
0	1	2	41.	Threatens to injure himself
0	1	2	42.	Touches or puts mouth on other person's sex parts
0	1	2	43.	Tries to involve others in sexual behaviour (describe):__________________
0	1	2	44.	Won't say when physically hurt

Please make sure you have answered each question

ID:
Child's name:
Child's age:
Your name:
Your relationship to the child: (e.g. mother, father, aunt, foster mother, grandfather)

Appendix 3

Assessment Checklist for Adolescents (ACA)

Girls' record form

ACA **Assessment Checklist for Adolescents** **GIRLS FORM**

PART 1 **Here are some statements that describe young people's behaviour and feelings.**

For each statement, please circle the number that best describes your child in the **last 4 to 6 months**.

→ circle **0** if the statement is **not true** for this young person in the last 4 to 6 months.
→ circle **1** if the statement is **partly true** for this young person in the last 4 to 6 months.
→ circle **2** if the statement is **mostly true** for this young person in the last 4 to 6 months.

Please do not check your answers with your child, as they may cause distress or embarrassment.

0	1	2	1.	Adjusts slowly to changes
0	1	2	2.	Avoids eye contact, except if in 'trouble'
0	1	2	3.	Believes she is no good at anything
0	1	2	4.	Changes friends quickly
0	1	2	5.	Clingy
0	1	2	6.	Complains of not being likeable
0	1	2	7.	Confused about where, or with whom she belongs
0	1	2	8.	Constantly seeking excitement or 'thrills'
0	1	2	9.	Craves affection
0	1	2	10.	Dislikes herself
0	1	2	11.	Distrusts adults
0	1	2	12.	Distrusts friends
0	1	2	13.	Does not cry
0	1	2	14.	Does not share with friends
0	1	2	15.	Does not show affection
0	1	2	16.	Does not speak up for herself
0	1	2	17.	Easily discouraged at home
0	1	2	18.	Easily discouraged at school
0	1	2	19.	Eats secretly (e.g. in the middle of the night)
0	1	2	20.	Eats too much
0	1	2	21.	Fears she might do something bad
0	1	2	22.	Fears you (or other adults) will reject her (describe):________________
0	1	2	23.	Feels ashamed
0	1	2	24.	Feels victimised or misunderstood
0	1	2	25.	Feels worthless or inferior
0	1	2	26.	Finds it hard to make decisions
0	1	2	27.	Gives up too easily
0	1	2	28.	Gorges food
0	1	2	29.	Has a low opinion of herself
0	1	2	30.	Hides feelings
0	1	2	31.	Hides or stores food
0	1	2	32.	Impulsive (acts rashly, without thinking)
0	1	2	33.	Is convinced that friends will reject her
0	1	2	34.	Is fearful of being harmed
0	1	2	35.	Lacks confidence
0	1	2	36.	Lacks guilt or empathy
0	1	2	37.	Low self-esteem
0	1	2	38.	Manipulates or 'uses' friends
0	1	2	39.	Nightmares about specific events or people
0	1	2	40.	Possessive, can't share friends
0	1	2	41.	Precocious (talks or behaves like an adult)
0	1	2	42.	Prefers to be with adults rather than peers
0	1	2	43.	Prefers to mix with older youths
0	1	2	44.	Refuses to talk
0	1	2	45.	Relates to strangers as if they were family
0	1	2	46.	Resists being comforted when hurt
0	1	2	47.	Risks physical safety, fearless
0	1	2	48.	Says friends are against her
0	1	2	49.	Says she is "bad", or "no good"
0	1	2	50.	Seems alone in the world (not connected to people or places)
0	1	2	51.	Seems insecure
0	1	2	52.	Shows intense and inappropriate anger
0	1	2	53.	Startles easily ('jumpy')
0	1	2	54.	Steals food
0	1	2	55.	Suspicious
0	1	2	56.	Thinks other young people are better than her
0	1	2	57.	Threatens to withdraw love (e.g. "I won't love you anymore unless … ")
0	1	2	58.	Too compliant (over-conforms)
0	1	2	59.	Too dramatic (false emotions)
0	1	2	60.	Too friendly with strangers
0	1	2	61.	Too independent
0	1	2	62.	Too jealous
0	1	2	63.	Treats you as though you were the child, and she was the parent
0	1	2	64.	Tries too hard to please other young people
0	1	2	65.	Turns friends against each other
0	1	2	66.	Uncaring (shows little concern for others)
0	1	2	67.	Upsets most people (without good reason)
0	1	2	68.	Wary or vigilant (over-alert to danger)
0	1	2	69.	Withdrawn
0	1	2	70.	Won't attempt new activities

Please turn over to complete part 2

ACA Assessment Checklist for Adolescents

GIRLS FORM

PART 2

Please note that the instructions are different on this page.

On this page only

→ circle **0** if the behaviour **did not occur** in the last 4 to 6 months.
→ circle **1** if the behaviour **occurred once** in the last 4 to 6 months.
→ circle **2** if the behaviour **occurred more than once** in the last 4 to 6 months.

0 1 2 71. Appears dazed, 'spaced out' (like in a trance)
0 1 2 72. Attempts suicide
0 1 2 73. Can't get scary thoughts or images out of her head (not due to watching a scary movie)
0 1 2 74. Can't tell if an experience is real or a dream
0 1 2 75. Causes injury to herself (describe):___________________
0 1 2 76. Describes how she would kill herself
0 1 2 77. Distressed or troubled by traumatic memories
0 1 2 78. Does not show pain if physically hurt
0 1 2 79. Dramatic changes in eating (e.g. dieting then over-eating)
0 1 2 80. Extreme emotional reaction to minor event (or for no obvious reason)
0 1 2 81. Extreme reaction to losing a friend, or being excluded by other young people (describe): ___________________
0 1 2 82. Feels like things, people or events aren't real
0 1 2 83. Forces or pressures other youth or children into sexual acts
0 1 2 84. Has eating binges (bouts of excessive eating)
0 1 2 85. Has panic attacks (when?)____________
0 1 2 86. Has periods of amnesia (e.g. has no memory of what has happened in the last hour)
0 1 2 87. Hits head, head-banging
0 1 2 88. Hugs men, other than a relative or male carer
0 1 2 89. Inappropriately shows genitals to others (in person, or through video or photo)
0 1 2 90. Intense reaction to criticism
0 1 2 91. Intentionally harms herself with knife or sharp implement (describe):__________
0 1 2 92. Rocks back and forth (describe):___________________
0 1 2 93. Says her life is not worth living
0 1 2 94. Says she feels 'empty' or without emotions
0 1 2 95. Seems overly preoccupied with sex (e.g. crude sexual talk, inappropriate sexual comments)
0 1 2 96. Sexual behaviour not appropriate for her age (describe):___________________ ___________________
0 1 2 97. Sexual relations with an adult (describe):___________________ ___________________
0 1 2 98. Sudden or extreme mood changes
0 1 2 99. Talks about suicide
0 1 2 100. Threatens to injure herself
0 1 2 101. Threatens to kill herself
0 1 2 102. Throws herself against walls, onto floors, etc (describe):___________________ ___________________
0 1 2 103. Touches or puts mouth on other person's genitals or breasts
0 1 2 104. Tries to involve others in sexual behaviour (describe):___________________ ___________________
0 1 2 105. Uncontrollable rage

Please make sure you have answered each question on both sides of the page

ID:
Young person's name:
Young person's age:
Your name:
Your relationship to this young person: (e.g. mother, father, aunt, foster mother, grandfather)

Appendix 4

Assessment Checklist for Adolescents – Short Form (ACA-SF)

Boys' record form

ACA-SF Assessment Checklist for Adolescents – Short Form BOYS FORM

PART 1

Here are some statements that describe young people's behaviour and feelings.
For each statement, please circle the number that best describes your child in the **last 4 to 6 months**.

→ circle **0** if the statement is **not true** for this young person in the last 4 to 6 months.
→ circle **1** if the statement is **partly true** for this young person in the last 4 to 6 months.
→ circle **2** if the statement is **mostly true** for this young person in the last 4 to 6 months.

Please do not check your answers with your child, as they may cause distress or embarrassment.

0 1 2 1. Craves affection
0 1 2 2. Does not show affection
0 1 2 3. Eats secretly (e.g. in the middle of the night)
0 1 2 4. Eats too much
0 1 2 5. Gorges food
0 1 2 6. Hides feelings
0 1 2 7. Hides or stores food
0 1 2 8. Impulsive (acts rashly, without thinking)
0 1 2 9. Precocious (talks or behaves like an adult)
0 1 2 10. Prefers to be with adults, rather than peers
0 1 2 11. Prefers to mix with older youths
0 1 2 12. Refuses to talk
0 1 2 13. Relates to strangers as if they were family
0 1 2 14. Resists being comforted when hurt
0 1 2 15. Says friends are against him
0 1 2 16. Seems alone in the world (not connected to people or places)
0 1 2 17. Startles easily ('jumpy')
0 1 2 18. Steals food
0 1 2 19. Too friendly with strangers
0 1 2 20. Tries too hard to please other young people
0 1 2 21. Withdrawn

PART 2

For each of the following statements:

→ circle **0** if the behaviour **did not occur** in the last 4 to 6 months.
→ circle **1** if the behaviour **occurred once** in the last 4 to 6 months.
→ circle **2** if the behaviour **occurred more than once** in the last 4 to 6 months.

0 1 2 22. Appears dazed, 'spaced out' (like in a trance)
0 1 2 23. Can't get scary thoughts or images out of his head (not due to watching a scary movie)
0 1 2 24. Can't tell if an experience is real or a dream
0 1 2 25. Extreme reaction to losing a friend, or being excluded by other young people (describe):_ ______________________________
0 1 2 26. Feels like things, people or events aren't real
0 1 2 27. Forces or pressures other youth or children into sexual acts
0 1 2 28. Has panic attacks (when?)_____________
0 1 2 29. Has periods of amnesia (e.g. has no memory of what happened in the last hour)
0 1 2 30. Hits head, head-banging
0 1 2 31. Inappropriately shows genitals to others (in person, or through video or photo)
0 1 2 32. Intense reaction to criticism
0 1 2 33. Says his life is not worth living
0 1 2 34. Seems overly preoccupied with sex (e.g. crude sexual talk, inappropriate sexual comments)
0 1 2 35. Sexual behaviour not appropriate for his age (describe):_________________________
0 1 2 36. Tries to involve others in sexual behaviour (describe):_________________________
0 1 2 37. Uncontrollable rage

Please make sure you have answered each question

ID:
Young person's name:
Young person's age:
Your name:
Your relationship to this young person: (e.g. mother, father, aunt, foster mother, grandfather)

Appendix 5

Brief Assessment Checklist for Children (BAC–C) record form

BAC-C Brief Assessment Checklist for Children (ages 4 to 11)

Child's name .... Boy / Girl

Child's age ....

Your relationship to this child .... (e.g. mother, father, aunt, foster mother, grandfather)

Here are some statements that describe children's behaviour and feelings.
For each statement, please circle the number that best describes your child in the **last 4 to 6 months**.

→ circle **0** if the statement is **not true** for your child in the last 4 to 6 months.
→ circle **1** if the statement is **partly true** for your child in the last 4 to 6 months.
→ circle **2** if the statement is **mostly true** for your child in the last 4 to 6 months.

1.	**0**	**1**	**2**	Can't concentrate, short attention span
2.	**0**	**1**	**2**	Craves affection
3.	**0**	**1**	**2**	Eats too much
4.	**0**	**1**	**2**	Fears you will reject her/him
5.	**0**	**1**	**2**	Hides feelings
6.	**0**	**1**	**2**	Is convinced that friends will reject her/him
7.	**0**	**1**	**2**	Lacks guilt or empathy
8.	**0**	**1**	**2**	Prefers to be with adults, rather than children
9.	**0**	**1**	**2**	Relates to strangers 'as if they were family'
10.	**0**	**1**	**2**	Seems insecure
11.	**0**	**1**	**2**	Startles easily ('jumpy')
12.	**0**	**1**	**2**	Suspicious
13.	**0**	**1**	**2**	Too dramatic (false emotions)
14.	**0**	**1**	**2**	Too friendly with strangers
15.	**0**	**1**	**2**	Too jealous
16.	**0**	**1**	**2**	Treats you as though you were the child and she/he was the parent
17.	**0**	**1**	**2**	Uncaring (shows little concern for others)

For each of the following statements:

→ circle **0** if the behaviour **did not occur** in the last 4 to 6 months.
→ circle **1** if the behaviour **occurred once** in the last 4 to 6 months.
→ circle **2** if the behaviour **occurred more than once** in the last 4 to 6 months.

18.	**0**	**1**	**2**	Distressed or troubled by traumatic memories
19.	**0**	**1**	**2**	Does not show pain if physically hurt
20.	**0**	**1**	**2**	Sexual behaviour not appropriate for her/his age

U.K. English version www.childpsych.org.uk

Office use		
ID:	Date:	Score:

Appendix 6

Brief Assessment Checklist for Adolescents (BAC-A) record form

BAC-A Brief Assessment Checklist for Adolescents (ages 12 to 17)

Young person's name .... Male / Female

Young person's age ....

Your relationship to this young person .... (e.g. mother, father, aunt, foster mother, grandfather)

Here are some statements that describe young people's behaviour and feelings.
For each statement, please circle the number that best describes your child in the **last 4 to 6 months**.

→ circle **0** if the statement is **not true** for this young person in the last 4 to 6 months.
→ circle **1** if the statement is **partly true** for this young person in the last 4 to 6 months.
→ circle **2** if the statement is **mostly true** for this young person in the last 4 to 6 months.

1.	**0**	**1**	**2**	Constantly seeking excitement or 'thrills'
2.	**0**	**1**	**2**	Craves affection
3.	**0**	**1**	**2**	Does not share with friends
4.	**0**	**1**	**2**	Does not show affection
5.	**0**	**1**	**2**	Feels victimised or misunderstood
6.	**0**	**1**	**2**	Gorges food
7.	**0**	**1**	**2**	Hides feelings
8.	**0**	**1**	**2**	Impulsive (acts rashly, without thinking)
9.	**0**	**1**	**2**	Lacks guilt or empathy
10.	**0**	**1**	**2**	Relates to strangers 'as if they were family'
11.	**0**	**1**	**2**	Resists being comforted when hurt
12.	**0**	**1**	**2**	Shows intense and inappropriate anger
13.	**0**	**1**	**2**	Too friendly with strangers
14.	**0**	**1**	**2**	Too jealous
15.	**0**	**1**	**2**	Tries too hard to please other young people
16.	**0**	**1**	**2**	Withdrawn

For each of the following statements:

→ circle **0** if the behaviour **did not occur** in the last 4 to 6 months.
→ circle **1** if the behaviour **occurred once** in the last 4 to 6 months.
→ circle **2** if the behaviour **occurred more than once** in the last 4 to 6 months.

17.	**0**	**1**	**2**	Appears dazed, 'spaced out' (like in a trance)
18.	**0**	**1**	**2**	Intense reaction to criticism
19.	**0**	**1**	**2**	Sexual behaviour not appropriate for her/his age
20.	**0**	**1**	**2**	Sudden or extreme mood changes

U.K. English version www.childpsych.org.uk

Office use		
ID:	Date:	Score:

Appendix 7

Assessment Checklist for Children Short Form (ACC–SF)

Girls' profile sheet

ACC-SF Assessment Checklist for Children – Short Form

Girls Profile Sheet (2012 version) **Reference group: 5-10 year-old girls in long-term alternate care**

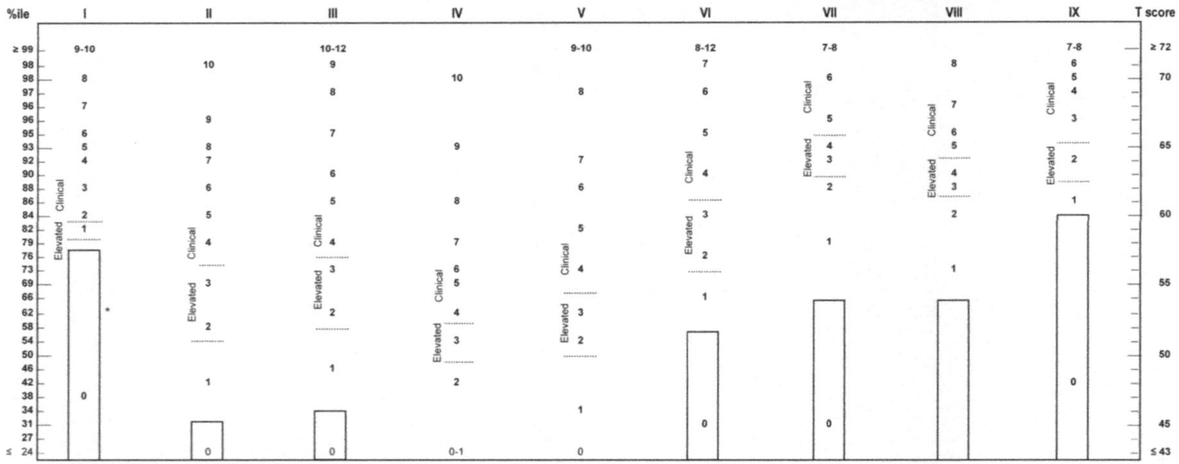

* Boxes show the percentile range for zero scores.

SHORT-FORM CLINICAL SCALES

I SEXUAL BEHAVIOUR	II PSEUDOMATURE	III NON-RECIPROCAL	IV INDISCRIMINATE	V INSECURE	VI ANXIOUS – DISTRUSTFUL	VII ABNORMAL PAIN RESPONSE	VIII FOOD MAINTENANCE	IX SELF– INJURY
___ 35. Describes / Imitates	___ 21. Precocious	___ 2. Avoid eye contact	___ 1. Attention-seeking	___ 4. Clingy	___ 5. Distrusts adults	___ 6. Does not cry	___ 9. Eats too much	___ 33. Bites self
___ 37. Forces / Pressures	___ 22. Prefers adults	___ 7. Doesn't share	___ 3. Changes friends	___ 12. Carer rejection	___ 10. Fears men	___ 19. Laughs if hurt	___ 13. Gorges food	___ 34. Self- injury
___ 40. Age-inappropriate	___ 23. Prefer older kids	___ 8. Affectionless	___ 15. Hugs men	___ 16. Peer rejection	___ 11. Fears bed-time	___ 36. Pain not shown	___ 14. Hides food	___ 39. Head-banging
___ 42. Touches others	___ 28. Independent	___ 18. Non-empathic	___ 24. Strangers as family	___ 25. Insecure	___ 17. Fears harm	___ 44. Won't say if hurt	___ 26. Steals food	___ 41. Threatens self-injury
___ 43. Tries to initiate sex	___ 29. Role reversal	___ 20. Manipulative	___ 27. Friendly strangers	___ 32. Worries for carer	___ 31. Wary or vigilant			
		___ 30. Uncaring			___ 38. Panic attacks			
___ Total I	___ Total II	___ Total III	___ Total IV	___ Total V	___ Total VI	___ Total VII	___ Total VIII	___ Total IX

Add scale scores

I ___
II ___
III ___
IV ___
V ___
VI ___
VII ___
VIII ___
IX ___

=

Total Clinical Score
(Transfer total score to next page)

ACC-SF Assessment Checklist for Children – Short Form   **Girls Profile Sheet** (2012 version)   **Reference group: 5-10 year-old girls in long-term alternate care**

ID:

Child's Name:

	Year	Month	Day
Date of Birth:	____	____	____
Date of Assessment:	____	____	____
Age:	____	____	____

Carer's name:
(the person who completed the ACC)

Carer's gender: Female ❑ Male ❑

Length of time carer has known child:___________

Carer's relationship to child
- ❑ Birth parent
- ❑ Step-parent
- ❑ Grandparent
- ❑ Other relative
- ❑ Adoptive parent
- ❑ Foster parent
- ❑ Group home staff
- ❑ Large residential staff
- ❑ Youth worker
- ❑ Other (describe): ______________________

Care Status
- ❑ Not in care (resides with parents)
- ❑ Adoption
- ❑ Kinship care (resides with relatives)
- ❑ Permanent or long-term foster care
- ❑ Temporary or short-term foster care
- ❑ Group or residential care
- ❑ Other (describe): ____________________

Referral Details:

Total Clinical Score =

Raw	T	%ile
Clinical range		
52-88	≥ 72	≥ 99
50-51	71	98
48-49	70	98
46-47	69	97
44-45	68	96
42-43	67	96
40-41	66	95
38-39	65	93
37	64	92
36	63	90
35	62	88
33-34	61	86
31-32	60	84
29-30	59	82
26-28	58	79
22-25	57	76
20-21	56	73
18-19	55	69
16-17	54	66
14-15	53	62
	52	58
Borderline clinical range		
13	52	58
11-12	51	54
10	50	50
Normal range		
9	49	46
8	48	42
7	47	38
6	46	34
	45	31
5	44	27
	43	24
4	42	21
	41	18
3	40	16
	39	14
	38	12
2	37	10
	36	8
	35	7
1	34	5
	33	4
	32	4
0	31	3
	30	2
	29	2
	≤ 28	1

Appendix 8

Assessment Checklist for Adolescents Short-Form (ACA-SF) profile sheet

ACA-SF Assessment Checklist for Adolescents – Short Form

Profile Sheet (boys & girls)

	I	II	III	IV	V	VI	TOTAL	
	6-12	8-16	5-14	6-12	8-10	5-10	18-74	*Marked*
CLINICAL ↑	3-5	5-7	3-4	4-5	6-7	3-4	12-17	*Indicated*
SUB-CLINICAL ↓	2	3-4	2	2-3	4-5	1-2	9-11	*Elevated*
	0-1	0-2	0-1	0-1	0-3	0	0-8	*Normative*

CLINICAL SCALES

I NON-RECIPROCAL

__ 2. Affectionless
__ 6. Hides feelings
__ 12. Refuses to talk
__ 14. Resists comfort
__ 16. Alone in the world
__ 21. Withdrawn

__ **Total I**

II SOCIAL INSTABILITY

__ 1. Craves affection
__ 8. Impulsive
__ 9. Precocious
__ 10. Prefers adults
__ 11. Prefer older youths
__ 13. Strangers as family
__ 19. Friendly strangers
__ 20. Please peers

__ **Total II**

III EMOTIONAL DYSREGULATION / DISTORTED SOCIAL COGNITION

__ 15. Friends against
__ 17. Startles easily
__ 23. Scary thoughts
__ 25. Reaction losing friend
__ 32. Reaction to criticism
__ 33. Life not worth living
__ 37. Uncontrollable rage

__ **Total III**

IV DISSOCIATION / TRAUMA SYMPTOMS

__ 22. Dazed
__ 24. Real or dream?
__ 26. Things aren't real
__ 28. Panic attacks
__ 29. Amnesia
__ 30. Head-banging

__ **Total IV**

V FOOD MAINTENANCE BEHAVIOUR

__ 3. Eats secretly
__ 4. Eats too much
__ 5. Gorges food
__ 7. Hides food
__ 18. Steals food

__ **Total V**

VI SEXUAL BEHAVIOUR

__ 27. Forces / Pressures
__ 31. Shows genitals
__ 34. Overly preoccupied
__ 35. Age-inappropriate
__ 36. Tries to initiate sex

__ **Total VI**

TOTAL SHORT FORM SCORE
(total score = sum of scale scores)

__ Scale I
__ Scale II
__ Scale III
__ Scale IV
__ Scale V
__ Scale VI
=
__ Total Short Form Score

ACA-SF scores should only be interpreted and reported by qualified child clinicians.

ACA-SF Assessment Checklist for Adolescents – Short Form

Profile Sheet (boys & girls)

ID:

Young person's name:

Referral Details:

	Year	Month	Day
Date of Birth:	____	____	____
Date of Assessment:	____	____	____
Age:	____	____	____

Carer's name:
(the person who completed the ACA)

Carer's gender: Female ☐ Male ☐

Length of time carer has known young person:____

Carer's relationship to young person

- ☐ Birth parent
- ☐ Step-parent
- ☐ Grandparent
- ☐ Other relative
- ☐ Adoptive parent
- ☐ Foster parent
- ☐ Group home staff
- ☐ Large residential staff
- ☐ Youth worker
- ☐ Other (describe): ______________________

Young Person's Care Status

- ☐ Not in care (resides with parents)
- ☐ Adoption
- ☐ Kinship care (resides with relatives)
- ☐ Permanent or long-term foster care
- ☐ Temporary or short-term foster care
- ☐ Group or residential care
- ☐ Other (describe): ______________________

Appendix 9

ACC scales with constituent items

A. CLINICAL SCALES

		Loading[a]	Item-rest[b]	Prevalence (%)[c]
I. Sexual Behaviour				
90	describes or imitates sexual behaviour	.68	.70	12
94	'flirts' with strangers	.49	.55	17
95	forces or pressures children into sexual acts	.80	.65	7
101	kisses with open mouth	.57	.52	8
108	sexual behaviour not appropriate for age	.72	.71	14
111	shows sex parts to children (other than siblings)	.51	.46	9
112	starts 'rude' conversations, tells jokes about sex	.37	.45	13
117	touches or puts mouth on other person's sex parts	.69	.51	4
118	tries to involve others in sexual behaviour	.86	.75	9
New items				
109	sexual intercourse with another young person			
110	sexual relations with an adult			
II. Pseudomature				
49	precocious (talks, behaves like an adult)	.68	.63	32
50	prefers to be with adults, rather than children	.66	.63	32
51	prefers to mix with older children	.59	.51	40
66	too 'dramatic' (false emotions)	.36	.58	35
68	too independent	.64	.51	27
69	too jealous	.35	.50	40
70	treats you as though you were the child, and he/she was the parent	.58	.54	26
73	turns friends against each other	.40	.42	14
III. Non-Reciprocal				
3	avoids eye contact	.56	.49	38
13	does not share with friends	.53	.50	40
14	does not show affection	.70	.49	23
42	lacks guilt or empathy	.64	.64	39
46	manipulates or uses friends	.52	.56	29
47	play includes violent or frightening themes	.45	.54	27
48	possessive, can't share friends	.41	.52	34
54	resists being comforted when hurt	.39	.36	13
58	secretive	.42	.59	37
62	suspicious	.37	.56	22
74	uncaring (shows little concern for others)	.74	.65	31
80	won't communicate with other children	.40	.45	15

		Loading[a]	*Item-rest*[b]	*Prevalence (%)*[c]
IV. Indiscriminate				
2	attention-seeking behaviour	.52	.60	74
6	changes friends quickly	.38	.51	36
7	clingy	.38	.41	52
9	craves affection	.53	.62	64
18	easily influenced by other children	.48	.45	72
38	hugs men (other than relatives or male carer)	.49	.46	20
53	relates to strangers 'as if they were family'	.63	.64	47
67	too friendly with strangers	.60	.54	68
V. Insecure				
26	fears you will reject him/her	.46	.52	31
36	hides feelings	.42	.59	37
39	is convinced that friends will reject him/her	.48	.59	20
44	lives in a fantasy world	.36	.42	25
52	refuses to talk	.41	.47	25
56	says friends are against her	.43	.47	25
59	seems insecure	.47	.63	44
60	startles easily	.44	.54	33
65	too compliant (over-conforms)	.53	.45	17
71	tries too hard to please other children	.57	.50	35
72	tries too hard to please you	.67	.49	35
78	withdrawn	.48	.53	18
81	worries something bad will happen to you	.42	.36	38
93	extreme reaction to losing a friend or to being excluded by children	.52	.42	15
VI. Anxious-Distrustful				
11	distrusts adults	.46	.53	27
22	fearful of men in general	.63	.45	11
23	fearful or nervous at bed-time	.59	.53	13
24	fears she/he might be molested	.32	.33	5
35	has nightmares	.33	.35	34
40	is fearful of being harmed	.55	.53	17
76	wants to be treated like a baby, or a toddler	.38	.36	27
77	wary or vigilant	.45	.50	19
91	distressed by traumatic memories	.37	.52	28
97	has panic attacks	.60	.42	8
VII. Abnormal Pain Response				
12	does not cry	.52	.46	24
43	laughs when injured or hurt	.56	.40	16
92	does not show pain if physically hurt	.76	.67	15
120	won't say when physically hurt	.58	.45	14
VIII. Food Maintenance				
21	eats too much	.65	.62	25
32	gorges food	.67	.65	23
37	hides or stores food	.68	.57	14
61	steals food	.69	.60	18

	Loading[a]	Item-rest[b]	Prevalence (%)[c]
IX. Self-Injury			
Self-injury index			
82 asks to be physically punished	.44	.42	4
84 bites him/herself	.49	.52	9
85 causes him/herself to vomit	.42	.31	4
86 causes injury to him/herself	.56	.55	10
87 cuts or pulls out own hair	.43	.41	8
88 cuts or rips own clothes	.46	.45	10
98 hits head, head-banging	.55	.51	10
99 intentionally harms her/himself with knives/implements	.64	.38	2
100 intentionally swallows dangerous substance to harm self	.77	.40	1
106 rocks back and forth	.42	.39	8
116 throws her/himself against walls, onto floors, etc	.36	.46	13
Pica index			
19 eats from garbage	.63	.49	7
20 eats things that are not food	.62	.42	8
119 unhealthy drinking (e.g. from discarded drink bottle, from toilet bowl)	.59	.51	5
X. Suicide Discourse			
83 attempts suicide	.34	.27	1
89 describes how he/she would kill themselves	.52	.51	2
105 requests to be harmed	.55	.48	2
107 says life is not worth living	.69	.50	5
113 talks about suicide	.84	.74	4
114 threatens to injure her/himself	.65	.62	3
115 threatens to kill him/herself	.77	.72	3

[a] Factor loading
[b] Item-rest correlation (correlation of the item score and the sum of all other items in the scale)
[c] Item prevalence (percentage of sample with item score of 1 or 2, n = 412)

B. OTHER CLINICAL ITEMS

	Prevalence (%)[a]
Inattentive items	
can't concentrate, short attention span	66
gets hurt a lot, accident prone	32
risks physical safety, fearless	21
picks at sores, or injuries	38
very forgetful	49
Dissociative items	
has an imaginary friend	9
has blackouts or periods of amnesia	2
thinks he/she is someone, or something else	8
Sexual items	
masturbates at home in view of others	9
masturbates at school, or in public	3

C. LOW SELF-ESTEEM SCALES

	Factor 1[b]	Factor 2[c]	Item-rest[d]	Prevalence (%)
I. Negative Self-Image				
believes he/she is no good at anything	.73	.09	.70	29
complains of not being likeable	.64	.04	.54	27
dislikes her/himself	.81	−.06	.71	19
fears he/she might do something bad	.60	.06	.54	14
feels ashamed	.63	−.05	.53	11
feels worthless or inferior	.85	.02	.80	20
has a low opinion of her/himself	.74	.17	.75	27
says she/he is 'bad', or 'no good'	.74	−.02	.65	15
thinks other children are better than him/her	.66	.07	.61	24
II. Low Confidence				
adjusts slowly to changes	−.08	.58	.42	46
does not speak up for her/himself	−.19	.68	.44	31
easily discouraged at home	.19	.60	.60	30
easily discouraged at school	.19	.58	.57	34
finds it hard to make decisions	.06	.73	.66	51
gives up too easily	.04	.74	.65	56
lacks confidence	.15	.69	.64	47
won't attempt new activities	−.03	.68	.54	29
Other Item				
low self-esteem	.53	.41	n.a.	38

[a] Item prevalence (percentage of sample with item score of 1 or 2, n = 412)
[b] Loading on Factor 1 on 2-factor model of low self-esteem
[c] Loading on Factor 2 on 2-factor model of low self-esteem
[d] Item-rest correlation (correlation of the item score and the sum of all other items in the scale)

Appendix 10

ACC short-form scales with constituent items

		Loading[a]	Item-rest[b]	Prevalence (%)[c]
I. Sexual Behaviour *(5 items, Cronbach's alpha = 0.84)*				
35	describes or imitates sexual behaviour	.71	.69	12
37	forces or pressures children into sexual acts	.82	.68	7
40	sexual behaviour not appropriate for age	.72	.70	14
42	touches or puts mouth on other person's sex parts	.65	.48	4
43	tries to involve others in sexual behaviour	.87	.77	9
II. Pseudomature *(6 items, Cronbach's alpha = 0.78)*				
21	precocious (talks, behaves like an adult)	.86	.65	32
22	prefers to be with adults, rather than children	.73	.60	32
23	prefers to mix with older children	.63	.53	40
28	too independent	.63	.48	27
29	treats you as though you were the child, and he/she was the parent	.65	.49	26
III. Non-Reciprocal *(6 items, Cronbach's alpha = 0.78)*				
2	avoids eye contact	.57	.48	38
7	does not share with friends	.49	.46	40
8	does not show affection	.78	.50	23
18	lacks guilt or empathy	.62	.59	39
20	manipulates or uses friends	.50	.53	29
30	uncaring (shows little concern for others)	.71	.64	31
IV. Indiscriminate *(5 items, Cronbach's alpha = 0.78)*				
1	attention-seeking behaviour	.40	.49	74
3	changes friends quickly	.57	.49	36
15	hugs men (other than relatives or male carer)	.65	.49	20
24	relates to strangers 'as if they were family'	.79	.70	47
27	too friendly with strangers	.76	.62	68
V. Insecure *(5 items, Cronbach's alpha = 0.72)*				
4	clingy	.50	.44	52
12	fears you will reject him/her	.78	.60	31
16	is convinced that friends will reject him/her	.51	.46	20
25	seems insecure	.62	.54	44
32	worries something bad will happen to you	.71	.40	38

		Loading [a]	Item-rest [b]	Prevalence (%) [c]
VI. Anxious-Distrustful *(6 items, Cronbach's alpha = 0.76)*				
5	distrusts adults	.44	.56	27
10	fearful of men in general	.63	.50	11
11	fearful or nervous at bed-time	.50	.47	13
17	is fearful of being harmed	.68	.52	17
31	wary or vigilant	.48	.51	19
38	has panic attacks	.69	.44	8
VII. Abnormal Pain Response *(4 items, Cronbach's alpha = 0.70)*				
6	does not cry	.49	.44	24
19	laughs when injured or hurt	.48	.38	16
36	does not show pain if physically hurt	.82	.69	15
44	won't say when physically hurt	.78	.48	14
VIII. Food Maintenance *(4 items, Cronbach's alpha = 0.81)*				
9	eats too much	.76	.63	25
13	gorges food	.73	.68	23
14	hides or stores food	.80	.58	14
26	steals food	.76	.61	18
IX. Self-Injury *(4 items, Cronbach's alpha = 0.67)*				
33	bites him/herself	.81	.55	9
34	causes injury to him/herself	.73	.55	10
39	hits head, head-banging	.48	.37	10
41	threatens to injure him/herself	.70	.46	3

[a] Factor loading
[b] Item-rest correlation (correlation of the item score and the sum of all other items in the scale)
[c] Item prevalence (percentage of sample with item score of 1 or 2, n = 347)

Appendix 11

ACA scales with constituent items

A. CLINICAL SCALES

		Loading[a]	*Item-rest*[b]	*Prevalence (%)*[c]	*ACA-specific*[d]
I. Non-reciprocal *(10 items, Cronbach's alpha = 0.83)*					
2	avoids eye contact	.52	.49	31	
13	does not cry	.53	.33	29	
14	does not share with friends	.50	.50	24	
15	does not show affection	.82	.62	31	
30	hides feelings	.56	.55	47	
44	refuses to talk	.47	.45	20	
46	resists being comforted when hurt	.64	.54	26	
50	seems alone in the world (not connected to people or places)	.59	.60	25	Yes
66	uncaring (shows little concern for others)	.50	.57	28	
69	withdrawn	.61	.55	23	
II. Social instability/behavioural dysregulation *(21 items, Cronbach's alpha = 0.92)*					
4	changes friends quickly	.60	.61	27	
8	constantly seeking excitement or 'thrills'	.54	.53	25	Yes
9	craves affection	.53	.55	38	
32	impulsive (acts rashly, without thinking)	.49	.65	57	Yes
36	lacks guilt or empathy	.42	.63	42	
38	manipulates or 'uses' friends	.59	.64	24	
40	possessive, can't share friends	.56	.65	17	
41	precocious (talks or behaves like an adult)	.62	.56	29	
42	prefers to be with adults, rather than peers	.59	.54	25	
43	prefers to mix with older youths	.63	.52	33	
45	relates to strangers as if they were family	.72	.63	26	
47	risks physical safety, fearless	.44	.48	24	
57	threatens to withdraw love (e.g. 'I won't love you anymore unless...')	.48	.52	10	Yes
59	too dramatic (false emotions)	.45	.56	28	
60	too friendly with strangers	.64	.54	42	
61	too independent	.42	.47	22	
62	too jealous	.44	.62	22	
64	tries too hard to please other young people	.63	.59	33	
65	turns friends against each other	.59	.45	11	
67	upsets most people (without good reason)	.59	.66	21	Yes
88	hugs men, other than a relative or male carer	.49	.43	10	

		Loading[a]	Item-rest[b]	Prevalence (%)[c]	ACA-specific[d]
III. Emotional dysregulation/distorted social cognition *(14 items, Cronbach's alpha = 0.90)*					
12	distrusts friends	.54	.51	21	Yes
24	feels victimised or misunderstood	.56	.63	31	Yes
33	is convinced that friends will reject him/her	.54	.55	24	
48	says friends are against him/her	.51	.61	23	
52	shows intense and inappropriate anger	.42	.68	39	Yes
53	startles easily ('jumpy')	.52	.48	17	
73	can't get scary thoughts or images out of his/her head (not due to watching a scary movie)	.54	.47	10	Yes
80	extreme reaction to minor event (or for no obvious reason)	.48	.66	24	Yes
81	extreme reaction to losing a friend, or being excluded	.53	.61	11	
90	intense reaction to criticism	.59	.67	34	Yes
93	says his/her life is not worth living	.62	.62	9	
94	says he/she feels 'empty' or without emotions	.58	.27	2	Yes
98	sudden or extreme mood changes	.64	.65	28	Yes
105	uncontrollable rage	.56	.76	23	Yes
IV. Dissociation/trauma symptoms *(7 items, Cronbach's alpha = 0.76)*					
39	nightmares about specific events or people	.52	.47	15	
71	appears dazed, 'spaced out' (like in a trance)	.52	.51	20	Yes
74	can't tell if an experience is real or a dream	.67	.60	10	Yes
82	feels like things, people or events aren't real	.75	.61	4	Yes
85	has panic attacks	.50	.46	11	
86	has periods of amnesia (e.g. has no memory of what has happened in the last hour)	.63	.52	10	
87	hits head, head-banging	.46	.37	7	
V. Food maintenance *(7 items, Cronbach's alpha = 0.87)*					
19	eats secretly (e.g. in the middle of the night)	.77	.71	20	Yes
20	eats too much	.75	.73	30	
28	gorges food	.66	.69	23	
31	hides or stores food	.75	.65	13	
54	steals food	.80	.73	15	
79	dramatic changes in eating (e.g. dieting then overeating)	.61	.39	5	Yes
84	has eating binges (bouts of excessive eating)	.70	.64	12	Yes
VI. Sexual behaviour *(7 items, Cronbach's alpha = 0.85)*					
83	forces or pressures other youth or children into sexual acts	.76	.71	3	
89	inappropriately shows genitals to others (in person, or through video or photo)	.56	.60	3	
95	seems overly preoccupied with sex (e.g. crude sexual talk, inappropriate sexual comments)	.56	.60	9	
96	sexual behaviour not appropriate for age	.67	.72	7	
97	sexual relations with an adult	.69	.43	1	
103	touches or puts mouth on other person's genitals or breasts	.72	.63	2	
104	tries to involve others in sexual behaviour	.75	.75	3	

	Loading[a]	Item-rest[b]	Prevalence (%)[c]	ACA-specific[d]
VII. Suicide discourse *(6 items, Cronbach's alpha = 0.88)*				
72 attempts suicide	.61	.57	3	
76 describes how he/she would kill him/herself	.86	.83	3	
91 intentionally harms him/herself with knife/implement	.57	.54	3	
99 talks about suicide	.81	.70	4	
100 threatens to injure him/herself	.87	.82	4	
101 threatens to kill him/herself	.79	.76	4	

B. OTHER CLINICAL ITEMS (15 items)

	Loading[a]	Item-rest[b]	Prevalence (%)[c]	ACA-specific[d]
5 clingy			19	
7 confused about where or with him he/she belongs			13	Yes
11 distrusts adults			21	
22 fears you (or other adults) will reject him/her			16	
34 is fearful of being harmed			14	
51 seems insecure			37	
55 suspicious			21	
58 too compliant (over-conforms)			16	
63 treats you as though you were the child, and he was the parent			33	
68 wary or vigilant (over-alert to danger)			10	
75 causes injury to him/herself			7	
77 distressed or troubled by traumatic memories			16	
78 does not show pain if physically hurt			13	
92 rocks back and forth			6	
102 throws him/herself against walls, onto floors, etc			4	

[a] Factor loading
[b] Item-rest correlation (correlation of the item score and the sum of all other items in the scale)
[c] Item prevalence = percentage of the CICS combined sample (n=230) with item score of 1 or 2
[d] Items that are specific to the ACA, i.e. not shared with the ACC

C. LOW SELF-ESTEEM SCALES

		Factor 1[e]	*Factor 2*[f]	*Item-rest*	*Prevalence (%)*
I. Negative Self-Image *(9 items, Cronbach's alpha = 0.91)*					
3	believes he/she is no good at anything	.59	.21	.65	30
6	complains of not being likeable	.79	.05	.70	17
10	dislikes him/herself	.78	.03	.74	15
21	fears he/she might do something bad	.71	.11	.56	13
23	feels ashamed	.77	.08	.64	10
25	feels worthless or inferior	.78	.10	.76	21
29	has a low opinion of him/herself	.70	.22	.75	35
49	says he/she is 'bad', or 'no good'	.81	.06	.70	14
56	thinks other young people are better than him/her	.72	.01	.65	22
II. Low Confidence *(8 items, Cronbach's alpha = 0.83)*					
1	adjusts slowly to changes	.02	.56	.46	52
16	does not speak up for her/himself	.06	.57	.40	30
17	easily discouraged at home	.23	.53	.57	29
18	easily discouraged at school	.17	.58	.57	39
26	finds it hard to make decisions	.08	.66	.61	46
27	gives up too easily	.08	.84	.66	53
35	lacks confidence	.38	.53	.63	53
70	won't attempt new activities	.10	.71	.51	31
Other Item					
37	low self-esteem	.54	.38	n.a.	37

[a] Factor loading
[b] Item-rest correlation (correlation of the item score and the sum of all other items in the scale)
[c] Item prevalence = percentage of the CICS combined sample (n=230) with item score of 1 or 2
[d] Items that are specific to the ACA, i.e. not shared with the ACC
[e] Loading on Factor 1 on 2-factor model of low self-esteem
[f] Loading on Factor 2 on 2-factor model of low self-esteem

Appendix 12

ACA short-form scales with constituent items

		Loading[a]	Item-rest[b]	Prevalence (%)[c]
I. Non-reciprocal *(6 items, Cronbach's alpha = 0.79)*				
2	does not show affection	.81	.58	31
6	hides feelings	.69	.57	47
12	refuses to talk	.60	.45	20
14	resists being comforted when hurt	.70	.54	26
16	seems alone in the world (not connected to people or places)	.61	.54	25
21	withdrawn	.73	.56	23
II. Social instability *(8 items, Cronbach's alpha = 0.84)*				
1	craves affection	.50	.54	38
8	impulsive (acts rashly, without thinking)	.51	.58	57
9	precocious (talks or behaves like an adult)	.82	.60	29
10	prefers to be with adults, rather than peers	.88	.62	25
11	prefers to mix with older youths	.78	.54	33
13	relates to strangers as if they were family	.52	.62	26
19	too friendly with strangers	.62	.58	42
20	tries too hard to please other young people	.53	.55	33
III. Emotional dysregulation/distorted social cognition *(7 items, Cronbach's alpha = 0.82)*				
15	says friends are against him/her	.60	.55	23
17	startles easily ('jumpy')	.49	.48	17
23	can't get scary thoughts or images out of his/her head (not due to watching a scary movie)	.76	.54	10
25	extreme reaction to losing a friend, or being excluded	.75	.62	11
32	intense reaction to criticism	.57	.60	34
33	says his/her life is not worth living	.79	.64	9
37	uncontrollable rage	.57	.65	23
IV. Dissociation/trauma symptoms *(6 items, Cronbach's alpha = 0.73)*				
22	appears dazed, 'spaced out' (like in a trance)	.49	.49	20
24	can't tell if an experience is real or a dream	.62	.58	10
26	feels like things, people or events aren't real	.53	.59	4
28	has panic attacks	.60	.46	11
29	has periods of amnesia (e.g. has no memory of what has happened in the last hour)	.52	.51	10
30	hits head, head-banging	.60	.39	7

	Loading[a]	Item-rest[b]	Prevalence (%)[c]
V. Food maintenance *(5 items, Cronbach's alpha = 0.87)*			
3 eats secretly (e.g. in the middle of the night)	.84	.73	20
4 eats too much	.77	.72	30
5 gorges food	.64	.67	23
7 hides or stores food	.83	.65	13
18 steals food	.85	.73	15
VI. Sexual behaviour *(5 items, Cronbach's alpha = 0.84)*			
27 forces or pressures other youth or children into sexual acts	.79	.67	3
31 inappropriately shows genitals to others (in person, or through video or photo)	.76	.62	3
34 seems overly preoccupied with sex (e.g. crude sexual talk, inappropriate sexual comments)	.68	.61	9
35 sexual behaviour not appropriate for age	.75	.70	7
36 tries to involve others in sexual behaviour	.92	.75	3

[a] Factor loading
[b] Item-rest correlation (correlation of the item score and the sum of all other items in the scale)
[c] Item prevalence = percentage of the CICS sample (n=230) with item score of 1 or 2

References

Achenbach, T. (1991) *Manual for the Child Behavior Checklist/4–18 and 1991 Profile*. Burlington, VT: University of Vermont.

Achenbach, T. and Edelbrock, C. S. (1978) The classification of child psychopathology: a review and analysis of empirical efforts. *Psychological Bulletin*, 85(6), 1275–301.

Achenbach, T., Howell, C., Quay, H. and Conners, C. (1991) National survey of problems and competencies among four- to sixteen-year-olds: parents' reports for normative and clinical samples. *Monographs of the Society for Research in Child Development*, 56(3).

Achenbach, T., McConaughy, S., Iyanova, M. and Rescorla, L. (2011) *Manual for the ASEBA Brief Problem Monitor (BPM)*. Burlington, VT: ASEBA.

Achenbach, T. and Rescorla, L. (2001) *Manual for ASEBA School-Age Forms and Profiles*. Burlington, VT: University of Vermont, Research Center for Children, Youth and Families.

Adams, J. and McClellan, J. (1995) Sexually inappropriate behaviors in seriously mentally ill children and adolescents. *Child Abuse and Neglect*, 19(5), 555–68.

Aiken, L. R. (1996) *Rating Scales and Checklists: Evaluating Behavior, Personality and Attitudes*. New York: Wiley.

Ali, Z. (2001) Pica in people with intellectual disability: a literature review of aetiology, epidemiology and complications. *Journal of Intellectual and Developmental Disability*, 26, 205–15.

American Psychiatric Association. (2000) *Diagnostic and Statistical Manual of Mental Disorders – text revision*, 4th edn. Washington, DC: American Psychiatric Association.

Armsden, G., Pecora, P. J., Payne, V. H. and Szatkiewicz, J. P. (2000) Children placed in long-term foster care: an intake profile using the child behavior checklist/4–18. *Journal of Emotional and Behavioral Disorders*, 8(1), 49–64.

Arnow, B. (2004) Relationships between childhood maltreatment, adult health and psychiatric outcomes and medical utilization. *Journal of Clinical Psychiatry*, 65(Suppl. 12), 10–15.

Asmundson, G., Wright, K. and Stein, M. (2004) Pain and PTSD symptoms in female veterans. *European Journal of Pain*, 8, 345–50.

Australian Institute of Health and Welfare (2004) *Child Protection Australia 2002–2003*. Canberra: AIHW (Child Welfare Series no. 34).

Australian Institute of Health and Welfare. (2007) *Child Protection Australia 2005–2006*. Canberra: AIHW (Child Welfare Series no. 40).

Ayoob, K., Kaminer, R. and Zawel, J. (1994) Chronic overeating without obesity in children with developmental disabilities: description of a new syndrome. *Mental Retardation*, 32(3), 194–9.

Baker, A., Kurland, D., Curtis, P., Alexander, G. and Papa-Lentini, C. (2007) Mental health and behavioral problems of youth in the child welfare system: residential treatment centers compared to therapeutic foster care in the Odyssey Project population. *Child Welfare*, 86(3), 97–123.

Becker, J. V. (1998) What we know about the characteristics and treatment of adolescents who have committed sexual offences. *Child Maltreatment*, 3, 317–29.

Bender, I. and Yarnell, H. (1941) An observation nursery: a study of 250 children on the psychiatric division of Bellevue Hospital. *American Journal of Psychiatry*, 97, 1158–74.

Benoit, J. L. and Kennedy, W. A. (1992) The abuse history of male adolescent sex offenders. *Journal of Interpersonal Violence*, 7, 543–8.

Bohus, M., Limberger, M., Ebner, U., Glocker, F., Schwarz, B., Wernz, M. *et al.* (2000) Pain perception during self-reported distress and calmness in patients with borderline personality disorder and self-mutilating behavior. *Psychiatry Research*, 95, 251–60.

Bonner, B. and Walker, C. E. (1999) *Children with Sexual Behavior Problems: Assessment and Treatment*: Final report for the National Center on Child Abuse and Neglect.

Bryant, F. and Yarnold, P. (1995) Principal-components analysis and exploratory and confirmatory factor analysis. In L. Grimm and P. Yarnold (eds) *Reading and Understanding Multivariate Analysis*. Washington, DC: American Psychological Association, pp. 99–136.

Burisch, M. (1984) Approaches to personality inventory construction. *American Psychologist*, 30, 214–27.

Burton, D. (2000) Were adolescent sexual offenders children with sexual behavior problems? *Sexual Abuse*, 12(1), 37–48.

Chaffin, M., Berliner, L., Block, R., Johnson, T. C., Friedrich, W., Louis, D., *et al.* (2008) Report of the ATSA task force on children with sexual behavior problems. *Child Maltreatment*, 13, 199–18.

Cheng, S., Foster, R. and Hester, N. (2003) A review of factors predicting children's pain experiences. *Issues in Comprehensive Pediatric Nursing*, 26, 203–16.

Cicchetti, D. and Rogosch, F. A. (1994) The toll of child maltreatment on the developing child. *Child and Adolescent Psychiatric Clinics of North America*, 3, 759–76.

Cicchetti, D., Toth, S. L. and Maughan, A. (2000) An ecological-transactional model of child maltreatment. In A. Sameroff and M. Lewis (eds), *Handbook of Developmental Psychopathology*, 2nd edn. Dordrecht, Netherlands: Kluwer Academic Publishers, pp. 689–722.

Claes, L., Vandereycken, W. and Vertommen, H. (2003) Eating disordered patients with and without self-injurious behaviours: a comparison of psychopathological features. *European Eating Disorders Review*, 11, 379–96.

Claes, L., Vandereycken, W. and Vertommen, H. (2006) Pain experience related to self-injury in eating disorder patients. *Eating Behaviors*, 7, 204–13.

Cohen, J. (1988) *Statistical Power Analysis of the Behavioral Sciences*, 2nd edn. New York: Academic Press.

Conners, C. K., Sitarenios, G., Parker, J. D. A. and Epstein, J. N. (1998) The revised Conners' Parent Rating Scale (CPRS-R): factor structure, reliability and criterion validity. *Journal of Abnormal Child Psychology*, 26(4), 257–68.

Coopersmith, S. (1981) *Manual for the Coopersmith Self-esteem Inventory*. Palo Alto, CA: Consulting Psychologist's Press.

Cosentino, C., Meyer-Bahlburg, H., Alpert, J., Weinberg, S. and Gaines, R. (1995) Sexual behavior problems and psychopathology symptoms in sexually abused girls. *Journal of the American Academy of Child and Adolescent Psychiatry*, 34(8), 1033–42.

Crittenden, P. M. (1997) Toward an integrative theory of trauma: a dynamic-maturational approach. In D. Cicchetti and S. L. Toth (eds), *The Rochester Symposium on Developmental Psychopathology, Volume 10: Risk, Trauma and Mental Processes*. Rochester, NY: University of Rochester, pp. 34–84.

Crittenden, P. M. (2006) A dynamic-maturational model of attachment. *Australian and New Zealand Journal of Family Therapy*, 27(2), 105–15.

Crone, M., Vogels, A., Hoekstra, F., Treffers, P. and Reijneveld, S. (2008) A comparison of four scoring methods based on the parent-report Strengths and Difficulties Questionnaire as used in the Dutch preventative child health care system. *BMC Public Health*, 8, 106.

D'Andrea, W., Ford, J., Stolbach, B., Spinazzola, J. and van der Kolk, B. (2012) Understanding interpersonal trauma in children: why we need a developmentally appropriate trauma diagnosis. *American Journal of Orthopsychiatry*, 82(2), 187–200.

de Kerdanet, M., Seveno, T. and Lecornu, M. (1993) Growth retardation of psychosocial origin: clinical and biological aspects in four cases. *Pediatrie*, 48(11), 783–7.

DeJong, M. (2010) Some reflections on the use of psychiatric diagnosis in the looked after or 'in care' child population. *Clinical Child Psychology and Psychiatry*, 15(4), 589–99.

Dekker, M., Nunn, R., Einfeld, S., Tonge, B. and Koot, H. M. (2002) Assessing emotional and behavioral problems in children with intellectual disability: revisiting the factor structure of the Developmental Behavior Checklist. *Journal of Autism and Developmental Disorders*, 32(6), 601–10.

Demb, J. (1991) Reported hyperphagia in foster children. *Child Abuse and Neglect*, 15(1), 77–88.

Demyttenaere, S., Finley, G., Johnston, C. and McGrath, P. (2001) Pain treatment thresholds in children after major surgery. *Clinical Journal of Pain*, 17(2), 173–7.

Doll, B. (1998) Test review of the Child Behavior Checklist. In J. Impara and B. Plake (eds), *Thirteenth Mental Measurements Yearbook*. Lincoln, Nebraska: Buros Institute of Mental Measurements, pp. 217–220.

Dowdy, E., Kamphaus, R., Abdou, A. and Twyford, J. (2012) Detection of symptoms of prevalent mental health disorders of childhood with the parent form of the Behavioral Emotional Screening System. *Assessment for Effective Intervention*, DOI: 10.1177/1534508412447009.

Drach, K., Wientzen, J. and Ricci, L. (2001) The diagnostic utility of sexual behavior problems in diagnosing sexual abuse in a forensic child abuse evaluation clinic. *Child Abuse and Neglect*, 25, 489–503.

Elander, J. and Rutter, M. (1996) Use and development of the Rutter parents' and teachers' scales. *International Journal of Methods in Psychiatric Research*, 6(2), 63–78.

Fanurik, D., Koh, J., Schmitz, M., Harrison, R. and Conrad, T. (1999) Children with cognitive impairment: parent report of pain and copings. *Journal of Developmental and Behavioral Pediatrics*, 20(4), 228–34.

Farmer, E. and Pollock, S. (2003) Managing sexually abused and/or abusing children in substitute care. *Child and Family Social Work*, 8, 101–12.

Fehrenbach, P., Smith, W., Montastersky, C. and Deisher, R. (1986) Adolescent sexual offenders: offender and offense characteristics. *American Journal of Orthopsychiatry*, 56, 225–33.

Felman, Y. and Nikitas, J. (1983) Sexually transmitted diseases and child sexual abuse. *New York State Journal of Medicine*, 83, 341–43.

Fergusson, D. and Lynskey, M. (1996) Adolescent resiliency to family adversity. *Journal of Child Psychology and Psychiatry*, 33, 1059–75.

Floyd, F. and Widaman, K. (1995) Factor analysis in the development and refinement of clinical assessment instruments. *Psychological Assessment*, 7(3), 286–99.

Fonagy, P. (2003) The development of psychopathology from infancy to adulthood: the mysterious unfolding of disturbance in time. *Infant Mental Health Journal*, 24(3), 212–39.

Friedrich, W. N. (1997) *Child Sexual Behavior Inventory: Professional Manual*. Odessa, FL: Psychological Assessment Resources, Inc.

Friedrich, W. N. (2005) Correlates of sexual behavior in young children. *Journal of Child Custody*, 2(3), 41–55.

Friedrich, W. N. (2007) *Children with Sexual Behavior Problems: Family-Based, Attachment-Focused Therapy*. New York: Norton.

Friedrich, W. N. and Grambsch, P. (1992) Child Sexual Behavior Inventory: Normative and clinical comparisons. *Psychological Assessment*, 4(3), 303-311.

Friedrich, W. N., Grambsch, P., Broughton, D., Kuiper, J. and Beilke, R. (1991) Normative sexual behavior in children. *Pediatrics*, 88(3), 456–64.

Friedrich, W. N., Fisher, J., Broughton, D., Houston, M. and Shafran, C. (1998) Normative sexual behavior in children: a contemporary sample. *Pediatrics*, 101(4), E91–E98.

Friedrich, W. N., Fisher, J., Dittner, C., Acton, R., Berliner, L., Butler, J. *et al.* (2001) Child sexual behaviour inventory: normative, psychiatric and sexual abuse comparisons. *Child Maltreatment*, 6(1), 37–49.

Friedrich, W. N., Davies, W., Feher, E. and Wright, J. (2003) Sexual behavior problems in preteen children: Developmental, ecological and behavioral correlates. *Annals of the New York Academy of Sciences*, 989, 95–104.

Friedrich, W. N., Baker, A., Parker, R., Schneiderman, M., Gries, L. and Archer, M. (2005a) Youth with problematic sexualised behaviors in the child welfare system: A one-year longitudinal study. *Sexual Abuse*, 17(4), 391–406.

Friedrich, W. N., Trane, S. and Gully, K. (2005b) Re: It is a mistake to conclude that sexual abuse and sexualized behavior are not related: a reply to Drach, Wientzen and Ricci (2001). *Child Abuse and Neglect*, 29, 297–302.

Gardner, J. (2000) Living with a child with fetal alcohol syndrome. *American Journal of Maternal/Child Nursing*, 25(5), 252–7.

Garwood, M. M. and Close, W. (2001) Identifying the psychological needs of foster children. *Child Psychiatry and Human Development*, 32(2), 125–35.

Gillberg, C. (1995) Endogenous opioids and opiate antagonists in autism: Brief review of empirical findings and implications for clinicians. *Developmental Medicine and Child Neurology*, 37, 239–45.

Gilmour, J. and Skuse, D. (1999) A case-comparison study of the characteristics of children with a short stature syndrome induced by stress (Hyperphagic Short Stature) and a consecutive series of unaffected 'stressed' children. *Journal of Child Psychology and Psychiatry and Allied Disciplines*, 40(6), 969-78.

Glaser, D. (2000) Child abuse and neglect and the brain – a review. *Journal of Child Psychology and Psychiatry*, 41(1), 97–116.

Gohlke, B., Khadilkar, V., Skuse, D. and Stanhope, R. (1998) Recognition of children with psychosocial short stature: a spectrum of presentation. *Journal of Pediatric Endocrinology*, 11(4), 509–17.

Goldfarb, W. (1949) Rorschach test differences between family-reared, institution-reared and schizophrenic children. *American Journal of Orthopsychiatry*, 1, 624–33.

Goodman, R. (2001) Psychometric properties of the Strengths and Difficulties Questionnaire. *Journal of the American Academy of Child and Adolescent Psychiatry*, 40, 1337–45.

Gray, A., Pithers, W., Busconi, A. and Houchens, P. (1999) Developmental and etiological characteristics of children with sexual behavior problems: treatment implications. *Child Abuse and Neglect*, 23(6), 601–21.

Green, J. (2003) Are attachment disorders best seen as social impairment syndromes? *Attachment and Human Development*, 5(3), 259–64.

Green, W., Campbell, M. and David, R. (1984) Psychosocial dwarfism: a critical review of the evidence. *Journal of the American Academy of Child and Adolescent Psychiatry*, 23(1), 39–48.

Grilo, C. and Masheb, R. (2001) Childhood psychological, physical and sexual maltreatment in outpatients with Binge Eating Disorder: frequency and associations with gender, obesity and eating-related psychopathology. *Obesity Research*, 9(5), 320–25.

Guadagnoli, E. and Velicer, W. (1988) Relation of sample size to the stability of component patterns. *Psychological Bulletin*, 103, 265–75.

Halfon, N., Mendonca, A. and Berkowitz, G. (1995) Health status of children in foster care. The experience of the Center for the Vulnerable Child. *Archives of Pediatrics and Adolescent Medicine*, 149(4), 386–92.

Haugaard, J. (2004) Recognizing and treating uncommon behavioral and emotional disorders in children and adolescents who have been severely maltreated: somatization and other somatoform disorders. *Child Maltreatment*, 9(2), 169–76.

Heckman, C. and Westefeld, J. (2006) The relationship between traumatization and pain: what is the role of emotion? *Journal of Family Violence*, 21(1), 63–73.

Heflinger, C. A., Simpkins, C. G. and Combs-Orme, T. (2000) Using the CBCL to determine the clinical status of children in state custody. *Children and Youth Services Review*, 22(1), 55–73.

Henry, D., Tolan, P. and Gorman-Smith, D. (2005) Cluster analysis in family psychology research. *Journal of Family Psychology*, 19(1), 121–32.

Hermann, C., Hohmeister, J., Demirakc, S., Zohsel, K. and Flor, H. (2006) Long-term alteration of pain sensitivity in school-aged children with early pain experiences. *Pain*, 125, 278–85.

Horan, S., Kang, G., Levine, M., Duax, C., Luntz, B. and Tasa, C. (1993) Empirical studies on foster care: review and assessment. *Journal of Sociology and Social Welfare*, 20(1), 131–54.

Howe, D. (2003) Attachment disorders: disinhibited attachment behaviours and secure base distortions with special reference to adopted children. *Attachment and Human Development*, 5(3), 265–70.

Howe, D. and Fearnley, S. (2003) Disorders of attachment in adopted and fostered children: recognition and treatment. *Clinical Child Psychology and Psychiatry*, 8, 369–87.

Jellinek, M. S., Little, M., Benedict, K., Murphy, J. M., Pagano, M., Poitrast, F., *et al.* (1995) Placement outcomes of 206 severely maltreated children in the Boston Juvenile Court system: a 7.5-year follow-up study. *Child Abuse and Neglect*, 19(9), 1051–64.

Johnson, T. C. (1993) Assessment of sexual behavior problems in pre-school and latency-aged children. *Child and Adolescent Psychiatric Clinics of North America*, 2(3), 431–50.

Kahn, T. and Lafond, M. (1988) Treatment of the adolescent sexual offender. *Child and Adolescent Social Work Journal*, 5, 135–48.

Kalland, M. and Sinkkonen, J. (2001) Finnish children in foster care: evaluating the breakdown of long-term placements. *Child Welfare. Special Issue: International Issues in Child Welfare*, 80(5), 513–27.

Kendall-Tackett, K. A., Williams, L. M. and Finkelhor, D. (1993) Impact of sexual abuse on children: a review and synthesis of recent empirical studies. *Psychological Bulletin*, 113(1), 164–80.

Kent, A., Waller, G. and Dagnan, D. (1999) A greater role of emotional than physical or sexual abuse in predicting disordered eating attitudes: the role of mediating variables. *International Journal of Eating Disorders*, 25, 159–67.

Klee, L., Kronstadt, D. and Zlotnick, C. (1997) Foster care's youngest: a preliminary report. *American Journal of Orthopsychiatry*, 67(2), 290–9.

Kozlowska, K. (2007) The developmental origins of conversion disorders. *Clinical Child Psychology and Psychiatry*, 12(4), 487–510.

Kreppner, J., O'Connor, T., Rutter, M., Beckett, C., Castle, J., Croft, C. *et al.* (2001) Can inattention /overactivity be an institutional deprivation syndrome? *Journal of Abnormal Child Psychology*, 29(6), 513–28.

Lambert, L., Essen, J. and Head, J. (1977) Variations in behaviour ratings of children who have been in care. *Journal of Child Psychology and Psychiatry and Allied Disciplines*, 18(4), 335–46.

Leslie, L. K., Gordon, J., Ganger, W. and Gist, K. (2002) Developmental delay in young children in child welfare by initial placement type. *Infant Mental Health Journal*, 23(5), 496–516.

Letourneau, E., Schoenwald, S. and Sheidow, A. (2004) Children and adolescents with sexual behavior problems. *Child Maltreatment*, 9(1), 49–61.

Levy, D. (1937) Primary affect hunger. *American Journal of Psychiatry*, 94, 643–52.

Lewis, D. O. (1992) From abuse to violence: psychophysiological consequences of maltreatment. *Journal of the American Academy of Child and Adolescent Psychiatry*, 31(3), 383–91.

Lieberman, A. F. and Zeanah, C. H. (1995) Disorders of attachment in infancy. *Child and Adolescent Psychiatric Clinics of North America*, 4(3), 571–87.

Liotti, G. (2006) A model of dissociation based on attachment theory and research. *Journal of Trauma and Dissociation*, 7(4), 55–73.

Lyons-Ruth, K., Dutra, L., Schuder, M. and Bianchi, I. (2006) From infant attachment disorganization to adult dissociation: relational adaptations or traumatic experiences? *Psychiatric Clinics of North America*, 29(1), 63–86.

McClellan, J., McCurry, C., Ronnei, M., Adams, J., Storck, M., Eisner, E., *et al.* (1997) Relationship between sexual abuse, gender and sexually inappropriate behaviors in seriously mentally ill youths. *Journal of the American Academy of Child and Adolescent Psychiatry*, 36(7), 959–65.

Melzack, R. (1999) From the gate to the neuromatrix. *Pain*, Supplement 6, S121–6.

Mian, M., Marton, P. and LeBaron, D. (1996) The effects of sexual abuse on 3- to 5-year-old girls. *Child Abuse and Neglect*, 20(8), 731–45.

Minde, K. (2003) Attachment problems as a spectrum disorder: implications for diagnosis and treatment. *Attachment and Human Development*, 5(3), 289–96.

Minnis, H. and Keck, G. (2003) A clinical/research dialogue on Reactive Attachment Disorder. *Attachment and Human Development*, 5(3), 297–301.

Minnis, H., Rabe-Hesketh, S. and Wolkind, S. (2002) Development of a brief, clinically relevant, scale for measuring attachment disorders. *International Journal of Methods in Psychiatric Research*, 11(2), 90–8.

Minnis, H., Everett, K., Pelosi, A., Dunn, J. and Knapp, M. (2006) Children in foster care: mental health, service use and costs. *European Child and Adolescent Psychiatry*, 15, 63–70.

Molinari, E. (2001) Eating disorders and sexual abuse. *Eating and Weight Disorders*, 6(2), 68–80.

Money, J. (1977) The syndrome of abuse dwarfism (psychosocial dwarfism or reversible hyposomatotropism). *American Journal of Diseases of Children*, 131(5), 508–13.

Money, J., Wolff, G. and Annecillo, C. (1972) Pain agnosia and self-injury in the syndrome of reversible somatotropin deficiency (Psychosocial dwarfism). *Journal of Autism and Childhood Schizophrenia*, 2(2), 127–39.

Nader, R., Oberlander, T., Chambers, C. and Craig, K. (2004) Expression of pain in children with autism. *Clinical Journal of Pain*, 20, 88–97.

Nakamura, B., Ebesutani, C., Bernstein, A. and Chorpita, B. (2009) A psychometric analysis of the Child Behavior Checklist DSM-oriented scales. *Journal of Psychopathology and Behavioral Assessment*, 31, 178–89.

O'Connor, T. and Rutter, M. (2000) Attachment disorder behavior following early severe deprivation: extension and longitudinal follow-up. *Journal of the American Academy of Child and Adolescent Psychiatry*, 39(6), 703–12.

O'Connor, T., Bredenkamp, D., Rutter, M. and the English and Romanian Adoptees Study Team. (1999) Attachment disturbances and disorders in children exposed to early severe deprivation. *Infant Mental Health Journal*, 20(1), 10–29.

Oliván, G. (2003) Catch-up growth assessment in long-term physically neglected and emotionally abused preschool age male children. *Child Abuse and Neglect*, 27(1), 103–8.

Paolucci, E., Genuis, M. and Violato, C. (2001) A meta-analysis of the published research on the effects of child sexual abuse. *Journal of Psychology*, 135(1), 17–36.

Patterson, G. R., DeBaryshe, B. D. and Ramsey, E. (1989) A developmental perspective on antisocial behavior. *American Psychologist*, 44(2), 329–35.

Pilowsky, D. (1995) Psychopathology among children placed in family foster care. *Psychiatric Services*, 46(9), 906–10.

Pithers, W., Gray, A., Busconi, A. and Houchens, P. (1998) Caregivers of children with sexual behavior problems: psychological and familial functioning. *Child Abuse and Neglect*, 22(2), 129–41.

Powell, G., Brasel, J. and Blizzard, R. (1967) Emotional deprivation and growth retardation simulating idiopathic hypopituitarism: I. Clinical evaluation of the syndrome. *New England Journal of Medicine*, 276, 1271–8.

Putnam, F. (2003) Ten-year research update review: child sexual abuse. *Journal of the American Academy of Child and Adolescent Psychiatry*, 42(3), 269–78.

Ricci, L., Drach, K. and Wientzen, J. (2005) Further comment on the lack of utility of sexual behavior problems as measured by the Child Sexual Behavior Inventory in diagnosing sexual abuse: a reply to Friedrich, Gully and Trane (2004). *Child Abuse and Neglect*, 29, 303–6.

Richters, M. M. and Volkmar, F. R. (1994) Reactive attachment disorder of infancy or early childhood. *Journal of the American Academy of Child and Adolescent Psychiatry*, 33(3), 328–32.

Romanelli, L., Landsverk, J., Levitt, J., Leslie, L. K., Hurley, M., Bellonci, C. *et al.* (2009) Best practices for mental health in child welfare: screening, assessment and treatment guidelines. *Child Welfare*, 88(1), 163–88.

Roy, P., Rutter, M. and Pickles, A. (2000) Institutional care: risk from family background or pattern of rearing? *Journal of Child Psychology and Psychiatry and Allied Disciplines*, 41(2), 139–49.

Rushton, A., Quinton, D., Dance, C. and Mayes, D. (1997) Preparation for permanent placement: evaluating direct work with older children. *Adoption and Fostering*, 21(4), 41–8.
Russ, M., Shearin, E., Clarkin, J., Harrison, K. and Hull, J. (1993) Subtypes of self-injurious patients with borderline personality disorder. *American Journal of Psychiatry*, 150(12), 1869–1871.
Rutter, M. (1999) Psychosocial adversity and child psychopathology. *British Journal of Psychiatry*, 174, 480–93.
Schmahl, C., Bohus, M., Esposito, F., Treede, R., Salle, F., Greffrath, W. *et al.* (2006) Neural correlates of antinociception in borderline personality disorder. *Archives of General Psychiatry*, 63, 659–67.
Schreck, K., Williams, K. and Smith, A. (2004) A comparison of eating behaviors between children with and without autism. *Journal of Autism and Developmental Disorders*, 34(4), 433–8.
Sedlak, A. and Broadhurst, D. (1996) *The Third National Incidence Study of Child Abuse and Neglect (NIS-3)*. Washington, DC: US Department of Health and Human Services.
Shephard, R., Greenough, A., Johnson, K. and Gerada, C. (2002) Hyperphagia, weight gain and neonatal drug withdrawal. *Acta Paediatrica*, 91, 951–3.
Silovsky, J. and Niec, L. (2002) Characteristics of young children with sexual behavior problems: a pilot study. *Child Maltreatment*, 7(3), 187–97.
Silver, H. and Finkelstein, M. (1967) Deprivation dwarfism. *Pediatrics*, 317, 317–24.
Simmonds, J. (2010) The making and breaking of relationships – organisational and clinical questions in providing services for looked after children? *Clinical Child Psychology and Psychiatry*, 15(4), 601–12.
Skuse, D., Albanese, A., Stanhope, R., Gilmour, J. and Voss, L. (1996) A new stress-related syndrome of growth failure and hyperphagia in children, associated with reversibility of growth-hormone insufficiency. *Lancet*, 348, 353–8.
Smith, S. and Howard, J. (1994) The impact of previous sexual abuse on children's adjustment in adoptive placement. *Social Work*, 39(5), 491–501.
Smyke, A., Dumitrescu, A. and Zeanah, C. H. (2002) Attachment disturbances in young children. I: the continuum of caretaking. *Journal of the American Academy of Child and Adolescent Psychiatry*, 41(8), 972–82.
St Claire, L. and Osborne, A. (1987) The ability and behaviour of children who have been 'in-care' or separated from their parents. *Early Child Development and Care*, 28, 187–354.
Statacorp. (2003) Stata statistical software (Version 8.0) [Statistical software]. College Station, Texas: Stata Corporation.
Steele, R. and Aylward, B. (2007) The use of cluster analytic techniques in developmental and behavioral research. *Journal of Developmental and Behavioral Pediatrics*, 28(4), 327–9.
Steinberg, M. (1996) Diagnostic tools for assessing dissociation in children and adolescents. *Child and Adolescent Psychiatric Clinics of North America*, 5(2), 333–49.
Stiegler, L. (2005) Understanding Pica behavior: a review for clinical and education professionals. *Focus on Autism and Other Developmental Disabilities*, 20(1), 27–3.
Stone, L., Otten, R., Engels, R., Vermulst, A. and Janssens, J. (2010) Psychometric properties of the parent and teacher versions of the Strengths and Difficulties Questionnaire for 4- to 12-year olds: a review. *Clinical Child and Family Psychology Review*, 13, 254–74.
Taitz, L. and King, J. (1988) Growth patterns in child abuse. *Acta Paediatrica Scandinavica – Supplement*, 343, 62–72.
Tarren-Sweeney, M. (2007) The Assessment Checklist for Children – ACC: a behavioral rating scale for children in foster, kinship and residential care. *Children and Youth Services Review*, 29, 672–91.
Tarren-Sweeney, M. (2008) Retrospective and concurrent predictors of the mental health of children in care. *Children and Youth Services Review*, 30, 1–25.
Tarren-Sweeney, M. (2010) It's time to re-think mental health services for children in care and those adopted from care. *Clinical Child Psychology and Psychiatry*, 15(4), 613–26.
Tarren-Sweeney, M. (2013a) The Assessment Checklist for Adolescents – ACA: a scale for measuring

the mental health of young people in foster, kinship, residential and adoptive care. *Children and Youth Services Review*, 35, 384–93.

Tarren-Sweeney, M. (2013b) An investigation of complex attachment- and trauma-related symptomatology among children in foster and kinship care. *Child Psychiatry and Human Development*. DOI: 10.1007/s10578-013-0366-x

Tarren-Sweeney, M. and Hazell, P. (2005) The mental health and socialization of siblings in care. *Children and Youth Services Review*, 27, 821–43.

Tarren-Sweeney, M. and Hazell, P. (2006) The mental health of children in foster and kinship care in New South Wales, Australia. *Journal of Paediatrics and Child Health*, 42, 91–9.

Tarren-Sweeney, M., Hazell, P. and Carr, V. (2004) Are foster parents reliable informants of children's behaviour problems? *Child: Care, Health and Development*, 30(2), 167–75.

Thompson, R., Authier, K. and Ruma, P. (1994) Behavior problems of sexually abused children in foster care: a preliminary study. *Journal of Child Sexual Abuse*, 3(4), 79–91.

van der Kolk, B. (2005) Developmental trauma disorder. *Psychiatric Annals*, 35(5), 401–8.

van Ijzendoorn, M. and Bakermans-Kranenburg, M. (2003) Attachment disorders and disorganized attachment: similar and different. *Attachment and Human Development*, 5(3), 313–20.

Vorria, P., Rutter, M., Pickles, A., Wolkind, S. and Hobsbaum, A. (1998) A comparative study of Greek children in long-term residential group care and in two-parent families: I. Social, emotional and behavioural differences. *Journal of Child Psychology and Psychiatry and Allied Disciplines*, 39(2), 225–36.

Walsh, T., McGrath, P. and Symons, D. (2008) Attachment dimensions and young children's response to pain. *Pain Research and Management*, 13(1), 33–40.

White, S., Halpin, B., Strom, G. and Santilli, G. (1988) Behavioral comparisons of young sexually abused, neglected and non-referred children. *Journal of Clinical Child Psychology*, 17, 53–61.

Wolff, G. and Money, J. (1973) Relationship between sleep and growth in patients with reversible somatotropin deficiency (psychosocial dwarfism). *Psychological Medicine*, 3, 18–27.

Wolkind, S. and Rushton, A. (1994) Residential and family foster care. In M. Rutter, E. A. Taylor and L. A. Hersov (eds) *Child and Adolescent Psychiatry: Modern Approaches*, 3rd edn. Oxford: Blackwell Scientific Publications, pp.252–66.

Woolf, C. and Salter, M. (2000) Neuronal plasticity: increasing the gain in pain. *Science*, 288, 1765–9.

World Health Organization (2002) *The World Health Report – 2002*. Geneva: World Health Organization.

Wyatt, D., Simms, M. and Horwitz, S. (1997) Widespread growth retardation and variable growth recovery in foster children in the first year after initial placement. *Archives of Pediatrics and Adolescent Medicine*, 151(8), 813–16.

Yule, W. and Raynes, N. V. (1972) Behavioural characteristics of children in residential care in relation to indices of separation. *Journal of Child Psychology and Psychiatry and Allied Disciplines*, 13(4), 249–58.

Zero to Three. (2005) *Diagnostic Classification of Mental Health and Developmental Disorders of Infancy and Early Childhood: Revised edition (DC: 0-3R)*. Washington, DC: Zero To Three Press.

Index